What they're saying about Nelson Mandela Speaks . . .

"Illuminating volume of speeches by one of South Africa's most remarkable political leaders. . . . These addresses help explain why Mandela commands so much respect across racial and ethnic lines both in South Africa and around the world." *St. Louis Post-Dispatch*

"A timely collection of speeches by the giant of world politics." *Caribbean Times* (London)

"Charts the way in which, through constant discussion, [the] process of revolutionary change has come about." Hilda Bernstein, *Southern African Review of Books*

"Belongs in every household." *Chicago Defender*

"Provides a remarkable insight into Mandela's politics." *An Phoblacht/Republican News* (Dublin)

"A man whose television delivery has captivated millions is as captivating on paper." *Baltimore Sun*

"Mandela answers many of the burning questions of politics, strategy, and tactics facing the revolutionary democratic movement in South Africa." *The Militant* (New York)

"Reveals both the moral vision and the political pragmatism that mark Mandela as an extraordinary political leader." *Choice*

"His talks are documents, steeped in history and chockfull of facts." Earl Caldwell, *New York Daily News*

"A valuable book, and not merely for the future historian." John S. Saul, *Globe & Mail* (Toronto)

"That Nelson Mandela could emerge from more than a quarter-century of political imprisonment to declare these views, and that he has succeeded in getting so many of his countrymen to go along with him, shows what might yet be achieved." *Independent* (London)

NELSON MANDELA SPEAKS

NELSON MANDELA SPEAKS

FORGING A DEMOCRATIC, NONRACIAL SOUTH AFRICA

MANDELA, NELSON

PATHFINDER

New York London Montreal Sydney

Edited by Steve Clark

Copyright ©1993 by Nelson Mandela and Pathfinder Press
All rights reserved

ISBN 0-87348-774-5 paper; ISBN 0-87348-775-3 cloth
Library of Congress Catalog Card Number 93-85689
Manufactured in the United States of America
First edition, 1993
Second printing, 1994

Cover and book design: Toni Gorton
Front cover photo: Andrew Mohamed/ANC Department of Information and
    Publicity. Back cover photo: Andrew Wiard

Permission to reprint material has been granted by:
    The Johannesburg Star, for interview published September 15, 1992. Time
    magazine, for interview published June 14, 1993, © 1993 Time, Inc.

Pathfinder
410 West Street, New York, NY 10014, U.S.A.
Fax: (212)727-0150 ■ CompuServe: 73321,414
    ■ Internet: pathfinder@igc.apc.org

Pathfinder distributors around the world:
Australia (and Asia and the Pacific):
    Pathfinder, 19 Terry St., Surry Hills, Sydney, N.S.W. 2010
    Postal address: P.O. Box K879, Haymarket, N.S.W. 2000
Britain (and Europe, Africa except South Africa, and Middle East):
    Pathfinder, 47 The Cut, London, SE1 8LL
Canada:
    Pathfinder, 4581 rue St-Denis, Montreal, Quebec, H2J 2L4
Iceland:
    Pathfinder, Klapparstíg 26, 2d floor, 101 Reykjavík
    Postal address: P. Box 233, 121 Reykjavík
New Zealand:
    Pathfinder, La Gonda Arcade, 203 Karangahape Road, Auckland
    Postal address: P.O. Box 8730, Auckland
Sweden:
    Pathfinder, Vikingagatan 10, S-113 42, Stockholm
United States (and Caribbean, Latin America, and South Africa):
    Pathfinder, 410 West Street, New York, NY 10014

CONTENTS

9   *Preface*

16   *Nelson Mandela*

17   *List of initials*

18   *Chronology*

23   **Now is the time to intensify the struggle**
Speech in Cape Town following release from prison
February 11, 1990

29   **Our struggle is against all forms of racism**
Speech in Harlem, New York, June 21, 1990

35   **Peace will not come to our country until
apartheid is ended**
Address to U.S. Congress, June 26, 1990

44   **We cannot afford to stand divided**
Address to Organization of African Unity, Kampala, Uganda
September 8, 1990

48   **The women's movement must play a central role**
Speech to ANC Constitutional Committee Workshop
November 1990

53   **The oppressed and exploited must lead South
Africa out of apartheid**
Keynote address to ANC Consultative Conference
December 14, 1990

68   **Our strategy is determined by objective reality**
Closing speech to ANC Consultative Conference
December 16, 1990

75   **Building a political culture that entrenches
political tolerance**
Speech to Johannesburg Press Club, February 22, 1991

85   **The violence has assumed a more organized and
systematic character**
Open letter to President de Klerk, April 5, 1991

92 **It is your sweat and blood that has created the wealth of South Africa**
Address to National Union of Mineworkers, April 27, 1991

99 **Our struggle has changed the balance of forces**
Opening address to ANC National Conference, July 2, 1991

118 **We will ensure that the poor and rightless will rule the land of their birth**
Speech to rally in Cuba, July 26, 1991

129 **The oppressed will be and must be their own liberators**
Address to conference of Umkhonto we Sizwe
August 9, 1991

146 **Codesa is the fruit of sacrifice and struggle**
Address at opening session of Convention for a
Democratic South Africa, December 20, 1991

153 **The National Party and the government talk peace while conducting a war**
Speech in reply to de Klerk, December 20, 1991

159 **We must all march together**
Message to the Jewish community, April 13, 1992

161 **An interim government is essential**
Speech at Institute of Foreign Policy, Sweden
May 20, 1992

166 **We are prepared to take responsibility for governing and reconstructing South Africa**
Address to ANC policy conference, May 28, 1992

174 **The National Party regime is killing our people**
Speech to residents of Boipatong, June 21, 1992

180 **For a democratically elected and sovereign constituent assembly**
Letter to President de Klerk, July 9, 1992

188 **A cold-blooded strategy of state terrorism**
Address to United Nations Security Council
July 15, 1992

199 **A decisive blow for peace and democracy**
Speech to demonstration at Union Buildings, Pretoria
August 5, 1992

204 **We must pull South Africa out from the morass**
Interview with 'Johannesburg Star,' published September 15,
1992

211 **1993 can be a year of decisive achievements**
Interview with 'Mayibuye,' published February 1993

217 **We are on the eve of great changes**
Speech at International Solidarity Conference, Johannesburg
February 20, 1993

219 **We have come to this region to start a peace
campaign**
Visit to Natal, March 12-14, 1993

235 **When we act together, with discipline and
determination, nothing can stop us**
Address to the nation following Chris Hani's assassination
April 13, 1993

238 **Apartheid must not be reformed; it must be
uprooted in its entirety**
Speech at funeral of Chris Hani, April 19, 1993

247 **We must act together to give birth to a new South
Africa**
Speech to members of British Parliament, May 5, 1993

257 **A landmark decision**
Interview with 'Time' magazine, published June 14, 1993

261 **New tasks on our common agenda**
Speech to NAACP convention, Indianapolis, July 10, 1993

269 *Notes*
281 *Glossary*
287 *Index*

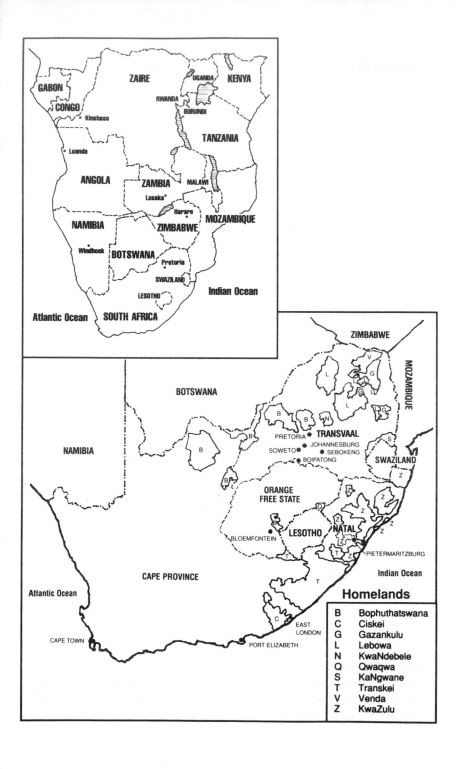

PREFACE

South Africa has long been a pariah among countries—the land of apartheid, of constitutionally entrenched racial oppression, of rule by a late twentieth-century "master race" plutocracy.

The apartheid system, consolidated under the National Party in 1948 following more than a century of white minority rule, has denied the most basic democratic and human rights to some 87 percent of the population. The majority of South Africans have been barred from the right to vote, to own land, to live outside specially designated "Bantustans" and urban "group areas," or to hold certain industrial and other jobs reserved for whites. Through these methods, brutally enforced by the army and police of the apartheid state, black working people are superexploited to benefit a handful of wealthy capitalist families. The framers of this modern "peculiar institution" promised it would last forever.

But today South Africa is at the threshold of a historic transformation. Working people and other supporters of freedom, social justice, and human progress the world over are anticipating a victorious outcome of the long, bloody, and courageously fought revolutionary struggle for a nonracial democratic republic. They recognize what a new South Africa will open up for tens of millions who for the first time will be equal citizens in the land where they live and work and whose social wealth they produce with their labor. Moreover, supporters of the antiapartheid struggle know the impulse such a triumph will give to those everywhere—regardless of skin color or national origin—who are fighting for a just and humane world.

A new chapter in the South African revolution was opened in February 1990 when Pretoria's ban was lifted on the African National Congress, together with other anti-apartheid, democratic, and socialist organizations, and ANC leader Nelson Mandela was freed after more than twenty-seven years in prison.

"We have entered the final decade of the twentieth century, and South Africa once again stands at a crossroads," Mandela told delegates to the ANC's December 1990 conference, the first held on its home ground since its banning thirty years earlier. "We now stand at the threshold of freedom. It is the solemn responsibility of the most oppressed and exploited to lead South Africa out of the morass and degradation of apartheid into a new era of freedom and democracy for all its people."

This book, through Mandela's own words, traces the accelerating development of the democratic revolution unfolding in South Africa during the opening years of the 1990s, up to the scheduling of the first one-person, one-vote elections ever to be held in that country, set for April 1994. What Nelson Mandela says in these pages is essential reading everywhere, because the political and social destiny of the South African people has been and continues to be bound up with prospects for the oppressed and exploited all over the world.

As Mandela reminds his listeners in his June 1993 speech to the National Association for the Advancement of Colored People (NAACP), the talk that closes this book, the ANC-led Defiance Campaign in the early 1950s gave heart to those struggling against Jim Crow segregation in the United States. The victories of the U.S. civil rights and black freedom struggle, in turn, and the ensuing movement against Washington's war in Vietnam encouraged a young generation of South African fighters during difficult years when their organizations were banned and many experienced leaders imprisoned or exiled. The rise of the fight for women's equality in the United States and other countries, combined with South African women's long record in resisting apartheid, led in 1990 to the ANC's explicit expansion of its central programmatic goal to that of a nonracial, democratic, and nonsexist South Africa.

Advances for national liberation in Asia, Latin America, and elsewhere in Africa have also been decisive in bringing about apartheid's demise. The 1988 defeat of South African troops at Cuito Cuanavale in Angola at the hands of Cuban, Angolan, and Namibian fighters altered the course of history in southern Africa. This reverse for Pretoria culminated the long fight that forced it to withdraw its troops from Angola and recognize Namibia's independence. As Mandela emphasized when he visited Cuba in 1991, the battle of Cuito Cuanavale was "a turning point in the struggle to free the continent and our country from the scourge of apartheid."

The student upsurge in Soweto in 1976 ignited a new rise of battles by South African workers and youth that the apartheid rulers have intermittently deflected through bloody repression and martial law, but have never been able to crush. Strengthened by the rising tide inside South Africa, solidarity with the antiapartheid struggle grew worldwide, compelling one government after another in the 1980s to stiffen economic and other sanctions on the apartheid regime. The effect of such measures, reinforced by spreading stagnation and sharpening competition in the world capitalist market, has sunk the South African economy in depression conditions for a decade.

Since 1990 the ANC has used the political space it has won to organize millions to participate in strikes, demonstrations, and other protests demanding the replacement of the apartheid regime by an interim government and democratically elected constituent assembly mandated to draft a new constitution. The ANC has looked to the organized power and discipline of the majority of the South African people—whether classified by Pretoria as African, Indian, Coloured, or white. It has led them in mobilizations and campaigns that have increased the self-confidence of a growing majority in their capacity to govern a new South Africa and to begin collectively changing the social conditions under which they live and work. Organizations of trade unionists, women, community residents, and youth have grown both in size and experience, as has the ANC itself.

Up to the beginning of the 1990s, the governing National

Party vowed it would never sit down at the same table with the ANC, which it labelled a "terrorist" organization. But Pretoria was forced into negotiations by the struggles of toilers and youth in the 1970s and 1980s and by its own international setbacks and isolation. Since then, the ANC-led democratic movement has won the repeal of apartheid laws segregating public facilities and housing, barring blacks from land ownership, and registering every resident under apartheid's reactionary "racial" classifications. Hundreds of political prisoners have been released, exiles have been allowed to return home, and much repressive legislation has been taken off the books.

At every point in the struggle, the National Party regime has sought to salvage what it can of white minority rule and privilege. In collusion with small sections of the black population based in the Bantustan administrations—social layers that feed off crumbs from apartheid's table—the Pretoria government has unleashed a bloody reign of terror in black townships and parts of the countryside. Thousands have been slaughtered in indiscriminate assaults on neighborhoods, commuter trains, and buses.

The aim of the regime is to limit effective political and trade union activity by South African working people, their mass organizations, and the ANC. Hypocritically blaming the deaths and maimings on the victims of these assaults, the rulers seek to exacerbate divisions within the oppressed majority while heightening fears and prejudices among whites.

In addition to covert involvement in massacres, Pretoria's cops and armed forces have killed many hundreds more by firing into crowds of demonstrators and strikers. Moreover, the officer corps of the regime's security forces provides a breeding ground—as well as a training school and arms depot—for ultrarightist paramilitary organizations with a base among a relatively small layer of whites.

In face of these enormous obstacles, the ANC has nonetheless retained the political initiative. It continues to draw new recruits into its branches and into a broadening alliance of democratic forces that encompasses the Congress of South African Trade Unions, the South African Communist Party, several Bantustan governments, and other organizations that have joined with the ANC in the Patriotic Front and in hundreds of ad hoc actions. As traced in the speeches by Mandela in these pages, the National Party regime has derailed negotiations time and again since early 1990, only to be forced back to the table under the pressure of mobilizations led by the ANC, other democratic organizations, and the trade unions.

Today, as this book goes to press, April 1994 has been set for the first nonracial elections in South African history, based on one person, one vote. Voters will elect a national assembly that will debate and draft the constitution of a nonracial democratic republic of South Africa. The ANC, still a banned organization barely three years ago, has launched an election campaign, with the goal of winning a decisive majority.

The day is closer than ever when it will be possible for a united South African nation to breathe political and social life into the historical fact asserted in the Freedom Charter adopted by the ANC and its allies in 1955: "that South Africa belongs to all who live in it, black and white." That will open the road to new efforts by South African working people, women, and youth to achieve a society free from all forms of oppression and exploitation. They will join with their brothers and sisters in many lands to resist the consequences on their lives and livelihoods of intensifying international competition for markets, the accelerating global economic and social crisis, and new wars and military aggression by the world's wealthiest and most powerful capitalist regimes.

*   *   *

Many of the speeches by Nelson Mandela published here were presented to mass rallies, community meetings, trade union conferences, student audiences, and other gatherings across South Africa. Others were presented to rallies in the

United States and Cuba, before the United States Congress and members of Parliament in Britain, and to meetings of the United Nations and Organization of African Unity. Also included are several press interviews given by Mandela both inside and outside South Africa, as well as letters and public appeals issued by him.

Two previous Pathfinder collections contain speeches by Mandela dating from his leadership of the ANC Youth League in the 1940s, to the struggles and frame-up trials of the 1950s and early 1960s, through the first months following his release from apartheid's prisons. These are *The Struggle Is My Life,* published in collaboration with the International Defence and Aid Fund for Southern Africa, and *Nelson Mandela: Speeches 1990.*

Pathfinder also publishes two Spanish-language books of the ANC leader's speeches: *Habla Nelson Mandela* and *Nelson Mandela: Intensifiquemos la lucha.* In addition, Pathfinder publishes, in English and Spanish, *How Far We Slaves Have Come! South Africa and Cuba in Today's World,* which includes the July 26, 1991, speeches by Nelson Mandela and Fidel Castro during a trip by Mandela to Cuba and other Latin American and Caribbean countries.

The ANC's Department of Information and Publicity provided many of the speeches and other documents in this collection, as did ANC offices in several other countries. The speeches from Mandela's March 1991 trip to Natal province were transcribed from tape recordings made while I was in South Africa earlier this year working on this book and reporting for the socialist newsweekly the *Militant;* other speeches in these pages have been transcribed from tape recordings as well. Interviews are reprinted by permission of the publications that first featured them.

Pathfinder gratefully acknowledges the assistance of Pallo Jordan, director of the ANC's Department of Information and Publicity, who helped compile many of the speeches for this collection; Jessie Duarte and Barbara Masekela of the ANC's Office of the President, who facilitated completion of this project; and Nigel Dennis and Andrew Mohamed of the Photo Unit of the ANC Department of Information and Publicity, who provided the cover portrait and many other photographs. Pathfinder would also like to thank Don Rojas, director of communications of the National Association for the Advancement of Colored People, for help in obtaining photographs.

Steve Clark
August 15, 1993

NELSON MANDELA

Born in 1918, Nelson Mandela joined the African National Congress in 1944. Together with Walter Sisulu, Oliver Tambo, and others, he helped form the ANC Youth League and was elected its general secretary in 1948 and its president in 1950.

He was a central organizer of the mass Defiance Campaign in 1952, in which thousands challenged the apartheid regime's internal passport laws and other measures. At the end of that year, Mandela was banned from attending public gatherings—a ban repeatedly renewed over the following nine years. Having been elected ANC deputy national president, Mandela was forced by the apartheid regime to resign officially from the ANC in 1953. Like many other ANC leaders, he was unable to attend the historic Congress of the People in 1955 that adopted the Freedom Charter. In 1956 Mandela and 155 others were arrested on charges of high treason; after four and a half years the defendants were acquitted.

After the ANC's banning in 1960, Mandela was forced to go underground in April 1961. In face of Pretoria's cutting off of all legal channels of protest and assembly, Mandela helped found Umkhonto we Sizwe (Spear of the Nation) late in 1961 to organize military training for armed operations against the apartheid regime.

In August 1962, after returning to South Africa from travels in Africa and Britain, Mandela was arrested on trumped-up charges and sentenced to five years' imprisonment. After other ANC leaders were arrested at Rivonia in 1963, Mandela—already in prison—was tried for sabotage. He was convicted and sentenced to life imprisonment along with seven others.

Held at the notorious Robben Island prison until 1982, Mandela was transferred to Pollsmoor and later Victor Verster prison. As the worldwide campaign for his freedom mounted, he was released without conditions on February 11, 1990.

Elected deputy president by the ANC National Executive Committee in March 1990, Mandela was chosen the organization's president at the ANC's 1991 national conference.

LIST OF INITIALS

ANC	African National Congress
APLA	Azanian People's Liberation Army
AWB	Afrikaner Weerstandsbeweging (Afrikaner Resistance Movement)
Azapo	Azanian People's Organisation
CCB	Civil Cooperation Bureau
Codesa	Convention for a Democratic South Africa
COSATU	Congress of South African Trade Unions
IFP	Inkatha Freedom Party
KZP	KwaZulu Police
MDM	Mass Democratic Movement
MK	Umkhonto we Sizwe (Spear of the Nation)
MPLA	Popular Movement for the Liberation of Angola
NAACP	National Association for the Advancement of Colored People
NEC	National Executive Committee (of ANC)
NP	National Party
NUM	National Union of Mineworkers
OAU	Organization of African Unity
PAC	Pan-Africanist Congress
PF	Patriotic Front
Renamo	Mozambique National Resistance
SACP	South African Communist Party
SADF	South African Defence Force (South Africa's army)
SAP	South African Police
UDF	United Democratic Front
UNITA	National Union for the Total Independence of Angola

CHRONOLOGY

1990

FEBRUARY 2—South African president F.W. de Klerk announces unbanning of ANC and other antiapartheid organizations and imminent release of Nelson Mandela.

FEBRUARY 11—Mandela is released from prison after more than 27 years.

MARCH 2—ANC National Executive Committee names Mandela ANC deputy president.

MARCH 21—Namibia wins independence from South African rule; Mandela attends ceremony in Windhoek.

MARCH 26—Police open fire on peaceful demonstration of 50,000 in Sebokeng, killing 17 and wounding over 400.

APRIL 5—Mandela meets with de Klerk to discuss ANC-government negotiations.

MAY 2-4—ANC and government delegations meet at Groote Schuur; reach agreement on removing obstacles to negotiations.

JUNE 7—State of emergency, in effect since 1986, is lifted in all but Natal province.

JUNE 19—Separate Amenities Act is repealed.

JUNE-JULY—Mandela undertakes six-week visit to 14 countries in Europe, North America, and Africa.

JULY 2—ANC and COSATU organize nationwide strike to protest violence organized by government and Inkatha.

JULY 22—A squad of Inkatha supporters, protected by heavily armed police and army units, attacks ANC supporters in Sebokeng, killing 30.

AUGUST 6-7—Meeting between ANC and government in Pretoria; government agrees to dates for release of prisoners, return of exiles, and repeal of repressive laws; ANC announces suspension of armed struggle.

SEPTEMBER 1—Official inquiry by Justice Richard J. Goldstone holds police responsible for March 1990 Sebokeng massacre.

OCTOBER 8—ANC initiates meeting with de Klerk to discuss government actions threatening negotiations.

OCTOBER 18—State of emergency is lifted in Natal.

DECEMBER 14-16—ANC holds consultative conference in Johannesburg.

1991

JANUARY 29—Mandela meets with Inkatha Freedom Party leader Mangosuthu Buthelezi. ANC and IFP agree to measures to end township violence.

FEBRUARY 1—ANC, PAC, and Azapo participate in joint protests demanding democratic elections on opening day of apartheid parliament.

APRIL 5—ANC announces it will pull out of constitutional talks unless the government takes steps to stop violence in the townships.

MAY 12—Hostel dwellers organized by Inkatha attack the Swanieville squatter camp near Krugersdorp, killing 27.

MAY 18—ANC breaks off talks with government until Pretoria takes measures to stop violence in the townships.

JUNE 5—Group Areas Act is repealed, along with Land Acts of 1913 and 1936.

JUNE 18—Population Registration Act is repealed.

JULY 2-7—ANC holds 48th National Conference. Mandela is elected ANC president.

JULY 19—Secret government funding to Inkatha is revealed ("Inkathagate").

JULY AUGUST Mandela visits Jamaica, Cuba, Mexico, Venezuela, and Brazil.

JULY 29—In response to Inkathagate exposures, Law and Order Minister Adriaan Vlok and Defense Minister Magnus Malan are relieved of their posts but retained in cabinet.

SEPTEMBER 14—National Peace Accord is signed between the government, ANC, Inkatha, and other forces.

OCTOBER 7—An armed attack on funeral for antiapartheid activist Sam Ntuli leaves 18 mourners dead in southern Transvaal.

OCTOBER 25-27—The Patriotic Front is formed at Durban conference of ANC, Pan-Africanist Congress, and other antiapartheid organizations.

NOVEMBER 4-5—ANC and COSATU organize two-day strike of 3.5 million workers against government imposition of value-added tax.

DECEMBER 20-21—The multiparty Convention for a Democratic South Africa (Codesa) meets; 17 organizations, including National Party government, issue Declaration of Intent for "a united, democratic, nonracial, and nonsexist state."

1992

MARCH 17—Whites-only referendum is held; a two-thirds majority endorses continued government negotiations on the country's future.

APRIL 23—Five police officers are found guilty of killing 11 in Trust Feed massacre of 1988.

MAY 15-16—Second meeting of Codesa is deadlocked by National Party demands for "power sharing" veto for white minority.

MAY 28-31—ANC holds policy conference.

JUNE 17—Over 45 are killed in massacre at Boipatong; evidence indicates government-Inkatha culpability.

JUNE 23—ANC suspends talks with government over Pretoria's involvement in violence against township residents; announces campaign of mass action.

JULY 15-16—United Nations Security Council holds special session on South Africa to discuss escalating violence; resolves to send special envoy.

JULY 26—Dr. Jonathan Gluckman, South African pathologist, reveals evidence of widespread police murder of prisoners.

AUGUST 3-9—ANC-led alliance culminates mass-action campaign to press demands on the white regime. Over two million participate in demonstrations and rallies throughout South Africa.

AUGUST 3-4—Four million workers observe the largest political strike in South African history.

AUGUST 5—Over 100,000 march on Union Buildings, seat of government in Pretoria.

SEPTEMBER 7—Troops in the Ciskei Bantustan open fire on ANC march of 70,000 in Bisho, killing dozens and wounding nearly 200.

SEPTEMBER 26—Record of Understanding is signed between Mandela and de Klerk, breaking the deadlock in negotiations.

OCTOBER—Mandela visits China.

OCTOBER 30—Over ANC objections, de Klerk pushes Indemnity Bill through Presidential Council, granting blanket amnesty to state officials involved in crimes.

NOVEMBER 16—Goldstone commission reveals pattern of overt and covert attacks by the South African army against the ANC.

DECEMBER 19—De Klerk announces dismissal of 23 officers, including six generals, but does not specify their actions or initiate any criminal proceedings.

1993

FEBRUARY 19-21—ANC-sponsored International Solidarity Conference in Johannesburg draws participants from 70 countries.

MARCH 5-6—Multiparty negotiations resume as 26 political parties meet in Johannesburg.

APRIL 10—ANC and Communist Party leader Chris Hani is assassinated by a white ultrarightist cadre.

APRIL 14—Millions strike to protest Hani assassination.

APRIL 24—ANC national chairperson Oliver Tambo dies.

JUNE 4—A meeting of parties and political organizations sets April 27, 1994, as tentative date for South Africa's first nonracial elections.

JUNE 25—Armed right-wing supporters break into building in Johannesburg where multiparty negotiations are taking place; police and security forces make no effort to halt the attack.

JULY 2—The April 27, 1994, election date is ratified by multiparty meeting.

JUNE 30-JULY 12—Mandela visits six U.S. cities to raise support for ANC election campaign.

Now is the time to intensify the struggle

SPEECH IN CAPE TOWN FOLLOWING RELEASE FROM PRISON, FEBRUARY 11, 1990

A mass rally at Cape Town's City Hall greeted Mandela on the day of his release from nearby Victor Verster prison. In addition to being heard by the tens of thousands in attendance, his address to the rally, published below, was televised and seen by millions throughout the world.

Amandla! [Power!] *i-Africa!*

Friends, comrades, and fellow South Africans:

I greet you all in the name of peace, democracy, and freedom for all. I stand here before you not as a prophet but as a humble servant of you, the people. Your tireless and heroic sacrifices have made it possible for me to be here today. I therefore place the remaining years of my life in your hands.

On this day of my release, I extend my sincere and warmest gratitude to the millions of my compatriots and those in every corner of the globe who have campaigned tirelessly for my release.

I extend special greetings to the people of Cape Town, the city which has been my home for three decades. Your mass marches and other forms of struggle have served as a constant source of strength to all political prisoners.

I salute the African National Congress. It has fulfilled our every expectation in its role as leader of the great march to freedom.

I salute our president, Comrade Oliver Tambo, for leading the ANC even under the most difficult circumstances.

I salute the rank-and-file members of the ANC. You have sacrificed life and limb in the pursuit of the noble cause of our struggle.

I salute combatants of Umkhonto we Sizwe, like Solomon Mahlangu and Ashley Kriel, who have paid the ultimate price for the freedom of all South Africans.

I salute the South African Communist Party for its sterling contribution to the struggle for democracy. You have survived forty years of unrelenting persecution. The memory of great Communists like Moses Kotane, Yusuf Dadoo, Bram Fischer, and Moses Mabhida will be cherished for generations to come.

I salute General Secretary Joe Slovo, one of our finest patriots. We are heartened by the fact that the alliance between ourselves and the party remains as strong as it always was.

I salute the United Democratic Front, the National Education Crisis Committee, the South African Youth Congress, the Transvaal and Natal Indian congresses, and COSATU [Congress of South African Trade Unions], and the many other formations of the Mass Democratic Movement.

I also salute the Black Sash and the National Union of South African Students. We note with pride that you have acted as the conscience of white South Africans. Even during the darkest days in the history of our struggle, you held the flag of liberty high. The large-scale mass mobilization of the past few years is one of the key factors which led to the opening of the final chapter of our struggle.

I extend my greetings to the working class of our country. Your organized strength is the pride of our movement. You remain the most dependable force in the struggle to end exploitation and oppression.

I pay tribute to the many religious communities who carried the campaign for justice forward when the organizations of our people were silenced.

I greet the traditional leaders of our country. Many among you continue to walk in the footsteps of great heroes like Hintsa and Sekhukhune.[1]

I pay tribute to the endless heroes of youth. You, the young lions, have energized our entire struggle.

I pay tribute to the mothers and wives and sisters of our nation. You are the rock-hard foundation of our struggle. Apartheid has inflicted more pain on you than on anyone else.

On this occasion, we thank the world community for their great contribution to the antiapartheid struggle. Without your support our struggle would not have reached this advanced stage.

The sacrifice of the Frontline States will be remembered by South Africans forever.[2]

My salutations will be incomplete without expressing my deep appreciation for the strength given to me during my long and lonely years in prison by my beloved wife and family. I am convinced that your pain and suffering was far greater than my own.

Before I go any further, I wish to make the point that I intend making only a few preliminary comments at this stage. I will make a more complete statement only after I have had the opportunity to consult with my comrades.

Today the majority of South Africans, black and white, recognize that apartheid has no future. It has to be ended by our own decisive mass action in order to build peace and security. The mass campaigns of defiance and other actions of our organization and people can only culminate in the establishment of democracy.

The apartheid destruction on our subcontinent is incalculable. The fabric of family life of millions of my people has been shattered. Millions are homeless and unemployed. Our economy lies in ruins and our people are embroiled in political strife.

Our resort to the armed struggle in 1961 with the formation of the military wing of the ANC, Umkhonto we Sizwe, was a purely defensive action against the violence of apartheid.

The factors which necessitated the armed struggle still exist today. We have no option but to continue. We express the hope that a climate conducive to a negotiated settlement will be created soon so that there may no longer be the need for the armed struggle.

I am a loyal and disciplined member of the African National Congress. I am therefore in full agreement with all of its objectives, strategies, and tactics.

The need to unite the people of our country is as important a task now as it always has been. No individual leader is able to take on this enormous task on his own. It is our task as leaders to place our views before our organization and to allow the democratic structures to decide on the way forward.

On the question of democratic practice, I feel duty-bound to make the point that a leader of the movement is a person who has been democratically elected at a national conference. This is a principle which must be upheld without any exceptions.

Today, I wish to report to you that my talks with the government have been aimed at normalizing the political situation in the country. We have not as yet begun discussing the basic demands of the struggle. I wish to stress that I myself had at no time entered into negotiations about the future of our country, except to insist on a meeting between the ANC and the government.

Mr. de Klerk has gone further than any other Nationalist president in taking real steps to normalize the situation. However, there are further steps as outlined in the Harare Declaration that have to be met before negotiations on the basic demands of our people can begin.[3]

I reiterate our call for, inter alia, the immediate ending of the state of emergency and the freeing of all, and not only some, political prisoners.

Only such a normalized situation which allows for free political activity can allow us to consult our people in order to obtain a mandate. The people need to be consulted on who will negotiate and on the content of such negotiations.

Negotiations cannot take place above the heads or behind the backs of our people. It is our belief that the future of our country can only be determined by a body which is democratically elected on a nonracial basis.

Negotiations on the dismantling of apartheid will have to address the overwhelming demand of our people for a democratic, nonracial, and unitary South Africa. There must be an end to white monopoly on political power and a fundamental restructuring of our political and economic systems to ensure that the inequalities of apartheid are addressed and our society thoroughly democratized.

It must be added that Mr. de Klerk himself is a man of integrity who is acutely aware of the dangers of a public figure not honoring his undertakings. But as an organization, we base our policy and strategy on the harsh reality we are faced with, and this reality is that we are still suffering under the policy of the Nationalist government.

Our struggle has reached a decisive moment. We call on our people to seize this moment so that the process towards democracy is rapid and uninterrupted. We have waited too long for our freedom. We can no longer wait. Now is the time to intensify the struggle on all fronts.

To relax our efforts now would be a mistake which generations to come will not be able to forgive. The sight of freedom looming on the horizon should encourage us to redouble our efforts. It is only through disciplined mass action that our victory can be assured.

We call on our white compatriots to join us in the shaping of a new South Africa. The freedom movement is the political home for you too.

We call on the international community to continue the campaign to isolate the apartheid regime. To lift sanctions now would be to run the risk of aborting the process towards the complete eradication of apartheid.

Our march to freedom is irreversible. We must not allow fear to stand in our way.

Universal suffrage on a common voters' roll in a united, democratic, and nonracial South Africa is the only way to peace and racial harmony.

In conclusion, I wish to go to my own words during my trial in 1964. They are as true today as they were then. I quote:

"I have fought against white domination, and I have fought against black domination. I have cherished the idea of a democratic and free society in which all persons live together in harmony and with equal opportunities. It is an ideal which I hope to live for and to achieve. But if needs be, it is an ideal for which I am prepared to die."[4]

Our struggle is against all forms of racism

SPEECH IN HARLEM, NEW YORK, JUNE 21, 1990

The following speech was given to a crowd of 100,000 in Harlem, New York, during an eight-city tour of the United States.

Chairman; distinguished guests:

We are very happy to be here this evening and it gives me immense pleasure to greet all of you on behalf of the leaders and members of the African National Congress and the Mass Democratic Movement.

It is with great joy that I speak to you this evening. My only regret is that I am not able to embrace each and every one of you.

Whilst my comrades and I were in prison, we followed closely your own struggle against the injustices of racist discrimination and economic inequality. We were and are aware of the resistance of the people of Harlem and continue to be inspired by your indomitable fighting spirit.

I am able to speak to you because of the mass resistance of our people and the unceasing solidarity of millions throughout the world. It is you, the working people of Harlem, that helped to make it happen. It is you, the clergy and believers, who helped to make it happen. It is you, the professionals and intellectuals, that helped to make it happen. It is you, the struggling women, who helped to make it happen.

The kinship that the ANC feels for the people of Harlem goes deeper than skin color. It is the kinship of our shared historical experience and the kinship of the solidarity of the victims of blind prejudice and hatred. To our people, Harlem symbolizes the strength and beauty in resistance, and you have taught us that out of resistance to injustice comes renaissance, renewal, and rebirth.

From the beginning of this century, we have been inspired by great antiracist freedom fighters like W.E.B. Du Bois, Sojourner Truth, Paul Robeson, Rosa Parks, Martin Luther King, Marcus Garvey, Fannie Lou Hamer, Adam Clayton Powell, Malcolm X, Harriet Tubman, and many others.[5]

At the turning of this century, W.E.B. Du Bois, with great foresight, predicted that "the problem of the twentieth century is the problem of the color line." As we enter the last decade of the twentieth century, it is intolerable and unacceptable that the cancer of racism is still eating away at the fabric of societies in different parts of our planet.

It remains one of the most important global issues confronting all humanity, black and white. It is a struggle that must involve people of all walks of life. It is a struggle that must involve people of different colors, religions, and creeds.

All of us, descendants of Africa, know only too well that racism demeans the victims and dehumanizes its perpetrators. Racism, we must emphasize, pollutes the atmosphere of human relations and poisons the minds of the backward, the bigoted, and the prejudiced.

On my way from the airport through the streets of New York yesterday, a slogan on the sweatshirt of a young woman moved me. It said, "Black by nature, proud by choice."

The oppressed people of South Africa—living in a country in which institutionalized racism permeates every pore of our lives and even in death, since we have segregated cemeteries—are acutely sensitive to pain and injuries suffered by people of color. It should therefore be clear that all antiracist fighters, wherever they may be, will always find a friend and ally in our people, in our movement—the ANC.

For us the struggle against racism has assumed the proportions of a crusade. We, all of us, black and white, should spare no effort in our struggle against all forms and manifestations of racism, wherever and whenever it rears its ugly head.

The revolt of our people continues in the land of apartheid. Our struggle is the struggle to erase the color line that all too often determines who is rich and who is poor; that all too often decides who lives in luxury and who lives in squalor; that all too often determines who shall get food, clothing, and health care; and that all too often decides who will live and who will die.

We continue to live in a country enslaved by apartheid. The vote, the land, economic wealth, and power remain a monopoly of the white minority. The only monopoly blacks have is the monopoly of ghettoes, of deprived and suffering children, the monopoly of millions of unemployed, the monopoly of urban slums, rural starvation, low wages, and the bullets and clubs of too many trigger-happy police.

But, my dear brothers and sisters, comrades and friends, I am here to report to you that due to the enormous sacrifices of our people and the solidarity and support of people like you and the international community, apartheid is nearing its end.

We are on the threshold of momentous changes. Last month, at the initiative of the ANC, we met with President de Klerk and his colleagues. It was not a meeting of master and servant. It was a meeting of equals. At that meeting we reached an agreement on removing those obstacles, harboring the creation of a climate conducive to negotiations. We are confident that the agreement can be implemented in full as a matter of urgency. Equally, we are confident that you will continue to support us in this fight.

Let me say, with all sincerity, that we do not doubt the integrity of President de Klerk and his colleagues. Equally, we welcome the moves to repeal certain racist legislation and the state of emergency in the greater part of our country.[6] Yet until the agreement has been implemented in full and there is profound and irreversible change, international pressure must be intensified and sanctions maintained. Keep the pressure on apartheid!

It is regrettable that in South Africa there is still a minority of a minority violently and vehemently opposed to a negotiated resolution of the conflict. Too many of them are heavily armed. Too many of them are to be found in the police force. Too many of them are mobilized and organized into paramilitary formations. They have the capacity, and it seems the will, to commit unspeakable atrocities.

But they will not deflect us from our chosen path. For our part, we understand and are sensitive to the fears about the future of many of our white compatriots. The ANC is profoundly committed and determined to do all we can to demonstrate that they have nothing to fear from a nonracial, nonsexist democracy. That indeed, only in a nonracial, nonsexist, united, and democratic South Africa will they be freed from the prison that is the apartheid system.

The ANC and the Mass Democratic Movement represent an unequaled diversity of cultures, languages, religion, tradition, and class. I am happy to report to you that there are increasing numbers of whites who not only realize that apartheid is unjust and a crime, but who are ready to be in the same trenches as their fellow black sisters and brothers.

As the struggle intensifies, the social base of the present government will be reduced, and more and more whites will join the ANC as equals, with equal duties, obligations, and responsibilities.

We are on the verge of victory. But the last mile of the freedom road could prove to be the most difficult and the most intractable. Thus our struggle cries out for organization, discipline, and unity. Struggle that does not strengthen organization can lead to a blind alley. Struggle without discipline can lead to anarchy. Struggle without unity enables the other side to pick us off one by one.

We are, therefore, deeply involved in trying to bring about the unity in action of all those opposed to apartheid. Any individual, any group, any organization that seeks genuine unity in action will find a ready partner in the ANC.

We are fighting for a democratic South Africa. This means first and foremost, one person, one vote on a nonracial voters' roll. On this there can be no compromise.

For us, political power should be the basis for the economic empowerment of people. It is outrageous that in the richest country on our continent, with its vast economic resources, that millions should be deprived of the basic necessities of life. The gap between the haves and the have-nots, black and white, is totally unacceptable. Any new democratic state must address this historic injustice as a matter of urgency. It also means that we are irrevocably committed to realizing a society in which the fruits of our people's labor shall be distributed equitably. That the striking imbalance between the wealth of the minority and the poverty of the majority has to be addressed.

To bring an end to this old, unjust, inequitable social order, and bring into being a new one characterized by the notions of justice and equity, requires that we address the questions of the enormous economic power wielded by and concentrated in the hands of a minority of a minority.

Brothers and sisters, comrades and friends, victory is in sight. The light at the end of the tunnel is now beckoning. But we are not yet there. To reach the end of the tunnel requires that we intensify the struggle on all fronts. It requires that we make the necessary sacrifices. It requires that we remain unrelenting in pursuit of our goals.

The masses of the people of our country are ready for the final battle. Let me assure you they will not flinch from that last battle. It is their heroism, courage, and unquenchable fighting spirit which has earned them the respect and admiration of the international community. Our people symbolize the spirit of resistance and no surrender.

Let me also assure you that the ANC will never be found wanting. Let me assure you that the ANC will never rest until we have accomplished our goals. This is a pledge that I make on behalf of all the freedom fighters in the ANC.

Brothers and sisters, comrades and friends, I am here to claim you because in the twenty-seven years of my imprisonment—indeed, throughout the life of the ANC—you have claimed our struggle. There is an umbilical cord that ties us together. So let us act in unity. Let us double and redouble our efforts to bring to a speedy end this shameful blot on humanity, this crime against humanity.

At the Rivonia trial, at which I was sentenced to life imprisonment, I said from the dock, "During my lifetime I have dedicated myself to this struggle of the African people. I have fought against white domination and I have fought against black domination. I have cherished the ideal of a democratic and free society in which all persons live together in harmony and with equal opportunities. It is an ideal which I hope to live for and to achieve. But if needs be, it is an ideal for which I am prepared to die."

To you, the wonderful citizens of New York, I declare that I stand by every word of my statement from the dock.

Death to racism!

Glory to the sisterhood and brotherhood of peoples throughout the world!

Thank you very much.

Peace will not come to our country until apartheid is ended

ADDRESS TO U.S. CONGRESS, JUNE 26, 1990

The speech below was given to a joint session of the U.S. Congress in Washington, D.C.

Mr. Speaker; Mr. President; esteemed members of the United States Congress; Your Excellencies, ambassadors and members of the diplomatic corps; distinguished guests; ladies and gentlemen:

It is a fact of the human condition that each shall, like a meteor—a mere brief passing moment in time and space—flit across the human stage and pass out of existence. Even the golden lads and lasses, as much as the chimney sweepers, come and tomorrow are no more.[7] After them all, they leave the people: enduring, multiplying, permanent—except to the extent that the same humanity might abuse its own genius to immolate life itself.

And so we have come to Washington, in the District of Columbia, and into these hallowed chambers of the United States Congress, not as pretenders to greatness, but as a parti-

cle of a people whom we know to be noble and heroic, enduring, multiplying, permanent—rejoicing in the expectation and
knowledge that their humanity will be reaffirmed and en-
larged by open and unfettered communion with the nations of
the world.

We have come here to tell you, and through you your own
people, who are equally noble and heroic, of the troubles and
trials, the fond hopes and aspirations of the people from
whom we originate. We believe that we know it as a fact, that
your kind and moving invitation to us to speak here derived
from your own desire to convey a message to our people, and
according to your humane purposes, to give them an opportunity to say what they want of you and what they want to
make of their relationship with you.

Our people demand democracy. Our country, which continues to bleed and suffer pain, needs democracy. It cries out
for the situation where the law will decree that the freedom
to speak of freedom constitutes the very essence of legality
and the very thing that makes for the legitimacy of the constitutional order.

It thirsts for the situation where those who are entitled by
law to carry arms, as the forces of national security and law
and order, will not turn their weapons against the citizens
simply because the citizens assert that equality, liberty, and
the pursuit of happiness are fundamental human rights
which are not only inalienable, but must, if necessary, be defended with the weapons of war.

We fight for and visualize a future in which all shall, without regard to race, color, creed, or sex, have the right to vote
and to be voted into all elective organs of state.

We are engaged in struggle to ensure that the rights of every individual are guaranteed and protected through a democratic constitution, the rule of law, an entrenched bill of
rights, which should be enforced by an independent judiciary, as well as a multiparty political system.

Mr. Speaker, we are acutely conscious of the fact that we
are addressing a historic institution, for whose creation and

integrity many men and women lost their lives in the War of Independence, the Civil War, and the war against nazism and fascism. That very history demands that we address you with respect and candor and without any attempt to dissemble.

What we have said concerning the political arrangements we seek for our country is seriously meant. It is an outcome for which many of us went to prison, for which many have died in police cells, on the gallows, in our towns and villages, and in the countries of southern Africa. Indeed, we have even had our political representatives killed in countries as far away from South Africa as France.

Unhappily, our people continue to die to this day, victims of armed agents of the state who are still determined to turn their guns against the very idea of a nonracial democracy. But this is the perspective which we trust Congress will feel happy to support and encourage, using the enormous weight of its prestige and authority as an eminent representative of democratic practice.

To deny any person their human rights is to challenge their very humanity. To impose on them a wretched life of hunger and deprivation is to dehumanize them. But such has been the terrible fate of all black persons in our country under the system of apartheid.

The extent of the deprivation of millions of people has to be seen to be believed. The injury is made more intolerable by the opulence of our white compatriots and the deliberate distortion of the economy to feed that opulence.

The process of the reconstruction of South African society must and will also entail the transformation of its economy. We need a strong and growing economy. We require an economy that is able to address the needs of all the people of our country; that can provide food, houses, education, health services, social security, and everything that makes human life human, that makes life joyful and not a protracted encounter with hopelessness and despair.

We believe that the fact of the apartheid structure of the South African economy and the enormous and pressing needs of the people make it inevitable that the democratic government will intervene in this economy, acting through the elected parliament. We have put the matter to the business community of our country that the need for a public sector is one of the elements in a many-sided strategy of economic development and restructuring that has to be considered by us all, including the private sector.

The ANC holds no ideological positions which dictate that it must adopt a policy of nationalization. But the ANC also holds the view that there is no self-regulating mechanism within the South African economy which will, on its own, ensure growth with equity.

At the same time, we take it as given that the private sector is an engine of the growth and development which is critical to the success of the mixed economy we hope to see in the future South Africa. We are accordingly committed to the creation of the situation in which business people, both South African and foreign, have confidence in the security of their investments, are assured of a fair rate of return on their capital, and do business in conditions of stability and peace.

We must also make the point, very firmly, that the political settlement, and democracy itself, cannot survive unless the material needs of the people, the bread-and-butter issues, are addressed as part of the process of change and as a matter of urgency. It should never be that the anger of the poor should be the finger of accusation pointed at all of us because we failed to respond to the cries of the people for food, for shelter, for the dignity of the individual.

We shall need your support to achieve the postapartheid economic objectives which are an intrinsic part of the process of the restoration of the human rights of the people of South Africa. We would like to approach the issue of our economic cooperation not as a relationship between donor and recipient, between a dependent and a benefactor.

We would like to believe that there is a way in which we could structure this relationship so that we do indeed benefit from your enormous resources in terms of your capital, technology, all-round expertise, your enterprising spirit, and your markets.

This relationship should, however, be one from which your people also derive benefit, so that we who are fighting to liberate the very spirit of an entire people from the bondage of the arrogance of the ideology and practice of white supremacy do not build a relationship of subservient dependency and fawning gratitude.

One of the benefits that should accrue to both our peoples and to the rest of the world should surely be that this complex South African society, which has known nothing but racism for three centuries, should be transformed into an oasis of good race relations, where the black shall to the white be sister and brother, a fellow South African, an equal human being—both citizens of the world.

To destroy racism in the world, we together must expunge apartheid racism in South Africa. Justice and liberty must be our tool, prosperity and happiness our weapon.

Mr. Speaker, distinguished guests, representatives of the American people:

You know this more than we do, that peace is its own reward. Our own fate, borne by a succession of generations that reach backwards into centuries, has been nothing but tension, conflict, and death. In a sense, we do not know the meaning of peace, except in the imagination. But because we have not known true peace in its real meaning, because for centuries generations have had to bury the victims of state violence, we have fought for the right to experience peace.

On the initiative of the ANC the process towards the conclusion of a peaceful settlement has started. According to a logic dictated by our situation, we are engaged in an effort which includes the removal of obstacles to negotiations. This will be followed by a negotiated determination of the mechanism which will draw up the new constitution.

This should lead to the formation of this constitution-making institution and therefore the elaboration and adoption of a democratic constitution. Elections would then be held on the basis of this constitution and, for the first time, South Africa would have a body of lawmakers which would, like yourselves, be mandated by the whole people.

Despite the admitted commitment of President de Klerk to walk this road with us, and despite our acceptance of his integrity and the honesty of his purposes, we would be fools to believe that the road ahead of us is without major hurdles. Too many among our white compatriots are steeped in the ideology of racism to admit easily that change must come.

Tragedy may yet sully the future we pray and work for if these slaves of the past take up arms in a desperate effort to resist the process which must lead to the democratic transformation of our country. For those who care to worry about violence in our country, as we do, it is at these forces that they should focus their attention, a process in which we are engaged.

We must contend still with the reality that South Africa is a country in the grip of the apartheid crime against humanity. The consequences of this continue to be felt not only within our borders but throughout southern Africa—which continues to harvest the bitter fruits of conflict and war, especially in Mozambique and Angola. Peace will not come to our country and region until the apartheid system is ended.

Therefore, we say we still have a struggle on our hands. Our common and noble efforts to abolish the system of white minority domination must continue.

We are encouraged and strengthened by the fact of the agreement between ourselves, this Congress, as well as President Bush and his administration, that sanctions remain in place. Sanctions should remain in place because the purpose for which they were imposed has not yet been achieved.

We have yet to arrive at the point when we can say that South Africa is set on an irreversible course leading to its transformation into a united, democratic, and nonracial country. We plead that you cede the prerogative to the people of South Africa to determine the moment when it will be said that profound changes have occurred and an irreversible process achieved, enabling you and the rest of the international community to lift sanctions.

We would like to take this opportunity to thank you all for the principled struggle you waged which resulted in the adoption of the historic Comprehensive Anti-Apartheid Act, which made such a decisive contribution to the process of moving our country forward towards negotiations.[8] We request that you go further and assist us with the material resources which will enable us to promote the peace process and meet other needs which arise from the changing situation you have helped bring about.

The stand you took established the understanding among the millions of our people that here we have friends, here we have fighters against racism who feel hurt because we are hurt, who seek our success because they too seek the victory of democracy over tyranny.

And here I speak not only about you, members of the United States Congress, but also of the millions of people throughout this great land who stood up and engaged the apartheid system in struggle, the masses who have given us such strength and joy by the manner in which they received us since we arrived in this country.

Mr. Speaker, Mr. President, senators and representatives:

We went to jail because it was impossible to sit still while the obscenity of the apartheid system was being imposed on our people. It would have been immoral to keep quiet while a racist tyranny sought to reduce an entire people into a status worse than that of the beasts of the forest. It would have been an act of treason against the people and against our conscience to allow fear and the drive towards self-preservation to dominate our behavior, obliging us to absent ourselves from the struggle for democracy and human rights, not only in our country but throughout the world.

We could not have made an acquaintance through literature with human giants such as George Washington, Abraham Lincoln, and Thomas Jefferson and not been moved to act as they were moved to act.

We could not have heard of and admired John Brown, Sojourner Truth, Frederick Douglass, W.E.B. Du Bois, Marcus
Garvey, Martin Luther King, Jr., and others, and not be
moved to act as they were moved to act.[9]

We could not have known of your Declaration of Independence and not elected to join in the struggle to guarantee
the people life, liberty, and the pursuit of happiness.

We are grateful to you all that you persisted in your resolve to have us and other political prisoners released from
jail. You have given us the gift and privilege to rejoin our people, yourselves, and the rest of the international community
in the common effort to transform South Africa into a
united, democratic, and nonracial country. You have given us
the power to join hands with all people of conscience to fight
for the victory of democracy and human rights throughout
the world.

We are glad that you merged with our people to make it
possible for us to emerge from the darkness of the prison cell
and join the contemporary process of the renewal of the
world. We thank you most sincerely for all you have done,
and count on you to persist in your noble endeavors to free
the rest of our political prisoners and to emancipate our people from the larger prison that is apartheid South Africa.

The day may not be far when we will borrow the words of
Thomas Jefferson and speak of the will of the South African
nation. In the exercise of that will by this united nation of
black and white people, it must surely be that there will be
born a country on the southern tip of Africa which you will
be proud to call a friend and an ally because of its contribution to the universal striving towards liberty, human rights,
prosperity, and peace among the peoples.

Let that day come now. Let us keep our arms locked together so that we form a solid phalanx against racism to ensure that that day comes now. By our common actions let
us ensure that justice triumphs without delay. When that has
come to pass, then shall we all be entitled to acknowledge the
salute when others say of us, "Blessed are the peacemakers."

Thank you for your kind invitation to speak here today and thank you for your welcome and the attention you have accorded our simple message. Thank you.

We cannot afford to stand divided

ADDRESS TO ORGANIZATION OF AFRICAN UNITY, SEPTEMBER 8, 1990

The following is the concluding section of a speech delivered to a meeting of the Organization of African Unity (OAU) in Kampala, Uganda. Earlier Mandela reviewed the escalating violence in South Africa's black townships and the government's responsibility for it, and reiterated the need to maintain international economic sanctions against the apartheid regime.

A matter which has been raised by the two previous speakers here is one of the unity of the blacks, the unity of the liberation movement. We regard this as very important, but our starting point is that in South Africa the people are united. Huge rallies that we have held since October last year have never been seen in the history of the country.

We have held a number of mass actions which have had a very important impact. We have defied apartheid in hospitals, hospitals which are reserved for whites. Our people have gone to these hospitals and demanded and got treatment. The result is that the government has now declared apartheid in hospitals dead, although in practice you still find white hospitals in which there is a great deal of reluctance to admit black patients. "There are not sufficient beds, there is not enough equipment and you are not so sick, please go home." But nevertheless, in rhetoric, apartheid in hospitals has been eliminated.

Our people have staged strikes which have been very successful from the point of view of the conservative press. If they have been reported even, figures indicate the response of the masses of the people to these calls sometimes 100 percent, other times 90 percent. An organization which is able to have such an impact has actually succeeded in uniting the people.

There is no country anywhere in the world which hasn't got various parties. There is an instance of different parties in the liberation movement of South Africa today. It does not indicate that the people of South Africa are not united. We are united, but we take into account the fact that there are other political organizations whose members have sacrificed like all of us. We feel it is only fair to recognize their contributions and to seek unity with them.

But there is a problem. We can only approach these organizations and ask them to join us that we should work together. We can't do more. We have approached these organizations—some of them are here—and said to them: Let's pool our resources. The situation in the country today is such that we can't afford to stand divided.

They don't grasp the importance of us pooling our resources at the present moment. I, as an individual, have made several efforts to see the leaders of these organizations. Some, of course, have responded very well. We are discussing with them. We have formed joint structures with them.

But there are others here who have persistently taken up the attitude of refusing to sit down to talk with us. On the contrary, they are using the mass media, the white mass media, to air differences amongst us without coming to us to say: "Here are our differences—can we resolve them?" It is that type of attitude, where organizations which are part of the liberation movement go to the mass media to try and solve the problems facing the liberation movement for mere publicity stunts and attacking other organizations in the mass media.

We have warned against this. And some other organizations have heeded the warning, but others have not. They don't understand what I am telling you today: that in South Africa we have the rise of the Renamo movement. They just don't appreciate that. Their ferocity is directed almost exclusively on the ANC and allied organizations, and our appeals that we should sit together to examine our problem together fall on deaf ears.

When I returned from overseas, we invited all organizations in the country—political, labor organizations, religious organizations, academic, and others—[to a meeting] in order to give them [a report on our campaign] to maintain sanctions and for resources. We are keen not only to share experiences at what the international community said in regard to sanctions; we are even prepared to share resources, because we are in a far better position to get resources from the international community. We are prepared to share even that.

All these organizations turned up except one, and only one: the PAC [Pan-Africanist Congress]. They refused, and their reason for refusing was difficult to understand, because among the reasons they advanced was the fact that we have invited other organizations as well, and they couldn't participate in that type of invitation.

We stretch out our hands of friendship to them. We say: Let us forget the past. We are brothers, we are sisters, we are one flesh and blood; our community is in danger, our people are being killed every day. If there is anything which can be dangerous to the future of South Africa, it is the fact that we should be squabbling amongst ourselves when Rome is burning.

I appeal to them, as I have done on many occasions in South Africa, to forget the past. Let us hold our hands, let us address this problem together. If we stand together, victory of the liberation movement is assured, because what has happened in other countries where faceless elements have destabilized those countries, their political system, their economic organization, is because there were individuals who were prepared to shout in the mass media to oppose the established government of those countries. And when that happened, reactionary forces throughout the world put all their resources in the hands of those elements.

There is no country which faces as much danger in this regard as South Africa, and it is therefore imperative for the liberation movement as a whole to pool their resources. That is our message. That is the spirit in which I make this appeal to them.

Thank you very much.

The women's movement must play a central role

The following remarks were made at the opening of the ANC's Constitutional Committee Workshop on Gender, entitled "Today and Tomorrow Towards the Women's Rights Charter."

Comrade chair; distinguished guests; delegates and friends:

For me it is a privilege to be accorded this opportunity of opening the Workshop on Gender Issues. I am humbled and honored by this gesture on the part of the ANC's Women's League and the Constitutional Committee.

Many a time we have stated that the balance of forces has changed in favor of the progressive forces. The regime has finally realized that it can no longer continue to impose its rule on the majority of our people without their consent. This realization has been brought about by the heroic struggle that has been waged by our people over many decades. Therefore, as we begin to devise a new constitution for our country, it is fitting and proper for us to pay tribute to all those patriots whose contribution has made this possible.

Throughout the history of our struggle, women have

played a prominent role. To mention but a few: our stalwarts such as Charlotte Maxeke, Dora Tamana, Ruth First, Annie Silinga, Mary Moodley, Lilian Ngoyi, Kate Molale, and Florence Mophosho. Their fighting spirit lives on in the contribution of such eminent women as Mrs. M. Zihlangu, Frances Baard, Helen Joseph, Ray Simons, Dorothy Nyembe, Gertrude Shope, and many others.

We salute the mothers of the cadres of Umkhonto we Sizwe, whose children have fallen in battle both inside and outside South Africa. We pay tribute to the mothers of all those who died in the course of struggle for freedom and against the apartheid system. We commend also those white mothers who stood by their sons for refusing to be conscripted into the apartheid army. We salute the wives and mothers whose husbands and sons still remain in prison despite the solemn undertakings of the apartheid regime. We salute those brave daughters of this country who are presently in prison for their commitment to a just, nonracial, and democratic South Africa. Special mention should be made here of those on death row. To them we vow: we shall not rest until all political prisoners have been released. We call upon the government to release all these people unconditionally—today and not tomorrow!

The South African society is profoundly patriarchal. While ultimate responsibility falls squarely on the shoulders of the ruling circles of this country, we men, both black and white, including many in the ANC, should accept our share of responsibility for the sexist stereotyping of women in our society and in our homes. This degradation of women finds reflection in every sphere of life.

Women in South Africa constitute the majority population; yet, in general, their status is one of powerlessness. They are underrepresented in all sectors of our society, except its lower reaches. This, unfortunately also applies to the leadership of the ANC and all democratic organizations of this country. Can we seriously claim to be democrats when in our practices we continue to treat women as underlings? Is it not time that we began seriously to address the inequalities that exist between men and women?

I am pleased to say that, though we still need to do a great deal, the African National Congress is in the process of addressing this issue. The timing of this workshop is a conscious effort on the part of the ANC to give prominence to the gender question. The past and present constitutions of South Africa have been based on discrimination, thereby denying the majority of our people their fundamental rights, which should be basic in modern democracies.

For decades institutionalized racism has been applied by the apartheid state to effect the most brutal forms of social engineering known to humanity. Need I remind anyone at this workshop that millions of black women remain illiterate in the age of advanced education and technology? That black women, in thousands, occupy the lowest ranks in employment? That black women are underpaid and are most brutally exploited as farm laborers and domestic workers? For generations, black women have been the most oppressed group in our society.

The majority of the African people are to be found in settlements of the homeless. I have found that the majority of the households in these settlements are made up of female-headed families. As single parents, these women have the added burden of bringing up children in conditions of extreme deprivation and squalor.

This workshop is charged with the task of addressing gender inequalities in the context of the actual situation of women under apartheid and developing the best possible mechanism for redressing the problems women presently experience. We must begin to discuss these issues in greater detail. I am aware that these debates commenced two years ago, after the ANC issued its constitutional guidelines. The working document on a bill of rights, released for discussion recently by the ANC's Constitutional Committee, should be tested against the actual demands the women of this country are making. This workshop is the first that has been organized since its publication.

The ANC, as well as other progressive organizations, should ensure that the women's movement in our country is not only strong but also united so that it can play a central role in the affairs of the organization and the country. From our experiences in the ANC, and lessons learnt from other parts of the world, we have come to realize that it is not just the provisions contained in the constitution that bring about true equality between men and women in a society. It is rather a preparedness to struggle on the part of the women's movement and all democrats.

The constitution should guarantee the equality between men and women and should seek to create conditions which entrench and establish these rights. We must explore whether the principles we wish to see enshrined in the constitution would not be enriched by a charter of women's rights, focusing on all the concrete areas where the law and public policy can play a role in affecting women's lives. We in the ANC, as democrats, should not be found wanting in promoting true equality in our lives, daily practices, as well as in the home.

I am informed that women from the various regions are represented at this workshop. I have been advised that progressive scholars are to participate at this workshop and that representatives of the workers are also present. I am therefore convinced that the deliberations and findings of this workshop are bound to impact profoundly on the process of constitution making.

Without prejudicing the discussions that will take place in this workshop, I would like to put forward, for your consideration, the following proposals:

1. That the constitution for a new South Africa should unequivocally state that South Africa should not only be unitary, nonracial, and democratic, but should also be a nonsexist state.

2. That all laws which place women in a disadvantageous position be abolished and be declared unconstitutional.

3. That constitutionally entrenched criteria and mecha-

nisms be established to break through the layers of prejudice and historical inequalities experienced by women.

4. That the laws and the constitution of a democratic South Africa should enable women to articulate their demands, their priorities, and expectations.

5. That the constitution should ensure a strong female presence in all decision-making processes of the new South Africa.

I place these before you not to dictate your agenda, but as issues that deserve urgent attention as we make our transition to democracy.

I wish you well in your deliberations. With these words I declare this workshop open.

Amandla!

The oppressed and exploited must lead South Africa out of apartheid

KEYNOTE ADDRESS TO ANC CONSULTATIVE CONFERENCE, DECEMBER 14, 1990

The following speech was given at the opening session of the ANC's National Consultative Conference, held in Johannesburg. The meeting was attended by 1,600 delegates.

Comrade president; comrade members of the National Executive Committee of the ANC; comrade leaders of the South African Communist Party, COSATU, and the UDF [United Democratic Front]; Your Excellencies, members of the diplomatic corps; distinguished guests; comrades and compatriots:

It is a signal honor for me to be addressing you on the occasion of the first ANC conference inside the borders of South Africa after thirty-one years. I am particularly moved because this conference also marks a reunion on our home ground with you, comrade president, a distinguished leader of our people and a close comrade-in-arms with whom I have shared many a historic trench.

I want to begin my remarks today with a personal tribute to the brilliant contribution you have personally made to the arrival of this day, a day on which the ANC once again firmly plants its standard on the soil of our country as one of the principal actors in determining the future of South Africa.

Comrade Oliver Reginald Tambo, president of the ANC for the past twenty-three years, deserves a special place in the annals of our struggle for liberation both because of the longevity of his service in the ranks of the ANC and for his outstanding stewardship during the most difficult and trying phase.

In 1967, when our late president, Comrade Albert Luthuli passed away, our movement was in grave difficulties. The underground headquarters of our movement had been uncovered four years earlier in Rivonia. The leaders of that underground were spending their fourth year in prison after their arrest. The second layer of the underground leadership had been tracked down and imprisoned in 1965. Hundreds of our movement's activists had been rounded up, subjected to harrowing tortures before being condemned to lengthy terms of imprisonment.

Those were indeed hard times for any person to assume the reins of the presidency of the ANC! The road ahead looked dark and daunting. What communication there was between the movement abroad and the home base was slender and irregular.

You took up the challenge boldly and creatively. From that winter of 1967, under your guidance and unwavering leadership, the ANC rebuilt its strength. From the crippling reverses our movement had sustained in the early 1960s, you labored to rekindle the fighting spirit of our people. Today our people are ready as never before to use their organized strength to destroy apartheid, thanks to you and the team of men and women you led.

The reconstruction of the weakened organizational capacity of the ANC and its underground from the few scattered units that existed in 1967 rates as no less a feat. The countless unsung heroes and heroines who painstakingly undertook this task will one day have the opportunity to tell their story. Many others, equally courageous and unmindful of the risks to themselves, made their contribution but have not survived to tell the tale. Some fell in the field of battle facing the enemy; others perished at the hands of their torturers and tormentors in the regime's security police. Building on these many years of bitter and extremely costly experience, it was under your personal supervision that we carried out the formidable task of slowly reassembling our internal organization, the most recent example being Operation Vulindlela, which despite the arrest of its leading personnel, will always rank high among our many efforts to build an effective and secure underground of the ANC.[10]

Nineteen sixty-seven, the year in which you took the helm, also marked the baptism in fire of the combatants of our people's army, Umkhonto we Sizwe. Those battles are in the best tradition of the ANC, which since its birth has fought the enemy in deeds and not in mere words. It is a matter of pride that many of the commanders and rank-and-file fighters who served in that campaign are still in harness and are among the seasoned MK veterans who trained and inspired later generations of combatants. The building, maintenance, and constant improvement of the ANC's military capacity, for three decades, has been a matter close to your heart. Under you, as the commander-in-chief of MK, the enemy was repeatedly challenged in combat. During 1967, in battles along a front that stretched from the Wankie game reserve in the west, to Sipolilo in the east, the combatants of the Luthuli Detachment proved themselves skilled and determined fighters.[11] In an escalating offensive which began in 1976, inside our country, the armed actions conducted by our fighters played a key role in providing the inspiration for the political upsurge which developed with increasing intensity during the decade of the 1980s.

It is thanks also to these qualities of leadership, your statesmanship, and your wisdom that you became universally recognized as the most outstanding spokesman of the struggling people of our country, highly respected by friend and opponent alike. In the councils of the OAU, the Frontline States, the UNO [United Nations Organization], the ILO [International Labor Organization], the Nonaligned Movement, and other international bodies where we sought to marshal international solidarity, your thoughts and opinions were highly valued and sought after. This external pressure played a vital role in deepening the crisis of apartheid and forcing the regime to move towards dialogue.

In paying tribute to our comrade president, I am addressing not only the unrivaled qualities and achievements of the individual, Oliver Tambo; I am addressing also the man as the crystallization and personification of what the ANC is and became under his leadership. When we assess the processes that brought about the watershed events of February 1990, we should never underrate the great importance of the individual personality in determining the pace at which matters moved to that turning point.

I call upon you all, comrades, to please join me in a salute to this great son of our people, Comrade Oliver Tambo, president of the ANC!

Viva Comrade President Tambo, viva!
Viva Comrade President Tambo, viva!

None of these achievements would have been possible had our president not had at his side a team of very able and talented colleagues and lieutenants. It was this remarkable group of men and women, which contained comrades of the caliber of J.B. Marks, Yusuf Dadoo, Florence Mophosho, Moses Kotane, and Duma Nokwe—all of whom are no longer with us—that held together our movement during those difficult times and kept the final goal in clear focus despite the odds. Our movement owes a great debt of gratitude to these departed comrades and also to the other serving members of the National Executive.

Undaunted by the burdens it imposed and the deprivations it visited upon their peoples, the newly independent states of Africa gave their unstinting support to our struggle for all those years. The price the Pretoria regime exacted for this solidarity can be counted in the infrastructure destroyed and devastated in punitive cross-border raids; in the economic and trade sanctions South Africa imposed against the countries who demonstrated their commitment to the destruction of colonialism by supporting our struggle; and in the thousands of their citizens killed and maimed by both the SADF [South African Defence Force] and its surrogates operating in these countries. Thirty years in the life of a young nation is a long time. Much as the people of South Africa bled for freedom, the Frontline States bled in equal measure so that we might meet in this manner today. Words cannot express our profound appreciation for the solidarity, succor, and support we received and continue to receive from the sister nations of Africa.

Comrade president:

February 1990 marked a political watershed in the history of our country and our struggle. Beginning with his opening of Parliament, the leader of the National Party—the architects of apartheid who had misgoverned and abused the people of South Africa for forty-two years—was compelled to admit failure. Through decades of hard-fought struggle we had forced that party whose political platform was outright racism to face the truth that its policies had led our country into a profound crisis for which they had no prescription.

Viewed strategically, the events of February constitute a defeat for the policies of apartheid, national oppression, and colonialism. From that moment on, the forces of race domination, as represented by the National Party and all the political formations to its right, have been placed on the defensive by the advances registered by the forces of national liberation and democracy. While recognizing these momentous changes wrought by the struggle, we should not forget that the February events, though of decisive importance, do not in themselves imply that apartheid has surrendered. Indeed, many of the government's actions since February are designed to limit the damage inflicted on its policies. Many more battles still lie ahead of us before we can say that the seal of permanence has been placed on the processes of ending race domination.

After consultations, the ANC accepted the need to enter into discussions with the National Party government with a view to insisting on the removal of the obstacles to a negotiated end to apartheid. We went to Groote Schuur in May 1990 to set in motion procedures which both sides had come to accept as necessary.[12] From that summit there arose joint government-ANC working groups, charged with translating various elements of the Groote Schuur Minute into legislative measures. Even before the respective working groups had completed their tasks, the ANC sought and secured the August 6 summit in order to accelerate the pace. As a token of our commitment to exploring every opportunity of achieving a peaceful transition to democracy, the ANC entered that August summit ready to declare a suspension of all armed action.

The decision to suspend armed action before all the obstacles to negotiations had been removed was not taken lightly by the ANC. We resolved to pursue this path in order to exploit all reasonable possibilities of keeping the peace process on course.

The Pretoria Minute, the outcome of the second summit, includes a series of solemn undertakings made by the government to ensure that by April 1991 all political prisoners and detainees are freed, all exiles are in a position to return home, and that the host of repressive laws on the South African statute books are repealed. The processes leading up to this final date were to commence as from September 1.

Related to the ANC's suspension of armed activity, the Pretoria Minute also includes provision for a working group to define the modalities of its execution.

Since the signing of the Pretoria Minute, we have come to recognize that our own commitment to see the process move along as swiftly as possible is not yet matched by that of the government. It is becoming increasingly clear that in spite of our initiative, the government is dragging its feet in carrying out its undertakings to clear away the obstacles in the path to real negotiations.

We have seen a plague of violence descend upon the PWV region [Pretoria–Witwatersrand–Vaal Triangle area, including Johannesburg] and spread like wildfire in all directions, so that no part of our country is now safe from this scourge. We cannot count it as coincidence that the week during which this wave of violence began was scheduled for the launching of a number of ANC branches in the affected townships. It is necessary for us to understand and correctly characterize this plague so that we may grasp the motives behind it.

Conventional wisdom, served up in our media every day, holds that the violence is the outcome of political rivalry among the organizations of the oppressed. While such rivalry accounts for some of the violence, it is our firm conviction, based on a study of the facts and a close monitoring of the events, that such rivalry accounts for a tiny fraction of the carnage. The massacres of commuters on the trains in Johannesburg; the raids on the hostels in Sebokeng; the massacres in the East and the West Rand; and the most recent spate of killings in Bekkersdal, Zonk'izizwe, Phola Park, and other squatter settlements are neither the outcome of political rivalry nor the expression of political intolerance among the oppressed.

This endemic violence is a continuation of the bloodletting that has already decimated our people in Natal for the past four years. These are all examples of an orchestrated campaign of counterrevolutionary violence which has a predetermined objective. As it has unfolded and taken hold over the past three months, it is evident that it is targeted at the ANC. It is our members, including Youth Leaguers, whose homes are systematically attacked. It is our supporters who are systematically being singled out for murder. Even when, as it often does, assume an indiscriminate character, the mayhem is conducted with the ANC in its sights. Its clear purpose is to destroy our capacity to provide leadership to our people in struggle. The authors of this carnage count on the outcome being a loss of mass confidence in the ANC and its leadership. They hope by these means to create a political vacuum into which their political allies could be maneuvered.

Let there be no mistake! We have through our struggle stripped the apartheid state and its repressive organs of their former capacity to repress the mass movement by detentions, jailings, and executions. The number of our supporters is such that it has rendered these conventional methods ineffective. In response, elements within the apartheid power bloc who are opposed to the peace process are resorting to acts of widespread terror and carnage against the people. These killings have a dual aim: to weaken the ANC and to discredit the concept of disciplined mass action.

Needless to say, anarchy and a scenario of random murders accompanied by retaliatory killings will not be conducive to any sort of negotiations. Its aim is to force those at the receiving end of the violence to become more amenable to authoritarian rule.

What is being played out is the double agenda pursued by elements within the South African government. While de Klerk and his colleagues have had to accept and go along with the ANC's initiative for a peaceful solution, there is a simultaneous attempt taking place whose purpose is to destabilize, undermine, and, if possible, crush the ANC and its allies. It is disturbing that the most senior ministers of government, including participants in the Groote Schuur and Pretoria summits, have misrepresented both the content of those meetings and the minutes arising from them.

At neither the Groote Schuur nor the more recent Pretoria summit did our delegation agree to the circumscription or proscription of the political activities of the people. Indeed, we rejected out of hand all government suggestions that we make such an undertaking. The stated purpose of both meetings was to explore the means of removing the obstacles to negotiations. These obstacles were identified as the state of emergency (then still in force), the continued incarceration of political prisoners, detention without trial, the continued exile of thousands of patriots, and the presence of repressive laws on the law books of this country.

The distortions, misrepresentations, and outright lies that have been spread are designed to create the impression that the ANC surrendered the people's right to engage in normal political activity. The purpose of these lies is to win moral support for attempts to illegalize and curtail perfectly acceptable political practices.

The democratic alliance—comprising the core of the forces of national liberation as represented by the ANC, the SACP [South African Communist Party], and COSATU—has also been viciously attacked both by government spokesmen and a section of the mass media. Those who imagine that they will cause a rift among us have understood neither the character of this alliance nor its historic role in our struggle for freedom. The ANC, like its allies, remains fully committed to the preservation and the strengthening of our alliance, and no amount of pressure will shake our resolve.

We have repeatedly made it plain that in the eyes of the 83 percent of the South African population who were born black, this government and its predecessors since Union,[13] based on the will of a minority, have no moral claim on authority. That being the case, it is our absolute and inalienable right to employ every legitimate device to ensure that they transfer power to the people as speedily as possible. The ANC shall under no circumstances compromise this universally recognized right of our people.

More insidious are the attempts to extend the meaning of the ANC's undertakings regarding the suspension of armed actions so as to cast us in the role of a surrendering belligerent. Cease-fires, whether bilateral or unilateral, are by their nature temporary measures. There is a recognized right, in international law, of belligerents to maintain their forces in combat readiness and replace any wastage in personnel and matériel. To enhance the prospects of peace, we voluntarily gave up our right to reequip and resupply our forces inside South Africa. The time is long overdue that the government gave some recognition to these concessions we have made, instead of reading them as signs of weakness to be exploited for its short-term advantage.

It must be understood too that the ANC's suspension of the armed struggle was conditional.[14] We expected and continue to expect the government to deliver on its undertakings. We will, therefore, constantly test the validity of that option against the government's actions.

The outcome of the government's attitude is that after seven months of discussions, two summits, and a number of smaller meetings, not enough has been achieved by way of practical results. With the exception of the state of emergency, many of the obstacles we set out to remove in May remain in place and the government seems determined to postpone their removal as long as possible.

This fact, combined with the carnage that has been unleashed, poses grave dangers for the peace process and the future stability of our country. We sound these warnings not to cause alarm, but rather to stress that in the eyes of our people, many of the government's actions appear to have no regard for the future of South Africa. We shall hold the government fully accountable for any breakdown in the peace process.

In the course of this year alone, some three thousand people have lost their lives as a result of the violence, in which the government's own forces are deeply implicated. In addition, three hundred people have been killed directly by the government's security services. Let us all rise in silent tribute to the thousands of our people who have perished. [*All rise and observe a moment's silence*]

We cannot accept the government's threadbare alibi for not apprehending and prosecuting the criminals responsible for these deaths. It is evident that a total disregard for the lives of black people, which is of the essence of apartheid, continues to hold sway at the highest reaches of the government.

The only response the government has thus far been able to muster against these outbreaks of violence are cynical pleas of impotence and more repression. The permissiveness with which it reacts to the provocative behavior and pronouncements of the white ultraright paramilitary formations also betrays a continued commitment to racist double standards. The rallying call of the day, to all our members wherever they are deployed, is: remain at your posts!

Continuing pressure from the international community and the weight of mass mobilization at home remain key factors in compelling the government to honor the agreements reached. These must be maintained!

The ANC, once again and unequivocally, commits itself to exploring every avenue to a negotiated solution to our country's problems. We shall also endeavor to bring an end to the carnage that has brought such misery to our people, and we reiterate our willingness to enter into discussions with any party or group that shares that objective. Platitudes about peace will not assist this process. All that is required is a genuine commitment and the will to act on that commitment.

The ANC is emerging from the shadows of thirty years of underground existence and is engaged in establishing itself once more as a legal political movement. The problems relating to this transition are innumerable. We have been obliged to reconstruct an entire organization—from the smallest local branch unit to the national leadership structures during a period of very rapid change and high expectations in our country. That the process has been uneven should not dismay or alarm us. That it is fraught with new and unique problems was to be expected. That we do not all see the problems in the same light was inevitable given the differing strands of experience that have shaped our membership, from its leading bodies to the branch level.

There are at least four clearly defined groups of comrades who bring different strands of experience to our effort to revive the legal ANC.

Firstly, we have amongst us those who have been steeled by years of combat experience and sacrifice in the ranks of

Umkhonto we Sizwe. These are comrades who have served the cause of liberation selflessly for many decades. They bring to their tasks an ironclad discipline and sense of duty of incalculable value.

Secondly, there are those of us who shared the harsh experience of long terms in jail. Prison is itself a tremendous education in the need for patience and perseverance. It is above all a test of one's commitment. Those who passed through that school have all acquired a firmness, tempered by a remarkable resilience.

Thirdly, there are the comrades who have been shaped by the experience of exile. They have worked for many years outside their home environment but have managed to keep a finger on the popular pulse. A number of these comrades reached political maturity in exile, contributing in various capacities to the continuity and survival of our movement. Exile afforded them the opportunity to acquire skills and a high level of political training, which the movement has harnessed to great advantage.

Lastly, there are the comrades whose experience derives from work in the mass democratic formations. These comrades are probably the most attuned to the popular mood, whose chief role was to discover the legal political spaces that could be utilized in an overall context of repression. We are filled with admiration for the creative manner in which they responded to and fended off this relentless state repression, including multiple states of emergency, detentions, assassinations, and other forms of harassment. It is to them that we owe our demonstrated ability for mass mobilization.

These four strands of experience have the potential of enriching our movement greatly, provided we recognize the value of each and work towards weaving them into a robust cord so that they are mutually reinforcing.

The gravest danger to the movement and its capacity to grow is posed by complacency. If we are to translate the evident mass support we enjoy into a mass membership we cannot afford to rest on our laurels. We should neither take our membership for granted nor can we forget that we must at all times hold ourselves accountable to the people. This requires that we build, at every level of our movement, a firmly rooted democratic tradition and practice.

This spirit of democracy must extend also to the manner in which we relate to other political formations working within our communities and to our people. Coercive methods might appear to yield easy and quick results, but in the long term will prove destructive and counterproductive. The ANC must, at every stage, earn the title of leader of our people by its sensitivity to their aspirations and by timeously responding to their needs and demands. We will achieve this by building the ANC as an instrument of the masses' struggle for liberation. The ANC will flourish or fail to the extent that the exploited and the oppressed see it as their movement, championing their rights, and as the embodiment of their will.

The transitional problems we are encountering have at times been obstacles in the way of full consultation and accountability. It is essential, especially in the run up to the negotiation process we are working towards, that we involve the masses of our people at all stages and give a regular account of our work through report-back meetings and regular consultations. The attempts by the government, parties representing vested interests, and others to exclude the masses from the negotiation process must be firmly rebuffed and resisted.

Mass involvement requires us to locate negotiations correctly as an aspect of our multipronged strategy. We must strike the right balance between negotiations, as one of the numerous terrains of our struggle, and the others, especially mass mobilization. This should not be read as implying that there will not be moments when one or the other assumes a higher profile. That is inevitable in any struggle provided we exercise the requisite vigilance that will ensure that we always proceed from the recognition that these various aspects are inseparable.

The ANC has already begun building a broad-based Patriotic Front to draw in actual and potential allies in the struggle for freedom. We have invited every political trend among the broad antiapartheid forces to enter into a dialogue with us for this precise purpose. Ironically, we find that some of those who shout the loudest their commitment to a united front have shunned such contact and consistently turn down our invitations. We cannot compel anyone to take up our invitations, but we shall keep the door open in the hope that wiser counsels will prevail.

In pursuance of this broad front, we have entered into a continuing exchange with the authorities in all the so-called homelands, including the nominally independent.[15] We have at the same time made it clear that the ANC will not serve as an umbrella to shelter discredited homeland administrations from the wrath of the people. We have noted with satisfaction that a number of these politicians have definitively parted company with the racist policies embodied in the Bantustan scheme. The challenge that faces all those who became entangled in the structures of the apartheid system is to transform themselves into patriotic leaders who not only identify with the struggle for freedom, but are prepared to make their individual contribution to it. There is a golden opportunity for them all to become part of the future instead of being forever associated with the past. Homeland leaders, acting individually or collectively, could begin by dismembering the repressive regimes inherited from Pretoria and firmly establishing basic democratic rights in the territories that they administer.

A Patriotic Front for freedom should draw to its ranks all political formations, parties, organizations, and bodies that are committed to the eradication of apartheid. Such unity, in our view, can best be forged in the crucible of united struggle.

A durable front will not be built on the basis of pious resolutions, though these must be part of the process. The ANC shall continue to strive towards such a front in order to isolate the apartheid regime and all those who are defenders of the old order.

When this century dawned it found South Africa in the grips of a terrible and costly war, waged by Britain against the two Boer republics to determine which section of the white community shall dominate our country.[16] The first decade of the twentieth century witnessed the erection of the basic institutions of racial domination and colonialism, which form the basis of apartheid. At the end of that decade, the Boers composed their differences with British imperialism and gave their compact palpable form in the shape of the Union of 1910, institutionalizing racial domination in the constitution they imposed on our country.

We have entered the final decade of the twentieth century, and South Africa once again stands at a crossroads. We now stand at the threshold of freedom. It is the solemn responsibility of the most oppressed and exploited to lead South Africa out of the morass and degradation of apartheid into a new era of freedom and democracy for all its people. We extend our arms in friendship to our white compatriots and call upon them to embrace the cause of democracy in their thousands, as the only reliable guarantor of their future. The bright promise of a democratic South Africa demands that they shed their fears and step forward, boldly prepared to build a country we can all be proud to call our home.

The ANC, founded by our forebears in response to the Union, shall and will play a central role in that process of self-emancipation. As we begin our conference, let us turn to our tasks with a seriousness of purpose suited to this occasion. We are aware that there will be differences amongst us. That is as it should be in any democratic discourse. Let us take up our tasks with a clear resolve to arrive at a consensus that will bind us all and serve as the basis for our program of action.

Comrades, let us get down to work!

Our strategy is determined by objective reality

CLOSING SPEECH TO ANC CONSULTATIVE CONFERENCE, DECEMBER 16, 1990

Mandela responded to the discussion by delegates at the National Consultative Conference in his closing address, printed here according to the abridged text published by the ANC.

Comrades and distinguished guests:

This consultative conference has been called by the National Executive Committee to consult you on a variety of important issues and provide you with an effective platform where you sincerely express your own views, criticize the leadership for its weaknesses and mistakes, and commend them for the enormous achievements.

To enhance the significance of this conference, the NEC strongly felt that President Oliver Tambo should be asked to attend the conference in person.[17] This would give you the opportunity to see him in the flesh after three decades, witness the recovery he has made, and wish him a speedy and complete recovery. The response of the membership has been magnificent, and here today we have 1,600 delegates from inside and outside the country.

Two hours were set aside for a discussion on the president's address and that of the deputy president, but for reasons which are now well known to you all, that particular discussion did not take place. Nevertheless, for three full days you took part in one or another of the six commissions and in plenary discussions.

You spoke out frankly and brought to our attention a host of weaknesses and even mistakes in our work and made a wealth of suggestions to improve the position. There are weaknesses and mistakes and some of these are very serious in regard to the carrying out of our tasks both to our own membership and to the public.

In these discussions, delegates expressed serious reservations on the way in which we handled issues like negotiations, the suspension of armed action, the violence in which thousands of our people have been slaughtered, the neglect of our soldiers on whom the future of our country rests, the homeland system, and other matters.

The leadership has grasped the principle that they are servants of the people and that they must seek guidance from the masses in taking important positions and in the formulation of policy. We accordingly welcome the frank criticism that has been voiced during the last three days. We promise to look into all these criticisms honestly and objectively, and there are certain issues in regard to which we will have to make radical adjustments and even changes in the light of your criticism. Our basic response, therefore, is that we accept without qualification most of the criticisms that have been made against us, and we will do everything in our power to correct these mistakes.

But our organization has in the past dealt with a variety of weaknesses and mistakes on the part of our membership as well. Factions and cliques, men and women who used the platforms of the organization for unprincipled discussions. People who played to the gallery, whose aim in meetings of this nature is to prove how revolutionary they are. Persons who have no idea whatsoever of working in a mass move-

ment, who are totally incapable of putting forward constructive ideas, and who are quick to pull down what others have
built.

I do not know whether or not there have been such elements in this conference. I have the hope and confidence
that you will agree with me when I say I believe that there are
no such people amongst you. It is, however, for each and every one of you to judge. What I would like to stress is that
there are certain arguments which have been advanced here
which we totally reject. The overwhelming majority of our
people generally and the delegates here in particular support
negotiations between the ANC and the government.

There have been certain suggestions that have been made
which we fully accept, e.g., the suggestion that there should
be no discussions on the constitution until all the obstacles
to negotiations are removed. But there have also been statements to the effect that there should be no confidential discussions between some of us and members of the government.

This statement could only be made by those who do not
understand the nature of negotiations and the practical problems that face us on the ground. There would have been no
talks about talks today—no future prospect for negotiations—
if there were no confidential meetings between members of
the ANC and the government. Confidential discussions and
not secret meetings.

Confidential discussions we propose to continue having
with the government. We are not prepared to neglect our duties as the leadership because of views which, although we respect those who have uttered them, are totally unreasonable.
Such confidential discussions have been marked by frankness on the part of your representatives.

There are many examples to illustrate this, but let me give
you one example and that is the meeting of October 8 this
year. That meeting took place at our initiative. We called for it
because we were convinced that if we did not do so there was
a danger of the peace process being derailed. We met de

Klerk and his delegation and presented to him a document in which we frankly criticized him personally and some members of his delegation and government. The criticism was so sharp that the government asked us not to publish the document.

Some comrades have insisted that we should take no action without consulting the membership. If that statement is made with a qualification, then we may agree with it. But when, as has happened here over these three days, that statement is made without qualification, we totally reject it. And, I repeat, it can only be made by people who have no idea of the problems that face the leadership on the ground.

On July 22 I returned to my home at about seven in the evening and found the place full of Soweto community leaders. They then briefed me on the events that took place that day. I was so horrified when they outlined to me the actions of the South African Police.[18]

Although it was late in the evening I immediately telephoned Mr. Vlok and asked him to come to Soweto so that he could have the opportunity which I had of being briefed by the community leaders on what was happening in the townships. He came over with a number of top police officials, including the commissioner of police. For three hours they addressed him on the conduct of the police that day.

Then one of the last incidents: I heard that about eighteen of our people were detained at the airport. Delegates that came for this conference. I went to the airport and found no senior person to talk to. I went to see de Klerk. It was a Saturday. He argued that they could not be released before Monday and gave reasons for that. We insisted and they were released that night.

We have also been criticized for neglecting prisoners on death row. There are no people in this country who have been as concerned with the welfare of our people on death row as your National Executive. Several of them have visited our comrades on death row. I also, personally, went to the Central Prison and spoke to them.

I briefed them on the situation and assured them that we will do everything in our power to see them out with other prisoners because they are covered in the definition of political prisoners about which we agreed with the government. It is not correct, comrades, that we have neglected our comrades on death row.

Then quite a song has been made about the fact that I have referred to Mr. de Klerk as a man of integrity. Again, this may be due to lack of information on the part of our own comrades. I don't think that there is any mystery about it. The very first time I gave a report from prison to the National Executive and described Mr. de Klerk as a man of integrity, I went further. I said: "The strategies of an organization are not determined by the integrity or honesty of any particular individual, no matter what position in government they hold."

Our strategy is determined by objective reality. It is guided by the fact that de Klerk represents a party which introduced one of the most brutal systems of racial discrimination in this country. As long as that is the position, all our strategies will remain in place. They will be reviewed only when our demand for a nonracial South Africa is accepted. To merely shout that it was a mistake for me to do so is to take my remarks out of context. Please don't do so.

We have also been criticized for the appeal we have made to homeland leaders to join the liberation movement. Again, our whole position on this question has been taken out of context. We have discussed this matter very carefully and taken a very clear stand. We want to isolate the government, and one of the ways is to get the very people on which they have relied for the implementation of the apartheid policy on our side.

We are succeeding in doing that and many of these leaders are cooperating with us in settling their problems on the ground and in doing almost everything we ask them to do. We have made it clear that we are not going to serve as an umbrella for discredited leaders. We have said this on countless occasions. We say they must settle their problems with the people in their area, and if they don't, we will reject any association with them.

We must also be guided by what is happening on our borders. We heard some of our friends whose economies have been completely shut down by fighting with people who have no real political agenda, whose idea is merely to destroy the infrastructure of the country. They at first took up a position similar to yours: we have nothing to do with them and there can be no discussions with them. But after a lot of damage, after enormous damage has been done, our friends are now discussing with those very enemies to seek a solution for their country because war had not been able to bring about what they had hoped they would achieve.

I would have hoped that our comrades who are serious, who are members of a serious political organization, would take account of such experiences and take appropriate measures in our country in order to make sure that such tragedies do not befall us. Problems must be looked at from all sides. Whilst we are free to criticize, to point out mistakes, we must at the same time be able to see the good politics of the same comrades that we criticize.

One of the most disappointing features of our discussion here is that there was hardly a word of praise for our comrades in the National Executive—the men who, with our comrade president here, have put this organization in a dominant position in the politics of this country. They have preserved and given us an organization which is making a tremendous impact both internally and externally, and whatever weaknesses we have detected in their work the most evident feature is that they have placed this organization on a new level altogether.

Nevertheless, all those comrades, even though we do not agree with them in regard to the issues I have identified, they are very good comrades whose bona fides and sincerity we accept without qualification. They are our pride and we wish that we could have enough time to sit down with them and to press out the reservations they have. We sincerely hope that we will have that opportunity.

One of the features of this entire discussion is that as a result of frank criticism that has been leveled and the very positive response of the chairpersons who listened, and who guided these discussions, we are leaving this hall closer to one another than we were before the commencement of this conference. We have emerged from the conference stronger than we were before. For this we thank you from the bottom of our hearts.

I must remind you that today is the twenty-seventh anniversary of Umkhonto we Sizwe, the organization which has given the liberation struggle in this country such muscle. I think it is fitting that we should sing in honor of Umkhonto we Sizwe, "Hamba kahle [go well], Mkhonto." Please stand up and sing.

Finally I want to make an announcement which I hope will delight you. At the suggestion of some delegates here, the National Executive has decided to give our comrade president the honor of Isitwalandwe.[19]

I must inform you that on a previous occasion he has been offered this honor, but because of his humility he refused to accept it. Well he is my president, but on this particular occasion I am ordering him to accept it.

I am expressing the wishes of all of us when I say: This is one of our happiest moments. We have handled our problems as real comrades, and everyone here will leave this place feeling that he is a worthy comrade of whom we are very proud.

Building a political culture that entrenches political tolerance

SPEECH TO JOHANNESBURG PRESS CLUB, FEBRUARY 22, 1991

The remarks below were given at a ceremony to present the Johannesburg Press Club's "Newsmaker of the Year" award jointly to Mandela and F.W. de Klerk.

Mr. Chairman; Mr. State President and Mrs. de Klerk; distinguished guests; ladies and gentlemen:

I wish firstly to express my profound and heartfelt appreciation of this honor that the Johannesburg Press Club has deemed fit to bestow on me by electing me as one of the two Men of the Year.

It is a sign of the times our country is passing through that this prize this year is shared by two people who trace their respective political ideals to opposing poles on our national political spectrum. I am confident that this joint award signifies the growing and visible consensus that has begun to emerge amongst the overwhelming majority of South Africans, cutting across racial and political affiliations, that apartheid must be consigned to the dustbin of history now! The developing national mood that includes most South Africans is that we must collectively commence the task of building a nonracial democracy.

This consensus has had to be built up slowly and we have finally arrived at it by a route that was extremely painful and costly of our national resources, amongst which we must count human lives lost or broken. Perhaps history ordained that the people of our country should pay this high price because it bequeathed to us two nationalisms that dominate the history of twentieth-century South Africa. These two— African and Afrikaner nationalism—embody two fundamentally differing perspectives on the character and future of our country.[20] Because both nationalisms laid claim to the same piece of earth—our common home, South Africa—the contest between the two was bound to be both acrimonious and at times brutal.

It is our hope that the progress thus far achieved in the talks that have preoccupied both the ANC and the government over the past twelve months have laid the basis for an end to at least the more brutal aspects of this contest. It is unavoidable that we should continue to debate and ideologically contest each other's positions, because that is the nature of politics in any society. We as the ANC have unequivocally committed ourselves to confining this contest to the battlefield of ideas and peaceful political activity. The sooner other parties to the conflict do likewise, the better the prospects of peace in our country will become.

On this occasion I wish to give due recognition to the divergent approaches we have adopted in addressing the problems confronting our country. I do this, Mr. Chairman, not in order to emphasize these differences, but rather in order to clarify a standpoint which the ANC has embraced. A spokesman for the government called for frankness and candor in these matters a few days ago. It is in that spirit that I shall frame my remarks. If in the process I also manage to persuade a few more converts to our view, I will feel I have achieved my purpose.

The gulf that previously separated African and Afrikaner

nationalism has narrowed considerably during the past twelve months. If there is any convergence of these two opposing views, such convergence will depend in large measure on a clear understanding of the underlying values and principles that inform both these two movements. It shall require courage and vision on the part of all South Africans for us to grasp the challenge presented by this unique moment. It is an opportunity to move as swiftly and as painlessly as possible towards the goals we have increasingly come to share in common.

At its birth African nationalism in South Africa embraced a number of values, principles, and ideals as the key pillars of its political philosophy. These core values have of course undergone evolution with the march of time, but are nonetheless recognizable till this day as deriving from a specific tradition.

In 1912, when the ANC came into being as the first nationalist movement in sub-Saharan Africa, and 1913, the year in which the National Party was founded, few if any of the leading statesmen of Europe would have blushed at the term "imperialist." It is an index of the manner in which our political vocabulary has been transformed by the nationalism of formerly oppressed peoples that today "imperialist" is regarded as a term of abuse. We can, with a degree of hindsight, perhaps say that the struggle for self-determination has been the leitmotiv of twentieth-century history. That struggle has in most instances been linked to a second one, the struggle for democracy.

Between 1912 and the mid-1940s, the period during which I entered national politics, the world experienced two devastating world wars. As a direct consequence, the political value system with which the ANC identified changed and was greatly expanded. Few will dispute that the political culture of human rights, which underwent its severest test during the course of this century, was greatly enriched by the war against fascism. Equally important was the contribution made by the colonial peoples after 1945, in their struggle for independence. This culture of human rights is rooted in and inextricably linked to the political revolutions of the late eighteenth century and those that took place during the mid-nineteenth century. It was adopted by humanity as its common heritage in the Universal Declaration of Human Rights after the Second World War.

It is not a widely known fact that during the Second World War, after Churchill and Roosevelt concluded the Atlantic Charter, the then-president of the ANC, Dr. A.B. Xuma, appointed a blue-ribbon committee of African thinkers and political leaders to draw up a charter for Africa, applying the principles embodied in the Atlantic Charter to the African continent. That document, titled "The African Claims," remains one of the most important statements of the central values subscribed to by the ANC. Anyone who reads it, even today, will agree that it is one of the best contributions to this universal human rights culture emanating from our country.

African nationalism, as it has evolved in South Africa, embraced these ideals and has sought to make them part of the political culture of our country. The environment in which we have struggled to nurse this tender plant so that it takes root has been extremely hostile. We have nonetheless persevered, surrounded though it was by robust weeds of racial hatred, because these principles are enduring.

Reduced to their essentials, they are:

(a) that all governments must derive their authority from the consent of the governed;

(b) no person or group of persons should be subjected to oppression or domination by virtue of his/her race, gender, color, or religious belief;

(c) all persons should enjoy security in their persons and their goods against intrusions by secular or clerical authorities;

(d) all persons should enjoy the right to life, unfettered by impositions from either secular or clerical authorities;

(e) all persons should have the untrammeled right to hold and express whatever opinions they wish to subscribe to as long as the exercise of that right does not infringe on the rights of others.

It is in pursuance of these principles that we have waged a struggle, employing whatever means we deemed necessary, to attain the democratic empowerment of those in our country who historically have borne the burden of oppression and exploitation. It is because of our commitment to these ideals also that we have adamantly opposed any political arrangement that will result in domination of either the majority by the minority or the minority by the majority.

These five basic principles are in their essence liberatory. Any reevaluation and recasting of these cardinal values we have inherited, we would insist, must therefore serve that essential purpose—the empowerment of the individual citizen by increasing his/her capacity to cope with the complexities of life in the modern era.

It is in the light of such considerations that the ANC also adheres to the second generation of human rights. In the bleak townships, squatter camps, ghettoes, compounds, and hostels in which the majority of black South Africans are compelled, under pain of imprisonment, to reside in the urban areas, the right to life would be meaningless if it did not translate into an accessible, dependable, and free health service. Indeed, we would assert that this is the right of every citizen irrespective of earning power or individual circumstances. The health of the national should be regarded as a national task rather than an issue subject to the fickle whims of fortune.

In those desolate wastelands populated by the "surplus people" who were forcibly ejected from their homes so that the pipe dreams of the architects of apartheid could be realized, in the rural slums and on the overutilized lands of the Bantustans, the right to life would amount to pious words scribbled on some paper if it did not entail decent, affordable shelter for all.

Those who hunger and thirst for knowledge but have by law been consigned to educational backwaters to fulfill the cynical social engineering of Dr. Hendrik Verwoerd, know too that for this right to be meaningful they must be enabled to pursue their studies and rise to the limits to which their talents will take them. In practice this requires a system of equitable, free primary and secondary education and training in every aspect of human endeavor and a system of tertiary education backed up by strong support from the state.

We would place equal emphasis on the urgent need for a national commitment to secure creative and productive employment for the millions who daily trudge our streets in search of a livelihood. Without this, what meaning can we give to the right to security of one's person?

The commitment of the ANC to these values goes beyond their impact on the poor and the politically voiceless in our country. Consistent with our point of departure that these ideals are universal, we have stood up for human dignity no matter how or by whom it was threatened. Thus the ANC has identified with all those who have deliberately been disadvantaged on grounds of their race, religion, sex, or national origin. We have applied this principle with equal force whether the case in question is that of European Jewry threatened with genocide by the fascist regimes of Europe, or it is the Palestinians subjected to victimization and aggression by the State of Israel.

Can the National Party make the same claim?

The ANC has, with equal determination, stood up for the rights of Asians, whether they reside in the city of Durban or in Birmingham, England, who fear to walk the streets because of threats of harassment on account of their racial origin.

Can the National Party make the same claim?

We have stood for and fought alongside those who have been silenced by governments because their views incurred the wrath of some minister or petty official. Editors, writers, musicians, and others whose work has been suppressed and banned have always received the unstinting support of the ANC.

Can the National Party make the same claim?

It is precisely because we hold these values in such high

esteem that I wish to use this platform to unreservedly condemn the bully-boy tactics of some of those who have come out to demonstrate their support for my wife, Comrade Nomzamo Winnie Mandela, during her court appearances.[21] While we appreciate the zeal that sometimes leads to such action, I am duty-bound to stress that such zeal is misplaced and misdirected if its outcome is to compromise the integrity of our movement and violate the principles we hold dear.

These values, which the ANC and its supporters have espoused, bear an incredibly high price. We shall not today enumerate the hundreds who have lost their lives in an attempt to make them a reality. We shall for the moment leave unsaid the names of the thousands of families, the homes and the lives that have been wrecked so that we can realize them. Those who joined the struggle did so with their eyes wide open and under no illusion that the path that they had chosen entailed sacrifice, hazards, and torment. We all did so not for any personal gain or material rewards. We took this stand because these were goals we saw as worthy and virtuous. We do not now nor shall we ever regret having made that choice.

I would like, Mr. Chairman, to direct some remarks to the vexing problem of tolerance and the rights of the individual. In this regard I want to stress that tolerance is one of the core principles of the human rights culture the ANC advocates. When I employ the term "tolerance," I do not intend it to be understood as the grudging accommodation of an opinion one does not hold. I employ it to underscore that we must begin from the premise that truth is elusive and can only be derived from the untrammeled competition of differing opinions and thorough debate.

The search for truth, therefore, cannot be circumscribed within the bounds of certain dogmas and predetermined beliefs. We eschew political intolerance for this precise reason. But our admonition that force should not be harnessed to gain leverage over the political process applies in equal measure to parliamentary parties as it does to the extraparliamentary opposition and movements; we address it with equal force to the government as we do to those who stand opposed to the government. In this respect, "force" applies not only to the actual wielding of weapons, stones, and other physical objects. It must be understood to cover also the employment of such devices as repressive laws, emergency powers, and other legal instruments that have the effect of forcibly compelling those who hold an opposing viewpoint to remain silent. I need not recount here the regularity with which the weapons of war have been used by the state to enforce its particular viewpoint.

The mischief these practices have already wrought on the political culture of our country can be measured by the evident inability of many of us to engage in sober debate without recourse to threats and even physical abuse. It cannot be considered unrealistic that we demand that, as a token of its own commitment to creating a climate conducive to a normal political climate, the government take expeditious measures to expunge such obnoxious laws from South Africa's statute books.

Tolerance cannot, nor has ever, meant that every idea, practice, or opinion shall be placed on the same moral plane. There can be no equivalence between the principle that human life is sacred and as such requires to be protected, and the misanthropic notions that encouraged the extermination of human beings. An appeal to tolerance cannot be invoked to legitimate the advocacy of murder, let alone its commission. Let me stress, however, that we suppress such advocacy and the commission of such acts not because of our absolute certainty that we are correct, but rather because of the universal recognition that such advocacy is absolutely wrong. It is by the same token that humanity has outlawed slavery in any form, though we continue to debate and haggle over the merits and demerits of other economic systems. Political tolerance, in our view, has always been qualified—qualified in the sense that human history and experience have already demonstrated that certain practices are intrinsically evil, and as such do not deserve to be tolerated.

We as the ANC shall continue to play our role in building a political culture that entrenches political tolerance. This does not mean, nor should it be understood as us withdrawing from the daily cut and thrust of politics and engagement with our opponents and critics. We shall, as we have always done in the past, conduct such debates with courtesy but with a firmness to principle that is apologetic to no one.

Mr. Chairman, I have dwelt at some length with the political values we hope to see achieved in our country. Before I sit down, there is one other matter which I feel we should raise. I chose the law as my professional career for a number of reasons. When I reflect on that choice today, one of the considerations that loomed largest in my mind was the manner in which the law was used in South Africa, not as an instrument to afford the citizen protection, but rather as the chief means of his subjection. As a young law student, it was one of my ambitions to try to use my professional training to help tilt the balance just a wee bit in favor of the citizen.

Unfortunately, it is well-nigh impossible, even with the best will in the world, to administer laws that are intrinsically unjust in a just fashion. Try as many of us did, we could not bring to bear any amount of legal expertise in favor of the citizen because the same process of lawmaking closed up the loopholes and ambiguities as quickly as we uncovered them.

This, unfortunately, is and shall remain the position in South Africa as long as we do not have a democratic system of government. If today many in our country hold the law in contempt, this is because of a widely held perception that it is oppressive and has been systematically used to deny millions rights which other people take for granted.

We might all agree that a society not governed by laws is barbarism of the worst order. We are today witnessing a crime wave of terrifying proportions, which, if it continues and escalates, could quickly reduce South Africa to a pile of ashes. I submit that the most effective means of building a law-abiding society is to cultivate respect for the law. The law in our country will only be deserving of respect to the extent that it serves the ordinary citizen and ceases to be a club wielded by the authorities to bludgeon us into submission or deprive us of our rights.

This relates directly to the issue of the legitimacy of the incumbent government and its administrative arm. Legitimacy is both a subjective judgment as well as an objective conclusion which can be adduced from generally accepted principles. When we say that the incumbent government has no moral right to govern, we say this not to heap insults or offer offense to anyone. We are merely stating a judgment which any democrat must make if he/she subscribes to basic democratic norms.

It is because of our concern to commence, as soon as possible, the reconstruction of a law-abiding society that we have called for an interim government. Obedience to the law should not be based on fear, but rather on respect for the law as the expression of commonly held societal values and shared goals. I fear that the longer we postpone the installation of a government that enjoys the confidence of all sections of our society, so long shall we be condemned to endure this steady drift towards lawlessness, with all the dangers that entails. Peace and freedom are today indivisible; we shall not have one without the other!

In conclusion, Mr. Chairman, ladies and gentlemen, permit me once more to express my thanks to the Johannesburg Press Club. The challenges that face us as an emergent nation are not really that great if we give them due consideration. What is required of every South African today is the simple recognition that his/her fellow citizens, like himself, are at root, simple, uncomplicated human beings. We are all "warmed by the same summer" and "chilled by the same winter," and it is recognition of that common humanity that shall bond us into a nation.

The violence has assumed a more organized and systematic character

OPEN LETTER TO PRESIDENT DE KLERK, APRIL 5, 1991

This document, addressed to President de Klerk and his cabinet, was issued by the ANC National Executive Committee.

1.0. Since the outbreak of violence that began in Natal, the country has witnessed a scale of bloodletting hitherto unknown.[22] Estimates provided by agencies who have been monitoring the situation place the numbers of those who have lost their lives in excess of five thousand.

Since the signing of the accord between the ANC and the Inkatha Freedom Party on 29 January 1991, the scale of violence has not diminished.[23] On the contrary, it has assumed a more organized and systematic character. In many parts of Natal the violence has taken on a random character, to an extent that it can be regarded as directed against the community itself.

Death and the destruction of homes and property on such a scale would be considered a national disaster in any sane society. The scale of the human tragedy alone provides sufficient motivation for us to address you with our grave concerns.

1.1. Throughout the period in question, there have been clearly discernible patterns in this unfolding violence that indicate disturbing features which by now should have been noted and be preoccupying the attentions of the authorities. We are, like many others, alarmed at the degree of inaction on the part of the authorities.

1.2. In almost every instance of violence that has erupted on the Reef,[24] for example, the following pattern has emerged: A group of individuals, drawn from a specific area of the country, sharing a common language, and publicly identifying themselves with a specific political party have established control over a migrant laborers' hostel through acts of intimidation. Those who would not submit to such pressure are subsequently driven out of the hostel. These individuals constitute themselves into a group, with insignia for common identification (usually a red headband). Supported by others of like purpose, bused in from other areas, they then stage a provocative armed demonstration through the township, escorted by the police.

1.3. Without exception, the townships that have suffered armed demonstrations did not previously have any visible presence of the Inkatha Freedom Party. In all the cases in question, the majority of participants in such demonstrations have been bused in from other localities. Instances when the police have averted attacks or deterred the perpetrators of such attacks are extremely rare. Even among cases where the assailants have been identified, the number of them who have been arrested or charged is derisory.

1.4. In at least five separate incidents, all of which occurred on the Reef during the past nine months, armed gangs of men have launched well-organized and coordinated attacks against commuters on the trains between the townships and Johannesburg city center, on the homes of bereaved families during funeral vigils, and on selected hostels. Those responsible for these actions are distinguished by their remarkable capacity to evade detection by the police and

Left: concert in Johannesburg greeting Mandela shortly after his release in February 1990. Above: rally for Mandela in Bisho, March 1990.

"February 1990 marked a political watershed in the history of our country and our struggle."

Facing page: Mandela being greeted in New York City, June 1990. Above: at Wembley Stadium, London, April 1990; bottom: at U.S. Congress, June 1990.

GREG McCARTAN/MILITANT

"Our struggle, and the leadership of the ANC within it, represents hope to democrats and struggling people throughout the world."

This page: gold mine workers; Mercedes Benz auto plant in Ciskei. Facing page, top: townships, squatter settlements, and rural areas inhabited by black South Africans; bottom: farm workers in Transvaal.

LEFT AND ABOVE: MARGRETHE SIEM/MILITANT — NIGEL DENNIS/ANC DIP

NIGEL DENNIS/ANC DIP — NIGEL DENNIS/ANC DIP

"Our people are still the hewers of wood and the drawers of water; in the decades of apartheid rule, we were reduced to beggars in our own land."

MARGRETHE SIEM/MILITANT

SAMSON SELEPE

Workers' hostels, where thousands are forced to live.

"In the bleak townships, squatter camps, ghettoes, compounds, and hostels in which the majority of black South Africans are compelled to reside in the urban areas, the right to life would be meaningless if it did not translate into an accessible, dependable, and free health service, affordable shelter for all, equitable and free primary and secondary education, and creative and productive employment for the millions."

Women workers demonstrate in Port Elizabeth, August 1991; inset, June 1992 meeting of ANC Women's League in Durban.

"For generations, black women have been the most oppressed group in our society. . . . The ANC should ensure that the women's movement plays a central role in the affairs of the organization and the country."

ANDREW COURTNEY/IMPACT VISUALS INSET: NIGEL DENNIS/ANC DIP

Top, left to right: Soweto demonstration, March 1990; march to Parliament to protest conditions of farm workers, April 24, 1992; striking food workers, July 1991. Right: workers demonstrate for trade union rights, Johannesburg, June 1992.

"It is your sweat and blood that has created the vast wealth that white South Africa enjoys."

TOP PHOTOS: MARGRETHE SIEM / MILITANT

"The South African government has never relented in its war against the democratic movement in our country."

Top left: funeral of four young men killed by police in Ntuzama, near Durban, March 24, 1990; top right: police patrol streets of Ciskei after ANC rally, March 31, 1990. Right: police at Cape Town demonstration to protest Chris Hani assassination, April 16, 1993.

RODGER BOSCH/IMPACT VISUALS

ANC National Conference,
July 2-6, 1991, Durban.
Bottom right: Mandela,
Oliver Tambo, Walter Sisulu.

"The ANC must stand out as an unchallenged example of a real people's movement, in touch with the masses, responsive to their needs, capable of drawing them into action in their millions, and enjoying their genuine allegiance and voluntary support."

Top: Mandela visits burned-out house of Sipho Mkhize, killed in attack by Inkatha supporters in southern Natal, June 1992.
Middle: Inkatha rally in Natal, March 1990.
Bottom: Mandela meeting with Inkatha leader Mangosuthu Buthelezi, January 29, 1991.

NIGEL DENNIS/ANC DIP

MARGRETHE SIEM/MILITANT

NIGEL DENNIS/ANC DIP

"Members of Inkatha should not allow themselves to be pawns of the National Party in its crusade to destroy the democratic movement."

other security services. In each of these instances the authorities were advised well in advance to take precautionary measures, but they failed to do so.

Authorities commit acts of violence

1.5. Since 22 July 1990, on at least three separate occasions when the authorities were summoned to assist or to avert violence, they have themselves committed acts of violence that have resulted in death. A case in point is that of Sebokeng. Thirty-eight (38) people had been killed in a pre-dawn attack on a hostel in Sebokeng. A judicial inquiry subsequently found that members of the South African Defence Force, who had been called to the scene to contain a potentially explosive situation, opened fire on a crowd, killing four persons and inflicting grave injuries on several others.

An equally disturbing case is that which occurred in Daveyton, Benoni, on 24 March 1991. The known facts indicate that after a large number of persons were bused into Daveyton, a provocative armed demonstration was staged from the hostels to a nearby stadium to hold a rally. The police had been advised of the probability of violence by township residents and were patrolling the streets. A group of residents, concerned because of the armed demonstration, assembled on an open space to discuss their response. The police opened fire on this group in an unprovoked attack, causing the deaths of at least twelve persons.

Every effort had been made by the local civic association to gain the cooperation of the police. An agreement had even been reached that no armed demonstration will be permitted and that those bearing any weapons would be disarmed. The police did not honor this agreement and permitted an armed demonstration. And rather than building on the spirit of trust, established through previous negotiations, they fired on an unoffending crowd. A number of those injured in this incident have subsequently been arrested, some taken from their hospital beds, and are in detention.

The police have made counterclaims to the effect that they were under attack. Based on previous experience, we have no reason to place confidence in these claims.

An alarming feature of the violence is the role being played by the KwaZulu Police in support of armed groups in launching attacks on specific areas. In January 1991 a large contingent of armed men, reinforced by the KwaZulu Police, invaded the Ndwendwe area of Osindisweni and made off with thirty head of cattle.

1.6. There has been a startling increase in the use of automatic weapons, assault rifles, and other firearms on the Reef since September 1990. Despite repeated efforts on the part of the ANC, civics, and other democratic bodies to assist the police and other government intelligence services with information pertaining to these arms and the trade in arms, not a single arrest has been made and not a single arms cache uncovered, nor has the supply line been interrupted. The apparent incapacity of the South African authorities in this regard beggars description.

Violence coincides with ANC campaigns

2.0. It is evident from our observation and that of others that the peaks in these waves of violence coincide uncannily with ANC-launched campaigns and with mass campaigns launched by other elements of the democratic movement.

Recent pronouncements by a political figure serving in the antidemocratic and unpopular structures foisted on the African urban population by the government, indicate that it is their intention to resist expressions of opposition to these bodies by a resort to armed intimidation and violence. Direct links between such expressed intentions and the acts of violence that have occurred have been drawn by this same individual. The concerted effort to draw councillors into the ranks of the Inkatha Freedom Party with the promise that it will protect them against mass pressure, also suggests the intention of using violence to ward off demands that councillors resign.[25]

It is the considered opinion of the ANC that it is inconceivable that the authorities lack the capacity or the skill to prevent the violent deeds we have enumerated. We suspect that, at best, the feeble response on the part of the state betrays an absence of will to take measures adequate to avert violence, detect and bring the guilty parties to justice, because the perpetrators of this violence are providing a line of defense for government institutions that would otherwise have been rendered dysfunctional.

2.1. Since the outbreak of this current cycle of violence, there has been an avalanche of charges of police partiality, connivance, and complicity in acts of violence. Apart from shrill denials from the relevant ministry, no adequate explanation has been forthcoming regarding the acts or omissions of the authorities.

It is evident that the killings, maimings, and beatings that have occurred have greatly inflamed feelings of ethnic antagonism among various sections of the African people; have distracted public attention from the root causes of poverty, hunger, deprivation, and want in our country; and have rendered it more difficult to achieve united action among the African people for generally accepted and commendable goals.

Those responsible for fomenting this violence have the clear intention of sowing divisions and stoking up a psychosis of fear, insecurity, and mutual distrust among the African people. At the same time, they hope to prey on the worst fears and prejudices of our white compatriots and thus make them more apprehensive about a democratic transformation.

We are persuaded that the government's evident reluctance to act with expedition and vigor against the instigators of this violence betrays a hope that their actions will rebound to the government's favor in the short and intermediate term.

2.2. The impact of this cycle of violence is that it has raised the costs/risks entailed in being a member of or of being identified with the ANC and its allies. In certain cities and rural areas it has resulted in "no-go areas" from which ANC members, activities, and symbols are excluded, not by the law but by gangs of hoodlums and vigilantes. This is designed to weaken the credibility of the ANC, limit its scope for growth, and disintegrate its new legal structures.

This has proved a far more effective means of political repression than the legal measures previously employed by the state to crush the democratic opposition. Its aim is to inflate the image of the Inkatha Freedom Party from that of a minor to the rank of the third major player on the political arena.

The ANC demands

2.3. The ANC is of the view that the government's equivocal attitude to the cycle of violence reflects either an attitude of cynical irresponsibility or is evidence of connivance at acts of organized terror in the hope that they will succeed in destroying or seriously crippling the ANC.

The government's inaction calls into serious question its true intentions and sincerity regarding the entire peace process and the democratization of South Africa. In view of this, the ANC demands:

• That the government take legislative measures during the current session of Parliament to outlaw the carrying of weapons, traditional or otherwise, at public assemblies, processions, rallies, etc.

• The dismissal of ministers Adriaan Vlok and General Magnus Malan from public office and the rustication of all the officers of the SADF and SAP who bear direct responsibility for the setting up, management, the crimes and misdemeanors of the CCB [Civil Cooperation Bureau] and other hit squads.

• The visible, public dismantling and disarming of all special counterinsurgency units such as the Askaris, Battalion 32, the CCB, Koevoet, the Z Squad, etc., and the establishment of a multiparty commission to oversee this process.[26]

• The immediate suspension from duty of all police officers and constables who were implicated in the massacres at Sebokeng on 22 June 1990 and the commencement of legal proceedings against them; the immediate suspension from duty of all the police officers and constables responsible for the shootings in Daveyton, Benoni, on 24 March 1991, pending a commission of inquiry into that incident.

• Satisfactory assurances that in future the SAP, SADF, and other security organs will employ acceptable and civilized methods of crowd control; and that the issuance of live ammunition to the police on such occasions shall be disallowed.

• Effective steps are taken to begin the process of phasing out the hostels and other labor compounds and transforming them into family units and single-occupancy flats.

• The establishment of an independent commission of inquiry to receive, investigate, and report on all complaints of misconduct by the police and other security services.

2.4. If by 9 May 1991 these demands have not been met the ANC shall:

(a) Suspend any further discussion with the government on the all-party congress; and

(b) Suspend all exchanges with the government on the future constitution of our country.

It is your sweat and blood that has created the wealth of South Africa

ADDRESS TO NATIONAL UNION OF MINEWORKERS, APRIL 27, 1991

The following speech was given at the conclusion of the Seventh Congress of the National Union of Mineworkers (NUM), an affiliate of the Congress of South African Trade Unions (COSATU). The gathering, held in Johannesburg April 24-27, was attended by seven hundred delegates.

Comrade president of NUM, James Motlatsi; the general secretary of NUM, Comrade Cyril Ramaphosa; distinguished guests; fellow workers:

It is indeed an honor for me to address your Seventh Congress, which was opened by our secretary-general, Alfred Nzo. Please accept my sincere apologies for not being able to attend your important deliberations over the past days. Nevertheless, I look forward to a thorough discussion with the leadership of the NUM on the decisions your congress has taken.

There is an added significance for me in being here with you. This union has made me an honorary life president, a tribute that I highly value. Your support helped sustain me during the long years of imprisonment.

We warmly greet the international guests who are with us today—the president of the Miners' International Federation, representatives from the British National Union of Mineworkers, from Sweden, who have been most generous in their support of our union, and from the USA. Your struggles are legendary and have inspired our own. We all know how intertwined the ownership and control of mines are throughout the world. This expression of international solidarity of workers of the world enables us to learn from each other, to support each other and strengthen our ties in the face of multinational strategies for profit maximization and exploitation.

We greet the representatives from our neighbors—Zambia, Zimbabwe, Namibia, and Botswana—as brothers. Many of your members have been migrant workers in South Africa and know the tyranny of apartheid. Your countries have provided immeasurable support and refuge to thousands forced to flee, despite Pretoria's military and economic aggression. We are in your debt and look forward to the future, when the whole region can prosper in a postapartheid era.

The ANC recognizes that the mining industry is facing a crisis of unprecedented magnitude. Johannesburg, the "city of gold," bears the scars of decades of burrowing deep underground for that most precious of metals, gold. The dust that blows into the townships comes from the mine dumps that have become a geographical feature of this city. But the scars that cover the most painful wounds are those deep inside every mine worker in this country.

You know what it is to work in the heat deep in the bowels of the earth. You know the fear of being buried alive underground. You know the humiliation of body searches and being treated like worthless cattle. You know the loneliness of hostel life, the control of your every move. You know the painful death that comes from inhaling the dust that destroys your lungs, that kills your children when they play in dumps of blue asbestos waste.

Yet it is your sweat and blood that has created the vast

wealth that white South Africa enjoys. You dig for diamonds, platinum, gold—the precious metals that adorn the rich. Yet in times of crisis, such as the industry now faces, you are the first to be retrenched. In the recent past sixty thousand workers have lost their jobs. Thousands more are threatened.

We are told this is because of the low gold price, the slump in the gold jewelery industry, and the international cut in demand. This may well be the case, given the worldwide recession, but we still expect the mine owners and employers to look beyond job cuts as a solution to the problem. I fully endorse the decision taken by NUM to call for a summit of the decision makers of the industry and the government to tackle this issue.

Alternative solutions must be found that take into account you, the workers, without whom mining is impossible. The crisis is of such proportions that a national response is required. The consequences for the entire country of such retrenchment will be devastating. The rural areas, already impoverished, will be hard hit. Foreign exchange earnings will be dramatically reduced. We assure you that the ANC will do whatever is necessary to ensure that this crisis is addressed at the highest level.

But the crisis in the mining industry is not the only one facing us. The violence ravaging our country is of such proportions that we have presented the government with a set of demands and a deadline date of May 9, or else we will not proceed with the planned all-party congress nor hold any discussions on the future constitution for South Africa. There is also the April 30 deadline date agreed to in terms of the Pretoria Minute affecting the release of political prisoners and return of exiles.

It goes without saying that those of us who have spent so many wasted, lonely years in apartheid's prisons, and who have been released, have a special obligation and concern for the thousands of political prisoners still behind bars. The government has turned the Pretoria Minute, a political document mutually agreed upon, into a legal quagmire. We want to put the position squarely before the government, which has less than a week in which to meet its obligations.

April 30 was never merely a "target date," as the government spokesmen now claim. It was the date mutually agreed upon by the ANC and the government negotiators as the date by which all political prisoners would be released. Together, we hammered out a definition of what was a political prisoner. The ANC agrees with the Human Rights Commission figures, which indicate that there are 1,146 clearly identified political prisoners.

But at a meeting of an "audit committee," formed two weeks ago to try to agree on the number of political prisoners, General Monro of the Department of Corrective Services stated that they have a list of four thousand unrest-related prisoners. Of this total they are only prepared to consider 320 as possible political prisoners. Thus the total of prisoners remaining in jail could be well over five thousand. The government is trying to narrow the guidelines of what constitutes a political offense and draw a distinction between security prisoners and unrest-related prisoners. The definition of political offenses, mutually agreed with the government, makes no such distinction. This is a measure of the failure of the government to live up to its commitments made through agreements with the ANC.

I would like to spend a little time discussing with you our perspective of the violence and why we found it necessary to put demands before the government, including the dismissal of ministers Vlok and Malan.

The violence is designed to create division among the African people, especially between Zulu and Xhosa, hostel dweller and township resident. Mine workers have a very important role to play in defusing the tensions. Hostels have been identified as sources of violence, where guns are kept and weapons training takes place. This violence only serves to enslave us, turning brother against brother while white South Africa pretends to stand above the conflict. It presents the picture that South Africa can only know stability and prosperity with whites in control.

We call on all of you to organize in the hostels. Act together with the township residents to isolate those who bring death and destruction. Isolate the vigilantes, and act against the levies for the purchase of weapons. Refuse to be part of Pretoria's plans to decimate our people and your organization, the ANC. Expose, for all the world to see, the role of the warlords and who they serve. You can help bring an end to this bloodletting, which threatens the very future of our country.

It is also necessary to address the question of sanctions. We regret the decision of the European Community to unilaterally decide to lift sanctions.[27] We repeat that the time is not yet right for such action. De Klerk has come this far only because of pressure, including international action in the form of sanctions. To relax this pressure now means that the government will feel less compelled to fulfill its obligations. If anybody needs to be rewarded, it is the ANC for initiating the peace process.

This decision also once again shows clearly how Europe allies itself with white South Africa, and has no regard for the lives, the views, and the needs of black South Africa. We are the victims, yet they reward the jailer for letting a little more light into our hellhole. It is regrettable that race still plays such a significant part in decision making even as we enter the much-heralded twenty-first century.

We call on all our compatriots to look beyond the propaganda that seeks to portray de Klerk as a conquering hero on this issue. The reality is that the ability of South Africa to attract investment and to get access to world markets will only be enhanced by political resolution of the conflict. Those who are serious about the much-needed economic recovery for South Africa must be equally serious about political resolution. As the EC decisions to reward de Klerk delay resolution of our political problems, they are also delaying economic recovery. Therefore, what seems to be a victory for de Klerk is, in fact, a loss for our country and its future.

Therefore, we are particularly encouraged by the strong resolution taken by this congress on sanctions. Your decision to call for the maintenance of sanctions reflects the views of hundreds of thousands of working people, and should be listened to.

We have entered negotiations so that our country can know peace and freedom. The purpose of these negotiations is to ensure that we emerge with a democratic government, a new constitution, and a country which is governed by the people, for the people. We demand our rightful place in the land of our birth. We want one person, one vote in a united, nonracial, and democratic South Africa.

We feel that the way to achieve this is through the following steps:

• An all-party congress, which is as inclusive as possible, so that we try to get common agreement on the framework to guide our way forward.

• An interim government, to last a maximum of eighteen months, which oversees the whole process of free and fair elections to a constituent assembly. This must be an effective government with the means to control the security forces.

• A constituent assembly elected by one person, one vote, on the basis of proportional representation. It is this body that will draw up a new constitution for the country.

It is precisely this process that the violence and destabilization is designed to prevent.

The ANC national conference is a few weeks away. Delegates from across the country, representing hundreds of thousands of people, will gather in Durban in the first week of July. We hope that there will be a strong delegation from branches of the ANC that are in the mines. We want your views, your demands, and your interests to also inform our discussions and decisions. You have a major role to play in our attempts to create a country and a future where democratic practice is the norm and the rights of working people are respected. We want a national culture of respect for each other, for our customs and traditions, for our different skin colors and religions. We want this not only in law but in the very fabric of our society.

You are the motor force of our great country. Your congress has taken important decisions for the future of the whole industry, and therefore for the whole country. I want to appeal to those who control the mining industry to listen to your decisions and be prepared to engage with you in the process of restructuring the industry for the sake of the future of all our people. The challenges facing us are enormous, but acting in unity we can succeed and achieve our goals.

Long live the National Union of Mineworkers!

Long live the alliance between COSATU, the ANC, and the SACP!

Our struggle has changed the balance of forces

OPENING ADDRESS TO ANC NATIONAL CONFERENCE, JULY 2, 1991

On July 2-7, 1991, the ANC held its Forty-eighth National Conference at the University of Durban-Westville, attended by 2,301 delegates, and guests from thirty-five countries. The conference selected a new leadership, electing Mandela ANC president. The speech below was Mandela's address at the opening session.

Comrade chairperson; comrade president of our movement; esteemed guests and observers; fellow delegates:

I would like to join our president, Comrade O.R. Tambo, in welcoming you all to conference. As he has said, this is an historic occasion not only for the ANC but also with regard to the future of our country.

It is an incontestable fact that the millions of our people and many more internationally are looking forward to the results of this conference in the expectation that at the end we will convey to them all a message of hope that the long days of apartheid tyranny are about to end.

We shall not, through our own acts of omission or commission, disappoint these expectations by reducing the conference just to another event in the political calendar of our country. The week ahead of us is therefore very important.

Consequently, we are very pleased that we have present in this hall representatives of all the organized structures of the ANC, as well as observers from our allied organizations. During the few days ahead of us we will have to take very important decisions which may very well decide the fate of this country for many years to come.

It will therefore be required of each one of us that we approach all issues on our agenda with all due seriousness. We expect of all of us rational and constructive debate. Out of that debate must come equally rational, constructive, and realistic decisions, aimed at taking South Africa forward as quickly as possible to its destination as a united, democratic, nonracial, and nonsexist country.

The conference here today is the culmination of a singularly democratic process. It is a little over a year since the ANC began the task of reconstituting itself as a public organization in our country. You delegates have been chosen by close to one thousand branches to represent the views of our entire membership. Your branches have participated in rigorous discussions concerning our strategy, constitution, organization, and policy.

You have been elected by a thoroughly democratic process. The procedures that have brought you here are unique in this country. There are not many movements or organizations which can claim to measure up to these democratic standards. Certainly, outside the ranks of the mass democratic and trade union movement, such practices are virtually unheard of. The very process that brings us together here is an outstanding example of participatory democracy which augurs well for the future.

Let us continue to demonstrate in our debates here this week that we stand by the principles of freedom of expression. All views are entitled to be aired. It is through vigorous and constructive debate that together we will chart the path ahead.

We have convened as part of our continuing effort to make further inputs into the unstoppable offensive to end the criminal system of apartheid, to transform South Africa into a nonracial democracy, and to reconstruct it as a country of justice, prosperity, and peace for all our people, both black and white, in keeping with the objectives contained in the Freedom Charter.[28]

In this regard, the first point we would like to make is that it is the responsibility of our movement to be in the vanguard of the process leading to the democratic transformation of our country. We must both lead and learn from our people.

We make this point not out of any feeling of arrogance or superiority over any other political formation. We say it to make the point that the ANC is the repository of the aspirations of the overwhelming majority of our people. In terms of mass support and for reasons that are very easy to understand, we are the major political formation in this country.

Secondly, because it is the oldest formation among the forces that are fighting for the victory of the perspective of a nonracial democracy, the ANC contains within it a unique reservoir of experience of the struggle for democracy, equality, and an end to racism in all its forms.

The ANC has a proud record of struggle and resistance to the efforts of successive white minority regimes to entrench this system and make it an everlasting reality defining the nature and functioning of South African society.

It is precisely that struggle which has changed the balance of forces to such an extent that the apartheid system is now in retreat. Through the struggles of our people, the ANC has been unbanned and we are able to meet in our own country today. A regime whose ideology is based on a virulent anti-communism has been forced to unban our ally, the South African Communist Party, and remove provisions from the law prohibiting the propagation of communist ideas.

We have with us many of our friends from the rest of the world who, only a short while ago, would not have been able to enter this country. They have come here at the invitation of the ANC in order to demonstrate their continuing solidarity with our cause.

All of these developments represent important victories of the heroic struggle that the masses of our people have waged under the leadership of the ANC.

It is our movement that has the vision, the policies, the programs, and the mature leadership which will take our country from its apartheid past to its democratic future.

From this conference we must formulate the strategies and provide the leadership that can and will enable us to lead all the people of South Africa to the goal which the overwhelming majority seeks, that of justice, democracy, peace, and prosperity.

In a period of transition, in which we will experience many things for the first time, we are bound to make mistakes and experience failures. We must make sure that we recognize these quickly, assess them, criticize ourselves where necessary, learn what has to be learnt, and emerge from these stronger and better able to carry out our historic mission.

The ability to conduct struggle is gained in struggle. The ability to score victories is a function of experience that we gain in struggle. Experience also means mistakes and failures. It is by learning from these that we are able to struggle in a better way. Fear of mistakes and failures means only one thing. It means fear of engaging in struggle.

As a result of the struggle that we waged for decades, the balance of forces has changed to such an extent that the ruling National Party, which thought it could maintain the system of white minority domination forever, has been obliged to accept the fact that it has no strength to sustain the apartheid system and that it must enter into negotiations with the genuine representatives of the people. Negotiations constitute a victory of our struggle and a defeat for the ruling group, which thought it could exercise a monopoly of political power forever.

When we decided to take up arms, it was because the only other choice was to surrender and submit to slavery.

This was not a decision we took lightly. We were always ready, as we are now, to seize any genuine opportunity that might arise to secure the liberation of our people by peaceful means.

We are very conscious that the process could not be smooth since we are dealing with a regime that is steeped in a culture of racism, violence, and domination. We are dealing with a group of politicians who do not want to negotiate themselves out of power and representatives of the state who fear the impact of democratic change.

The point which must be clearly understood is that the struggle is not over, and negotiations themselves are a theater of struggle, subject to advances and reverses as any other form of struggle.

Despite our own heroic efforts, we have not defeated the regime. Consequently, we see negotiations as a continuation of the struggle leading to our central objective: the transfer of power to the people. There are therefore some issues that are nonnegotiable: among others our demands for one person, one vote; a united South Africa; the liberation of women; and the protection of fundamental human rights.

As a movement we recognize the fact that apart from ourselves there are other political formations in the country. These are as entitled to exist as we are. They have a right to formulate their own policies and to contest for support for their policies and organizations. We have agreed to enter into talks with all these, and have been talking to most of them, because we have no desire whatsoever to impose our views on everybody else.

We have never claimed that we have a monopoly of wisdom and that only our views and policies are legitimate. As a democratic movement we shall continue to defend the right of all our people to freedom of thought, association, and organization. It is precisely because of this that we have firmly committed ourselves to the perspective of a multiparty democracy.

We say all this to contribute to our preparations for the

period ahead of us, when we shall enter into negotiations which will determine the destiny of our country for the foreseeable future. We must participate in these processes with a clear vision of what we want to achieve, with a clear view of the procedures we must follow to ensure that our representatives are properly mandated and that they report back to us, and with a clear view of the process of negotiations.

Our demand is for freedom now! It can never be in our interest that we prolong the agony of the apartheid system. It does not serve the interests of the masses we represent and the country as a whole that we delay the realization of the achievement of the objective of the transfer of power to the people.

Therefore, it is necessary that we should have an idea of the time frame we visualize for the processes which must take us to the election of a parliament representative of all the people of our country.

What, then, are the principal steps that we foresee on the road to this goal? First of all, there remains the matter of the complete removal of obstacles to negotiations as spelt out in the Harare Declaration. This must now include the question of the ending of the campaign of terror against the people, in this province, in the Transvaal, and in the rest of our country.

When these issues have been attended to, we should then move to convene the all-party congress. Out of that congress must emerge a number of very important decisions. These will include agreed constitutional principles, the mechanism to draw up the new constitution, the establishment of an interim government, and the role of the international community during the transitional period.

We still have to grapple with the fact that the process of the removal of obstacles to negotiations has not yet been completed. We will discuss this question, bearing in mind both the progress achieved and what still remains to be done. One of the issues we must note carefully is the way in which the government has acted to discredit the process of negotiations, by dragging its feet in terms of implementing what has been agreed.

This has come as no surprise. It has never been on the agenda of the National Party to enter into negotiations with anybody other than those whom it had itself placed in supposed positions of power. It is also in this context that we should understand the use of violence to derail the peace process.

All of us present in this hall know that there are people within our country, and within state structures, who remain opposed to the transformation of our country into a nonracial democracy. Not only do these forces of reaction stand against the realization of that ultimate goal, they are also opposed to each and every step that has so far been taken to build towards the accomplishment of this objective.

They did not and do not like the fact that agreement was reached to release all political prisoners and detainees, to allow the free return of all exiles, to terminate political trials, to end the state of emergency, to review security legislation, and so on.

They took fright at the prospect of these agreements being implemented because they knew that sooner or later this process would lead to the democratization of political power in our country and, therefore, the creation of the possibility for the people themselves to dismantle the system of apartheid and create a society that would be in keeping with the genuine aspirations of all citizens of our country. That is precisely why there has been the escalation of public violence such as we have experienced during the last twelve months.

It was not because we were failing that they decided to shoot the people down. It was exactly because we are succeeding. The lesson from all this must surely be that as long as we make progress towards the achievement of our goals, so must we expect that those who fundamentally disagree with these goals will resort to violence and terror to deny us the possibility to move forward.

A heavy responsibility rests on the shoulders of the presently ruling National Party to demonstrate that it is, in practical terms, as committed to change as its statements suggest. This it cannot do by engaging in maneuvers designed to discredit the process of negotiations.

Neither can it expect that we will accept its good faith when it sits paralyzed as the security forces it controls themselves engage in violence against the people, permit such violence to occur, and remain immune from prosecution when there is clear evidence of their involvement in or connivance at the murder of innocent people.

Consequently, nobody should complain when we accuse the Pretoria regime of pursuing a double agenda, one of talking peace while actually conducting war. It is for this regime to demonstrate its good faith not by what it says but by what it does.

What is of strategic importance for us is that we must defend the lives of our people at the same time as we push the process forward leading to the transfer of power into their hands. We should not allow the situation whereby those who deliberately inject violence into our communities succeed in their intention of slowing down the process leading to the democratic transformation of our country through the use of such violence.

We must defend peace at the same time as we advance towards people's power. We must engage in successful defensive battles against the counterrevolution at the same time as we conduct successful offensive battles to defeat the apartheid system. This is a struggle we must fight on all fronts simultaneously.

Conference has a responsibility to consider these questions, which pose important strategic and tactical challenges. In this context, we will need to assess the correctness of the positions we have adopted, the effectiveness of the actions we have taken, the possibilities we face in the future, and arrive at decisions that will ensure that we do not submit to an agenda that has been set by the forces of counterrevolution but pursue our own agenda, whose core must always remain the speedy transfer of power into the hands of the people.

Conference will have to consider all issues which relate to the creation of a climate conducive to negotiations and take all the necessary decisions. I have no doubt that our struggle to create such a climate will succeed, as I am certain that our offensive to achieve the democratic transformation of our country will triumph.

Accordingly, in our planning we must proceed beyond the mere removal of obstacles, important as this issue might be. We must engage one another in serious discussion about how we should manage the period of transition which our country has entered.

From all that has happened so far, it seems clear that this period is likely to prove one of the most difficult, complex, and challenging in the entire life of our organization. It is therefore one which we must all approach with the greatest vigilance and firmness with respect to matters of principle, clarity with regard to strategy and timeousness, and flexibility with reference to tactical issues.

One of the first principal policy questions we are going to face during the transitional period, and in the context of the process of negotiations, is the issue of the all-party congress. With regard to this matter, we must evolve a clearer idea on such questions as the composition of this congress, its agenda, the manner of its functioning, and the length of time we propose that it should sit.

Conference should bear in mind the fact that we ourselves said that the all-party congress should convene when the obstacles to negotiations have been removed. Accordingly, we must calculate on the congress taking place sooner rather than later, and therefore approach all preparations for our own participation with some urgency.

Similarly, we must discuss the issue of constitutional principles which will be on the agenda of the all-party congress. Fortunately, we have a draft document on this issue, prepared some time ago by our Constitutional Committee and which we have been discussing in our branches and regions. I refer here to the documents dealing with constitutional principles and a bill of rights.

These are important documents, as they spell out our views on the framework and the broad character of the new constitution. We must ensure that these do indeed advance our fundamental perspective of the transformation of South Africa into a united, democratic, nonracial, and nonsexist country.

We must also discuss the issue of the mechanism to draw up the new constitution. As all of us know, we are convinced that this mechanism should be an elected constituent assembly and have made this into one of our major campaigning slogans.

The winning of the objective of a constituent assembly will not be achieved solely through the negotiation process. It will require the generation of mass support for this demand. We reject the regime's contention that mass mobilization stands in the way of the negotiating process. In the absence of voting rights, the only power we can exercise is the power and the strength of our organized people.

But we must also deal with other important matters which arise in the context of the constituent assembly. To have an elected constituent assembly means that we must have elections. For us to succeed in those elections we must prepare for them, bearing in mind the fact that throughout the period of its existence the ANC has never participated in general elections.

We must therefore take all the necessary decisions which will enable us to engage in this process successfully. Among other things, this means that we must have the necessary policies to present to the country at large and the organizational machinery to do this. It also means that we must have clear ideas about such questions as electoral systems and the demarcation of boundaries of constituencies.

As you are aware, another issue which belongs within the transitional period is the question of the interim government. The importance of the matter cannot be overemphasized. Among ourselves we are agreed that it would be incorrect and unacceptable that during this transitional period one of the parties to the negotiations, in this case the National Party, should continue to govern the country on its own.

An interim government will therefore have to be formed and constituted in such a manner that it is broadly acceptable to the various political formations in our country. To that extent, it will take on the character of a transitional government of national unity. Once this government is formed, we will have reached the situation whereby, for the first time this century, South Africa will cease to be ruled by a white minority regime.

In this regard we must provide the lead on all major questions that will affect the constitution of an interim government as well as its life span.

It would be important that we have some idea of the time frame within which the new constitution should be drawn up and adopted. We certainly do not want a long-drawn or endless process with regard to this matter. In the end, as we have said already, the sooner power transfers into the hands of the people the better.

The international community continues to be of vital importance to the future of our country. This will remain the case even after we have won our freedom. In both the Harare and UN Declarations,[29] it is visualized that a stage will be reached when this community will determine that we have arrived at an internationally acceptable solution to the South African question. This would then enable the rest of the world to welcome democratic South Africa as an equal partner among the community of nations.

But before we reach that stage, it would be important that we discuss the question of the possible role of the international community during the transitional period—the role it could play to expedite this process so that we move forward with minimum delay towards the accomplishment of our cherished goals. Conference will therefore have to deal with this matter as well.

Needless to say, the transitional period is not an end in itself. It constitutes the conveyor belt which should take us through to the goal of a democratic South Africa. At the end of this road and the beginning of another, is the question of the exercise of political power. I take it that we all agree that when the moment comes, the ANC will present itself to the country at large for the election into the new parliament.

It therefore seems obvious that we should continue the work we have been doing already of preparing our policy positions on all major questions of public life. We have already had to explain ourselves to the people as a whole, in terms of these various policy positions. The country has understood that we needed the time to work out these positions as we had to rebuild our movement after thirty years of illegality.

But obviously elaboration of policy cannot itself go on forever. We must begin to arrive at firm conclusions about what we would do with the country once we become the governing party. Conference should at least give the broad guidelines which will enable the movement as a whole to move forward and arrive at these basic policy positions as quickly as possible.

The matter should not be underestimated that all our people want to know how we would govern the country if they gave us this responsibility. They want us to speak with one consistent voice and put forward a clear vision.

It is clear from everything we have said that there are very many major tasks ahead of us. Their accomplishment will be of critical importance not only to the ANC and its allies but to the country as a whole and to the millions of people who are not necessarily members of our organization.

We must therefore closely scrutinize the issue of our organizational capacity to carry out these tasks. If we are weak, we will not be able to realize our goals. If we work in a confused manner, we will not be able to take the country forward.

The secretary-general will be presenting the report on the organization. Therefore, I will not go into any detail with regard to the issues that confront us in this area of our work. I would, however, like to draw your attention to a few issues which I am sure conference will have to discuss.

Organizationally, what do we need? We need a movement that is organizationally strong in terms of the membership that it attracts into its ranks. After seventeen months of legality, we have recruited 700,000 members. Even though the effort has been commendable, there is no room for complacency and much more work has got to be done to draw millions of all our people into the ANC.

We must also express concern at the proportionately low number of members that is drawn from rural areas. We must also do more to attract members from the middle strata.

We can ill afford to be content with the relatively low level of success that we are making with regard to drawing whites, Coloureds, and Indians into the organization.[30] We must ask ourselves frankly why this is so. In this context, we should not be afraid to confront the real issue that these national minorities might have fears about the future, which fears we should address.

We must remain a movement representative of all the people of South Africa — a people's movement, both in name and in reality. As we build our organization, we must therefore constantly watch this issue to ensure that we do not just concentrate on one sector of our population.

Apart from the ANC itself, our movement has three other important component parts. These are the youth and women's leagues, and the people's army, Umkhonto we Sizwe. The responsibilities that fall on the shoulders of the leagues are very heavy indeed. It is part of our task to ensure that they are themselves strong enough to carry out these responsibilities.

They, like the ANC itself, should understand the point clearly that they are charged with the task of leading not just their own members. They must, each in its own sector, lead the millions falling within their constituencies. Thus when we talk of mass action, it must be real mass action, which draws into struggle not just members but the masses of the people we represent.

At the same time, we need to pay better attention to our heroic army, Umkhonto we Sizwe, than we have done during the past year or so. MK has been at the center of our struggle in the past and delivered the telling blows that brought us to the point where a negotiated solution became possible.

It is proper that this conference should pay homage to all the commanders and combatants of MK who laid down their lives and made other invaluable sacrifices that have brought us to where we are today. We are very glad that some of those who survived during the course of that struggle are with us today.

Some of them were serving long sentences, but we managed to get them out, even to the point where the notorious Robben Island prison has at last been closed down. Some of them are serving commanders of the people's army, but we have succeeded to get them to be present at this, their conference. Of those that were sentenced to death, we have ensured that none will hang! Soon we shall have all of them among us, to continue the struggle for the victory of the people's cause.

We have suspended armed action, but have not terminated the armed struggle. Whether it is deployed inside the country or outside, Umkhonto we Sizwe therefore has a responsibility to keep itself in a state of readiness in case the forces of counterrevolution once more block the path to a peaceful transition to a democratic society.

New challenges will face MK in the context of the installation of the interim government. As we have said, this is one of the issues we will have to discuss, an important part of which will be the issue of the control of the security forces by such a government. It is clear that MK will have to play a vital role in these processes. Where it can, it must, of course, make its expertise available to those communities that are engaged in the process of establishing their self-defense units.

At the same time, MK must prepare itself to become part of the new national defense force we shall have to build as part of the process of the reconstruction of our country. The task of training this cadre cannot await the adoption of a democratic constitution but must be carried out now to ensure that, as happened in Zimbabwe and Namibia, when the time comes to rebuild our defense forces, we are ready to participate in these processes in defense of our democratic gains.

Such are some of the major tasks that confront MK during this period. To carry them out properly requires that all the necessary logistics be made available. But it also requires that MK continues to be an army that is committed to the democratic perspective that we represent.

We will also be discussing the new constitution of the ANC. Quite clearly we must ensure that we agree on a structure which enables the membership to participate in the formulation of policy and direction of the work of the movement while the leadership we will elect recognizes that it is accountable without compromising its ability to lead.

But whatever our constitution will say, it will only function properly if we all proceed from the position that we are all comrades, bound together by common goals, with all of us equally committed to make a contribution to the realization of those common goals. Much work remains to be done among us all to raise the level of political consciousness so that every cadre, however high the position they may occupy, is schooled in the policies of our movement, its character, its strategy and tactics.

Certainly, we must also resist the efforts of some among the media to encourage factions within the movement by suggesting there are groups locked in mortal combat, there is a division between the exiles and the internal group, the ex-prisoners and somebody else, the so-called militants and moderates.

We should not tolerate the formation of factions within the movement. The best means of ensuring this is through open democratic discussion within our ranks, so that no one feels excluded or denied the right to express his or her opinion.

Many people both inside and outside our country repeatedly raise the question of our relations with the Communist Party. We would therefore like to take this opportunity once more to reiterate the fact that we consider the South African Communist Party a firm and dependable ally in the common struggle to rid our country of the system of white minority rule. We will therefore rebuff all attempts to drive a wedge between our two organizations.

At the same time, the point must be borne in mind that the SACP is a separate organization which does not seek to dominate the ANC as the ANC. The ANC, for its part, does not seek to dominate the Communist Party. The policies of the ANC are not decided in the Communist Party as neither are the policies of the SACP decided in the ANC, regardless of the number of people who might be members of both organizations.

Both we and the Communist Party must be judged by the policies we espouse and the things we do to propagate and advance those views. We believe our detractors should outgrow the pathological anticommunism of the period of the cold war, stop the red-baiting, and live up to the commitment they all express in favor of a multiparty democracy.

The other member of our alliance is the Congress of South African Trade Unions. We would like to reaffirm our firm determination to respect the independence of the trade union movement and to act in a manner consistent with this position, both now and in the future. We are ready to act in support of positions that are put forward by this allied organization with regard to issues such as retrenchment, a living wage, and the workers' charter.

The incoming National Executive Committee will have to ensure that our tripartite alliance works better than it has done in the past. This will ensure that we use the collective strength represented by our respective organizations in a better way.

We have also advanced the perspective of a front of all patriotic forces. Undoubtedly a report will be presented to conference on this matter. The unity of our people, and the organizations that represent them, has always been central to both our thinking and to our practice. Unity remains important to this day. It must remain an essential part of our activities, from the branch upwards.

Our contact with various organizations has not been as strong as it should be. This, too, will have to be corrected.

Our strength lies in the masses of the people. We must therefore continue to pay the closest attention to the issue of our work among the masses. They must see the ANC as their organization, one that represents their aspirations and actually advances their interests.

We must ensure that these masses are in fact engaged in struggle and are drawn into the fundamental discussion which must now take place about the future of our country. To ensure that these do not remain mere slogans and pious wishes, we must pay attention to the importance of door-to-door campaigning and the value of small local meetings.

We must help entrench the culture of political tolerance amongst our people. We reiterate: it is absolutely impermissible for any one of us to use force against the people. As we continue to engage in mass struggles, we must ensure that the people join these struggles as a result of conviction and not because of intimidation.

We must stand out as an unchallenged example of a real people's movement, in touch with these masses, responsive to their needs, capable of drawing them into action in their millions, and enjoying their genuine allegiance and voluntary support. Hopefully conference will address this question as well and be unsparing in its analysis and criticism of where we might have failed to relate to the masses in the manner I have described, so that we do indeed strengthen our links with these masses.

The continued support of the international community remains vital for the victory of our cause. We also need further to strengthen our links with the rest of the world to ensure that the international community, so well represented here today, remains engaged not only in the struggle against apartheid, but also in the struggle for the democratic transformation of our country.

From this international community we shall therefore require continuing political and material support for the present phase of our struggle. But equally we will need to prepare these friendly nations to come to our aid as we carry out the enormous tasks that will face us during the period of the reconstruction of our country, as well as define the place of a democratic South Africa within that international community. These are matters of critical importance to our people as a whole and will have to be discussed bearing in mind this reality.

Undoubtedly, we will also continue our discussions of the sanctions question, which we began at our consultative conference last December. The challenge that faces us with regard to this question is that we should find ways and means by which we arrest the process of the erosion of sanctions and help create the situation whereby we do not lose this weapon which we will need until a democratic constitution has been adopted.

Let me take this opportunity once more to join our president in saluting our honored international guests who are with us today and pay tribute to them for everything they have contributed to the protracted struggle which has brought us to where we are today. We thank you most sincerely for your support and are confident that you will stay the course with us not only to end the system of apartheid but to help us rebuild this otherwise beautiful country.

While you are with us, we hope that you will see a little bit of it, talk to as many of our people as you can, and gain a better understanding of the challenges that the ANC and the rest of the democratic movement face.

The masses of our people will undoubtedly feel greatly strengthened that you were able to visit them directly to express your solidarity and to strengthen the bonds of friendship which must underpin the relations that a free South Africa will have with the rest of the world.

We would also like to thank all of our other distinguished

guests from within our country, including the members of the diplomatic corps, who took time off to be with us today. We deeply appreciate the interest you have shown in our conference and trust that you will accept its results as a contribution to the common concern we share of the speedy transformation of our country into a nonracial democracy.

I would like to thank all the comrades and friends who have been involved in the work of preparing this conference. They have had to attend to a lot of issues. To honor and respect their contribution to the struggle, we are called upon as delegates to go about the business of our conference with all due diligence and seriousness. I wish all of you success.

Finally, I would like to thank the vice chancellor of the University of Durban-Westville, Professor Reddy, and all other members of the university for making the university available for our historic conference.

We have no words to express our gratitude, but trust that the results of our conference will help to reinforce the work in which you yourselves are engaged, of transforming this center of learning and the educational system as a whole in keeping with our common aspiration to create a just society.

Thank you for your attention.

We will ensure that the poor and rightless will rule the land of their birth

SPEECH TO RALLY IN CUBA, JULY 26, 1991

The address that follows was given to a rally of tens of thousands in Matan-zas, Cuba, during a trip by Mandela to five Latin American and Caribbean countries. The rally marked the thirty-eighth anniversary of the opening of the Cuban revolution; speaking alongside Mandela was Cuban president Fidel Castro.[31] During the rally Castro awarded Mandela the José Martí medal, the highest honor bestowed by the Cuban government. The award is named for one of the principal leaders of Cuba's struggle for independence from Spain, killed in battle in 1895.

First secretary of the Communist Party, president of the Council of State and of the government of Cuba, president of the socialist republic of Cuba, commander-in-chief, Com-rade Fidel Castro;

Cuban internationalists, who have done so much to free our continent; Cuban people; comrades and friends:

It is a great pleasure and honor to be present here today, especially on so important a day in the revolutionary history of the Cuban people. Today Cuba commemorates the thirty-eighth anniversary of the storming of the Moncada. Without

Moncada the *Granma* expedition, the struggle in the Sierra Maestra, and the extraordinary victory of January 1, 1959, would never have occurred.[32]

Today this is revolutionary Cuba, internationalist Cuba, the country that has done so much for the peoples of Africa.

We have long wanted to visit your country and express the many feelings that we have about the Cuban revolution, about the role of Cuba in Africa, southern Africa, and the world.

The Cuban people hold a special place in the hearts of the people of Africa. The Cuban internationalists have made a contribution to African independence, freedom, and justice, unparalleled for its principled and selfless character.

From its earliest days the Cuban revolution has itself been a source of inspiration to all freedom-loving people. We admire the sacrifices of the Cuban people in maintaining their independence and sovereignty in the face of a vicious imperialist-orchestrated campaign to destroy the impressive gains made in the Cuban revolution.

We too want to control our own destiny. We are determined that the people of South Africa will make their future and that they will continue to exercise their full democratic rights after liberation from apartheid. We do not want popular participation to cease at the moment when apartheid goes. We want to have the moment of liberation open the way to ever-deepening democracy.

We admire the achievements of the Cuban revolution in the sphere of social welfare. We note the transformation from a country of imposed backwardness to universal literacy. We acknowledge your advances in the fields of health, education, and science.

There are many things we learn from your experience. In particular we are moved by your affirmation of the historical connection to the continent and people of Africa.

Your consistent commitment to the systematic eradication of racism is unparalleled.

But the most important lesson that you have for us is that no matter what the odds, no matter under what difficulties you have had to struggle, there can be no surrender! It is a case of freedom or death!

I know that your country is experiencing many difficulties now, but we have confidence that the resilient people of Cuba will overcome these as they have helped other countries overcome theirs.

We know that the revolutionary spirit of today was started long ago and that its spirit was kindled by many early fighters for Cuban freedom, and indeed for freedom of all suffering under imperialist domination.

We too are also inspired by the life and example of José Martí, who is not only a Cuban and Latin American hero but justly honored by all who struggle to be free.

We also honor the great Che Guevara, whose revolutionary exploits, including on our own continent, were too powerful for any prison censors to hide from us. The life of Che is an inspiration to all human beings who cherish freedom. We will always honor his memory.[33]

We come here with great humility. We come here with great emotion. We come here with a sense of a great debt that is owed to the people of Cuba. What other country can point to a record of greater selflessness than Cuba has displayed in its relations with Africa?

How many countries of the world benefit from Cuban health workers or educationists? How many of these are in Africa?

Where is the country that has sought Cuban help and has had it refused?

How many countries under threat from imperialism or struggling for national liberation have been able to count on Cuban support?

It was in prison when I first heard of the massive assistance that the Cuban internationalist forces provided to the people of Angola, on such a scale that one hesitated to believe, when the Angolans came under combined attack of South African, CIA-financed FNLA, mercenary, UNITA, and Zairean troops in 1975.[34]

We in Africa are used to being victims of countries wanting to carve up our territory or subvert our sovereignty. It is unparalleled in African history to have another people rise to the defense of one of us.

We know also that this was a popular action in Cuba. We are aware that those who fought and died in Angola were only a small proportion of those who volunteered. For the Cuban people internationalism is not merely a word but something that we have seen practiced to the benefit of large sections of humankind.

We know that the Cuban forces were willing to withdraw shortly after repelling the 1975 invasion, but the continued aggression from Pretoria made this impossible.

Your presence and the reinforcement of your forces in the battle of Cuito Cuanavale was of truly historic significance.[35]

The crushing defeat of the racist army at Cuito Cuanavale was a victory for the whole of Africa!

The overwhelming defeat of the racist army at Cuito Cuanavale provided the possibility for Angola to enjoy peace and consolidate its own sovereignty!

The defeat of the racist army allowed the struggling people of Namibia to finally win their independence!

The decisive defeat of the apartheid aggressors broke the myth of the invincibility of the white oppressors!

The defeat of the apartheid army was an inspiration to the struggling people inside South Africa!

Without the defeat of Cuito Cuanavale our organizations would not have been unbanned!

The defeat of the racist army at Cuito Cuanavale has made it possible for me to be here today!

Cuito Cuanavale was a milestone in the history of the struggle for southern African liberation!

Cuito Cuanavale has been a turning point in the struggle to free the continent and our country from the scourge of apartheid!

Apartheid is not something that started yesterday. The origins of white racist domination go back three and a half centuries to the moment when the first white settlers started a process of disruption and later conquest of the Khoi, San, and other African peoples—the original inhabitants of our country.

The process of conquest from the very beginning engendered a series of wars of resistance, which in turn gave rise to our struggle for national liberation. Against heavy odds, African peoples tried to hold on to their lands. But the material base and consequent firepower of the colonial aggressors doomed the divided tribal chiefdoms and kingdoms to ultimate defeat.

This tradition of resistance is one that still lives on as an inspiration to our present struggle. We still honor the names of the great prophet and warrior Makana, who died while trying to escape from Robben Island prison in 1819, Hintsa, Sekhukhune, Dingane, Moshoeshoe, Bambatha, and other heroes of the early resistance to colonial conquest.[36]

It was against the background of this land seizure and conquest that the Union of South Africa was created in 1910. Outwardly South Africa became an independent state, but in reality power was handed over by the British conquerors to whites who had settled in the country. They were able in the new Union of South Africa to formalize racial oppression and economic exploitation of blacks.

Following the creation of the Union, the passing of the Land Act, purporting to legalize the land seizures of the nineteenth century,[37] gave impetus to the process leading to the formation of the African National Congress on January 8, 1912.

I am not going to give you a history of the ANC. Suffice it to say that the last eighty years of our existence has seen the evolution of the ANC from its earliest beginnings aimed at uniting the African peoples, to its becoming the leading force in the struggle of the oppressed masses for an end to racism and the establishment of a nonracial, nonsexist, and democratic state.

Its membership has been transformed from its early days

when they were a small group of professionals and chiefs, etc., into a truly mass organization of the people.

Its goals have changed from seeking improvement of the lot of Africans to instead seeking the fundamental transformation of the whole of South Africa into a democratic state for all.

Its methods of achieving its more far-reaching goals have over decades taken on a more mass character, reflecting the increasing involvement of the masses within the ANC and in campaigns led by the ANC.

Sometimes people point to the initial aims of the ANC and its early composition in order to suggest that it was a reformist organization. The truth is that the birth of the ANC carried from the beginning profoundly revolutionary implications.

The formation of the ANC was the first step towards creation of a new South African nation. That conception was developed over time, finding clear expression thirty-six years ago in the Freedom Charter's statement that "South Africa belongs to all who live in it, black and white." This was an unambiguous rejection of the racist state that had existed and an affirmation of the only alternative that we find acceptable, one where racism and its structures are finally liquidated.

It is well known that the state's response to our legitimate democratic demands was, among other things, to charge our leadership with treason and, in the beginning of the 1960s, to use indiscriminate massacres. That and the banning of our organizations left us with no choice but to do what every self-respecting people, including the Cubans, have done—that is, to take up arms to win our country back from the racists.

I must say that when we wanted to take up arms we approached numerous Western governments for assistance and we were never able to see any but the most junior ministers. When we visited Cuba we were received by the highest officials and were immediately offered whatever we wanted and needed. That was our earliest experience with Cuban internationalism.

Although we took up arms, that was not our preference. It was the apartheid regime that forced us to take up arms. Our preference has always been for a peaceful resolution of the apartheid conflict.

The combined struggles of our people within the country, as well as the mounting international struggle against apartheid during the 1980s, raised the possibility of a negotiated resolution of the apartheid conflict. The decisive defeat of Cuito Cuanavale altered the balance of forces within the region and substantially reduced the capacity of the Pretoria regime to destabilize its neighbors. This, in combination with our people's struggles within the country, was crucial in bringing Pretoria to realize that it would have to talk.

It was the ANC that initiated the current peace process that we hope will lead to a negotiated transfer of power to the people. We have not initiated this process for goals any different from those when we pursued the armed struggle. Our goals remain achievement of the demands of the Freedom Charter, and we will settle for nothing less than that.

No process of negotiations can succeed until the apartheid regime realizes that there will not be peace unless there is freedom and that we are not going to negotiate away our just demands. They must understand that we will reject any constitutional scheme that aims at continuing white privileges.

There is reason to believe that we have not yet succeeded in bringing this home to the government, and we warn them that if they do not listen we will have to use our power to convince them.

That power is the power of the people, and ultimately we know that the masses will not only demand but win full rights in a nonracial, nonsexist, democratic South Africa.

But we are not merely seeking a particular goal. We also propose a particular route for realizing it, and that is a route that involves the people all the way through. We do not want a process where a deal is struck over the heads of the people and their job is merely to applaud.

The government resists this at all costs because the question of how a constitution is made, how negotiations take place, is vitally connected to whether or not a democratic result ensues.

The present government wants to remain in office during the entire process of transition. Our view is that this is unacceptable. This government has definite negotiation goals. It cannot be allowed to use its powers as a government to advance its own cause and that of its allies and to use those same powers to weaken the ANC.

And this is exactly what they are doing. They have unbanned the ANC, but we operate under conditions substantially different from that of other organizations. We do not have the same freedom to organize as does Inkatha and other organizations allied to the apartheid regime. Our members are harassed and even killed. We are often barred from holding meetings and marches.

We believe that the process of transition must be controlled by a government that is not only capable and willing to create and maintain the conditions for free political activity. It must also act with a view to ensuring that the transition is towards creating a genuine democracy and nothing else.

The present government has shown itself to be quite unwilling or unable to create a climate for negotiations. It reneges on agreements to release political prisoners and allow the return of exiles. In recent times it has allowed a situation to be created where a reign of terror and violence is being unleashed against the African communities and the ANC as an organization.

We have had ten thousand people murdered in this violence since 1984 and two thousand this year alone. We have always said that this government that boasts of its professional police force is perfectly capable of ending this violence and prosecuting the perpetrators. Not only are they unwilling, we now have conclusive evidence, published in independent newspapers, of their complicity in this violence.[38]

The violence has been used in a systematic attempt to advance the power of Inkatha as a potential alliance partner of the National Party. There is now conclusive evidence of funds provided by the government—that is, taxpayers' money—to Inkatha.

All of this indicates the necessity to create an interim government of national unity to oversee the transition. We need a government enjoying the confidence of broad sections of the population to rule over this delicate period, ensuring that counterrevolutionaries are not allowed to upset the process and ensuring that constitution making operates within an atmosphere free of repression, intimidation, and fear.

The constitution itself, we believe, must be made in the most democratic manner possible. To us, that can best be achieved through electing representatives to a constituent assembly with a mandate to draft the constitution. There are organizations that challenge the ANC's claim to be the most representative organization in the country. If that is true, let them prove their support at the ballot box.

To ensure that ordinary people are included in this process we are circulating and discussing our own constitutional proposals and draft bill of rights. We want these to be discussed in all structures of our alliance—that is, the ANC, South African Communist Party, and Congress of South African Trade Unions, and amongst the people in general. That way, when people vote for the ANC to represent them in a constituent assembly, they will know not only what the ANC stands for generally, but what type of constitution we want.

Naturally these constitutional proposals are subject to revision on the basis of our consultations with our membership, the rest of the alliance, and the public generally. We want to create a constitution that enjoys widespread support, loyalty, and respect. That can only be achieved if we really do go to the people.

In order to avoid these just demands, various attempts have been made to undermine and destabilize the ANC. The violence is the most serious, but there are other more insidious methods. At present there is an obsession in the press, amongst our political opponents, and many Western governments with our alliance with the South African Communist Party. Newspapers continually carry speculations over the number of Communists on our National Executive and allege that we are being run by the Communist Party.

The ANC is not a communist party but a broad liberation movement, including amongst its members Communists and non-Communists. Anyone who is a loyal member of the ANC, anyone who abides by the discipline and principles of the organization, is entitled to belong to the organization.

Our relationship with the SACP as an organization is one of mutual respect. We unite with the SACP over common goals, but we respect one another's independence and separate identity. There has been no attempt whatsoever on the part of the SACP to subvert the ANC. On the contrary, we derive strength from the alliance.

We have no intention whatsoever of heeding the advice of those who suggest we should break from this alliance. Who is offering this unsolicited advice? In the main it is those who have never given us any assistance whatsoever. None of these advisers have ever made the sacrifices for our struggle that Communists have made. We are strengthened by this alliance. We shall make it even stronger.

We are in a phase of our struggle where victory is in sight. But we have to ensure that this victory is not snatched from us. We have to ensure that the racist regime feels maximum pressure right till the end and that it understands that it must give way, that the road to peace, freedom, and democracy is irresistible.

That is why sanctions must be maintained. This is not the time to reward the apartheid regime. Why should they be rewarded for repealing laws which form what is recognized as an international crime? Apartheid is still in place. The regime must be forced to dismantle it, and only when that process is irreversible can we start to think of lifting the pressure.

We are very concerned at the attitude that the Bush administration has taken on this matter. It was one of the few governments that was in regular touch with us over the question of sanctions, and we made it clear that lifting sanctions was premature. That administration nevertheless, without consulting us, merely informed us that American sanctions were to be lifted. We find that completely unacceptable.

It is in this context that we value our friendship with Cuba very, very much. When you, Comrade Fidel, yesterday said that our cause is your cause, I know that that sentiment came from the bottom of your heart and that that is the feeling of all the people of revolutionary Cuba.

You are with us because both of our organizations, the Communist Party of Cuba and the ANC, are fighting for the oppressed masses, to ensure that those who make the wealth enjoy its fruits. Your great apostle José Martí said, "With the poor people of this earth I want to share my fate."

We in the ANC will always stand with the poor and rightless. Not only do we stand with them. We will ensure sooner rather than later that they rule the land of their birth, that in the words of the Freedom Charter, "The people shall govern." And when that moment arrives, it will have been made possible not only by our efforts but through the solidarity, support, and encouragement of the great Cuban people.

I must close my remarks by referring to an event which you have all witnessed. Comrade Fidel Castro conferred upon me the highest honor this country can award. I am very much humbled by this award, because I do not think I deserve it. It is an award that should be given to those who have already won the freedom of their peoples. But it is a source of strength and hope that this award is given for the recognition that the people of South Africa stand on their feet and are fighting for their freedom. We sincerely hope that in these days that lie ahead we will prove worthy of the confidence which is expressed in this award.

Long live the Cuban revolution!
Long live Comrade Fidel Castro!

The oppressed will be and must be their own liberators

ADDRESS TO CONFERENCE OF UMKHONTO WE SIZWE, AUGUST 9, 1991

This speech was given at the opening of a conference of Umkhonto we Sizwe (Spear of the Nation), the ANC's military wing, also known as MK. The meeting was held in Thohoyandou, Venda.

Comrade chairperson; Your Excellency, Colonel Ramusho-ane, head of state of Venda; Your Honors, the vice chancellor and members of the Senate and Council of the University of Venda; comrades, members of the NEC of the African National Congress; commanders, commissars, and combatants of Umkhonto we Sizwe; distinguished guests and friends; comrades-in-arms and fellow combatants:

I bring to this conference the greetings of the leadership of the ANC and indeed the entire membership of our movement, spread across the length and breadth of South Africa. It is a singular honor for me that I was assigned the task of giving the keynote address at this historic conference, the first of its kind on the soil of our motherland. Historic because in the year of the thirtieth anniversary of our people's army, we are gathered not in the cellars, safe houses, and hideouts of the

129

underground, but in full view of all, including the media, as a legal organization. It is thanks to the achievements of this army, Umkhonto we Sizwe, that we are able to meet, discuss, and plan our future not as fugitives but as a recognized military wing of the ANC.

I want to take this very first opportunity to express, on behalf of the ANC and the command of Umkhonto we Sizwe, our profound gratitude to the University of Venda, its faculty and its student body for having so generously lent us their campus for the occasion of this conference. Let me express our thanks also to the government and administration of Venda for the assistance they have rendered us to ensure that this conference is a success.

We have in our midst today comrades who were among the founding members of Umkhonto we Sizwe. These are men and women steeled in the struggles of the 1950s and early 1960s, who after a long tradition of nonviolent struggle had the courage to make the agonizing decision that there was no other way forward other than by taking up arms.

Amongst us also are those seasoned fighters who received their baptism in fire in the heat of battles along a front that stretched from Wankie in the west to Sipolilo in the east during the 1967 campaign undertaken by the Luthuli Detachment into then racist-ruled Rhodesia.

Here too are the veterans who braved the reverses and hardships, the failures and the mishaps, who refused to despair and surrender, and who year after year tried to make their way over numerous hazards into South Africa—by air, by ship, over land—in order to engage the enemy and to ensure that the armed struggle took root amongst our people.

As I scan the assembled faces here, I recognize also the generation of fighters who produced comrades of the caliber of Solomon Mahlangu and numerous others who had faced the armored might of the oppressor state with their bare fists and stones during the Soweto uprising: the generation of June 16 [1976] who took up arms and spat fire at the pride of the racist state's economic infrastructure at Sasol, Koeberg, and many other targets.[39]

We have too the veterans of the mass struggles of the 1980s, whose inexhaustible creativity spawned the first popular self-defense units, opening the way to a perspective of insurrection during that decade.

Four generations of fighters are assembled here today. They are drawn from every part of South Africa, and they speak every language and dialect that exists among our people, they are of every hue and color, and are from divergent religious backgrounds. Their bonds of comradeship were forged in the very crucible of combat, and their commitment has been tempered by the experience of battle and political struggles. This is a truly national army, an army of the people of South Africa! Today, on the soil of our motherland, we have come together to collectively chart the way forward for our army.

We are meeting at a time in our country's history pregnant with great possibilities for the realization of our people's most heartfelt aspirations, but at a time also fraught with the gravest dangers of reaction and counterrevolution. What we do and say in the next two days will and must have a crucial bearing on the entire future course of our people and our country. We have set ourselves an immense task. We dare not fail!

When the ANC met in national conference during July, among the decisions taken were a number with a direct bearing on MK. We resolved at our national conference that:

• MK should remain combat ready.

• MK should establish structures throughout the country at all levels.

• The ANC has the duty to maintain and develop MK as a fighting force until a democratic constitution has been adopted with a view to the integration of its personnel into a new defense force.

• MK should play a role in training and establishing popular defense units, under the control of community organizations, to defend our communities against state-sponsored violence and crime.

It is in pursuance of those decisions that we are gathered here today.

Comrade chairman:

To see the road ahead of us more clearly, it is perhaps necessary that we today recall the path our people's army has traveled to arrive at this historic conference.

Umkhonto we Sizwe was founded by the leadership of our revolutionary alliance thirty years ago in order to give coherence to the spontaneous revolutionary violence our people were beginning to assert in response to the repressive violence of the South African racist state. During the late 1950s, there had already been a number of armed uprisings in various parts of the country as the oppressed fought back to claim their rights, which were being ruthlessly suppressed by the Verwoerd regime. In the Northern Transvaal the peasants had risen against the imposition of the Bantustan system. In the Western Transvaal the rising of the peasants had been suppressed with great violence and whole communities had fled into then–British Botswanaland. In the Transkei the imposition of the Bantustan system had provoked the most sustained peasant rising in six decades, and in many portions of that region the rule of the puppet chiefs and the regime had been superseded by popularly elected peasants' committees.

The struggle in the urban areas had also reached a high-water mark. The massacres at Sharpeville and Langa in 1960, the slaughter of a peasant demonstration at Ngquza Hill in Pondoland in June 1960, and the massive armed response of the Verwoerd regime to our mass mobilization for a national general strike in May 1961,[40] all conspired to convince the leadership of our movement that the alternatives before us were either to surrender and accept slavery in perpetuity, or take up arms and fight for our freedom as all other peoples have done in the past and shall surely continue to do in the future when faced with intransigent and oppressive rulers.

The strategy of the ANC and its allies was based on the

recognition of five basic features of the system of apartheid and white domination. These are:

• That apartheid is a system of minority rule, rooted in the era of colonialism, in which the black majority are, by the basic law of the country, excluded from the political process. Except for a few delegated powers, political power is explicitly the monopoly of the white minority who base their claims to govern on race and the rights of conquest.

• That the South African state is based on the conquest and dispossession of the indigenous peoples of their land and its wealth. This dispossession itself has been institutionalized and formalized into law so that 87 percent of the land area of our country was, until a few months ago, set aside exclusively as the preserve of the whites, who at no time in the history of South Africa ever numbered more than 17 percent of the total population.

• That it is a system of labor coercion, underpinned by a host of extraeconomic measures, specifically designed to compel the African people to make themselves available as a source of cheap labor power.

• That it is a system in which access to productive capacity and property are racially defined, which has consequently produced a skewed social structure in which the property-owning classes are drawn almost exclusively from the white minority.

• That it is a system of repressive social control increasingly sustained by the exercise of brute force and violence against the oppressed.

These features of white domination have remained more or less constant in spite of the modifications that have been made from time to time to adapt the system to changing times. It is for this reason that we reject the simple equation of apartheid with specific laws and legal measures. We are dealing with a comprehensive system of domination which cannot be unpacked into discrete laws, which if repealed will imply its demise.

As a movement, we argued that the most visible and

dominant conflict in South Africa was that between the oppressed black majority and the oppressor state. And, as in other colonial situations, this conflict could not be resolved by the colonial state reforming itself out of existence. Only struggle to overthrow the system of colonial domination could lead to the resolution of the conflict. The singular difference was this: whereas in other colonial systems the colonizing state existed outside the borders of the colony, in our case the colonial state and the colonized lived within one territory. In South Africa, therefore, the struggle must result in the destruction of the colonial state and not only the system of colonialism.

Our struggle, consequently, is not merely a struggle to achieve universally recognized civil rights within the context of a white-controlled and -dominated state. It is essentially a struggle for national liberation and national self-determination like those of other colonized peoples. Civil rights, civil liberties, and the other universally accepted rights would be achieved by national liberation and not the other way around.

It followed from our analysis that the principal forces of national liberation are the oppressed black majority. Among this cluster of liberatory forces the African people, as the most brutally oppressed and exploited, are the main and decisive contingent. Freedom would come as the oppressed black masses themselves consciously engaged in struggle, and not as a gift from the oppressor. The oppressed, we said, will be and must be their own liberators.

It was on the basis of such understanding that we set out our strategy and tactics, described the lineup of social and political forces, and defined our allies. The foundation stone of the ANC's strategy is that no group of revolutionaries, acting on their own, no matter how courageous, disciplined, and self-sacrificing, can hope to overthrow the system of oppression. Victory in the national liberation struggle is dependent upon the active and conscious participation of the masses of the oppressed people, determining their own destiny, through struggle. In order for the ANC and its allies to secure that participation, the movement must be integrated with the masses, enjoy their confidence, and be capable of providing overall leadership to their many-sided struggle. It was always our view, therefore, that the armed liberation struggle was based on and grew out of the mass political struggles waged by the oppressed. It was those mass struggles that posed state power as the central issue of South African politics, after 1961. We argued that the transfer of power could only be realized by the all-round defeat of the white minority regime, the dismantling of the institutions of racial oppression, and the creation of a democratic state on the principles set out in the Freedom Charter.

Our strategy to attain this goal was based on four interpenetrating strategic tasks:

• The extension and consolidation throughout the country, among all races, classes, and strata, of an ANC underground machinery, capable of reaching, directing, and giving leadership to the majority of people of South Africa.

• The political mobilization of the masses of the people, especially the oppressed, into united, active struggle around local, regional, and national issues, while continuously educating the people into the recognition that without the transfer of power from the oppressor state to the people, no major problem of South African life could be satisfactorily solved.

• The assertion of the significance of revolutionary violence, as a permanent feature of our struggle, in order to smash the enemy's instruments of coercion and repression and thus deprive him of the capacity to dominate the political process.

• The mobilization of international solidarity to isolate the apartheid regime internationally and to persuade the majority of the international community to accept the national liberation movement as the true representative of the people of our country.

The ANC and the alliance of liberation forces that it heads, have always acted on the basis that it is in actual struggle that the masses will acquire the political experience to mould themselves into an effective and victorious political force. Strategically this dictated that the ANC must strive to shift the balance of strength within the country in favor of the liberation forces. In other words, the regime must find itself confronted with struggles throughout the country, involving the oppressed and carried out in a variety of ways—strikes, boycotts, mass rallies, civil disobedience campaigns, demonstrations, cultural and other manifestations—all directed at achieving the conscious unity of the masses.

Tactically, this required that the popular movement provide the conditions in which the ANC's underground politico-military structures could function and survive. But survive not merely as an end in itself but in order that they could multiply themselves by imparting to the masses the necessary political and military skills to wage the struggle more effectively. This was a perspective that envisaged that the advanced military detachments of our movement, represented by Umkhonto we Sizwe, would fuse with and generate popular military units.

The forces of national liberation and democracy were also to take full advantage of all the legal and semilegal opportunities that existed to encourage the formation of organizations of the oppressed to draw the greatest number of our people into active struggle. We were of the view that through struggle more legal space could be created and the ability of the movement to mobilize would thus be enhanced.

The fundamental strategic weakness of the oppressor state is its narrow social-political base. The forces of race domination and apartheid therefore continuously seek ways to undermine the strength and potential unity of the oppressed by encouraging ethnic, racial, linguistic, and religious distinctions amongst us. Parallel with such efforts they also embarked on attempts to create organizations and encourage movements and groups that represent sectional and other divisive interests. Traditionally the regime has relied on tribalism and a narrow ethnic chauvinism as the best means of drawing mass support away from the national liberation movement.

The renewal of organized, mass opposition and resistance to the institutions of racial domination is the central feature of South African politics during the 1980s. This was a period characterized by repeated cycles of mass revolt, at times assuming the proportions of near insurrection; the growth and consolidation of a Mass Democratic Movement; the unification of the democratic trade union movement under the banner of COSATU; and the proliferation of mass organs of struggle among all strata and in every field of endeavor amongst the oppressed.

The single most enduring facet of the upheavals that erupted during that decade was the emergence of a broad strategic alliance, embracing the leading elements of the Mass Democratic Movement and the national liberation alliance under the leadership of the ANC. Coalesced around the Freedom Charter as a common programmatic statement, this alliance gave leadership to the mass struggles of the period.

The completion of three wars of national liberation, crowned in 1988 by the ignominious defeat of an abortive invasion of Angola by the South African regime, created the preconditions for the implementation of UN Security Council Resolution 435 in Namibia, leading to the independence of that country in 1990.

The increased polarization of South African society itself, with one pole identifying with the cause of national liberation and democracy, while on the opposing side stood those of racism, reaction, and colonialism, created the conditions for the emergence of new progressive forces among the white population, who were increasingly attracted into the political orbit of the ANC. Our demonstrated capacity to challenge the regime militarily, plus the evident growing influence our movement could exercise amongst the mass of our people and the political interventions the ANC made in the political process, helped to concentrate the minds of the regime on the need for a peaceful resolution of the crisis.

The ANC has never on principle been opposed to the employment of negotiations as one of the means to arrive at our cherished goal. We always insisted that, depending on the level and intensity of the struggle, the Pretoria regime will one day find it advisable to seek negotiations. At the same time, we said also that negotiations cannot be regarded as a substitute for the national liberation struggle. They must and can only be an aspect of the movement's strategy, employed at a specific moment to attain our stated and historic objectives. It was from that perspective that the ANC entered into the process leading through the Harare Declaration to Groote Schuur and to the Pretoria Minute.

We took this path not because we had become tired of fighting. We took this path not because we thought we are incapable of defeating the enemy. We took this path not because we had been defeated militarily or politically. We took it because of our firm conviction that we should exhaust every opportunity to resolve by peaceful means the terrible crisis into which racism has plunged our country.

It is a matter of record that the ANC has loyally, scrupulously, and very faithfully observed the letter and the spirit of all the agreements entered into with the South African government.

Can President de Klerk and his cabinet make the same claim?

Despite the severe and trying provocations of state-sponsored violence, massive covert destabilization operations, the systematic assassination of our regional leaders and other supporters of the ANC, our movement has bent every endeavor to keep the peace process on track.

Can President de Klerk and his cabinet make the same claim?

In the teeth of the orchestrated covert campaign to finance, train, and sustain a legion of dummy organizations and bodies as an opposition to the ANC, our movement has exercised restraint and given due recognition even to these very creations of the security police as a token of our commitment to political pluralism.

Can President de Klerk and his cabinet, who have so assiduously plotted to destroy the ANC and its allies, make the same claim?

The recent disclosures, documenting the range of criminal and near-criminal activities the South African government has been prepared to stoop to, demonstrate in the clearest possible terms the pressing need for an interim government of national unity to preside over the entire transition from apartheid to democracy. As we have often stated, such a government should be constituted so as to enjoy the support of the overwhelming majority of South Africans. The modalities of its installation and its actual composition can be a matter for discussion and negotiation among all the players on the political arena. We would insist only on two principles. The first is inclusivity, so that no body of political opinion feels excluded. The second is a definite and unambiguous time frame. For an interim government to assume office will require that the incumbent government resign and hand over power to the transitional administration. The interim government would have to take charge of all armed and security forces in the country, adopt an interim bill of rights, supervise and conduct the elections for a constituent assembly, in addition to implementing other measures necessary to prepare the country for democracy.

Though we have suspended armed activity, though our commitment to the search for peace is beyond question, it is precisely because of our keen awareness of the dangers inherent in the minority regime's determination to cling on to power that we dare not relax our vigilance and we dare not permit this MK to disintegrate or wither away. We are called upon, as the bulwark of the people's interests and their champion against oppression and repressive violence, to assist the masses in devising the appropriate response to state-sponsored and vigilante violence.

As the custodians of the most treasured democratic traditions of the people of this country, we are called upon to prepare ourselves and to restructure MK so that its cadres can take their rightful place in the armed forces of a democratic South Africa.

As the one army that is truly above race, ethnicity, tribe, or language group, we are called upon to build on these principles so that they may be transmitted down to mould the single South African identity our new army must possess.

As the army that has embraced the spirit of disinterested internationalism, we must preserve these traditions to enrich the democratic culture that must be at the heart of the new South African army.

Comrade chairperson:

Thirty years ago, when a small tightly knit group of us took the inescapable decision to create and build Umkhonto we Sizwe, we were in many respects taking a step into the unknown. Since the last wars of conquest and dispossession, the successive white minority regimes that have ruled this country made sure that the African people learnt nothing about modern warfare. Even when this country seemed in danger of imminent invasion and occupation by hostile foreign powers, the white minority governments balked at imparting modern military skills to the African people. African soldiers called to serve in the armed forces of this country were armed with nothing more lethal than a knobkerrie [heavy, knobbed traditional weapon] or an assagai [spear]!

We were quite literally starting on a blank page.

In order to begin we had to seek the assistance of those who through word and deed had demonstrated their commitment to the struggle for freedom and the destruction of apartheid. I want to use this occasion to salute and address special words of thanks to all those friends and allies, from every part of the world, who assisted us in building, training, and maintaining our people's army.

We must mention in the first instance the countries of Africa, through the OAU Liberation Committee and Fund, who have been a source of moral and material support to all the liberation wars waged in southern Africa. In this regard, special mention must be made of the Democratic Republic of Algeria, which trained many of our earliest fighters and combatants and has over the years provided very generously towards the liberation army. We recall with especial warmth the sterling contribution made by the Frontline States, chief amongst them Angola and Tanzania, who have housed the combatants of Umkhonto we Sizwe within their borders and been compelled to fend off numerous acts of aggression as a result.

Amongst African countries we must count also Uganda, Ethiopia, Somalia, and Egypt, all of whom at one time or another made their own unique contribution to the growth and the development of our people's army.

The socialist countries made and continue to make an outstanding contribution to the training and upgrading of our army. It is no secret that without the assistance we and all the liberation movements of our region received from this quarter, colonialism and apartheid would still be dominant. We single out for special mention in this regard the USSR, Cuba, the GDR [German Democratic Republic], and the People's Republic of China.

There are few struggles in the world that have attracted as wide-ranging and ecumenical support as ours. Despite the attitude adopted by the majority of governments in the West, large numbers of people in Europe and North America, disgusted by the policies of their own governments, found ways and means to lend practical assistance to the liberation movement in this respect as well. The committed anti-apartheid fighters from countries such as Britain, the Netherlands, France, Greece, Canada, the USA, Belgium, Germany, etc., acting in the best traditions of democratic internationalism, who have risked life and limb to contribute directly to our struggle, are too numerous to mention. There will come a time, and it is not too distant, when we will be in a position to give these extremely courageous comrades-in-arms the recognition that is due to them.

The spirit of selfless assistance to the cause of human liberation which moved many others to lend their full support to the national liberation struggle in our country, also animates the average MK combatant. MK cadres were to be found in the trenches, together with their comrades from other movements in the region. At the height of South African aggression against Angola, numerous of our comrades laid down their lives in defense of Angolan independence. MK combatants were among those who helped defeat Portuguese colonialism in Mozambique. MK comrades fought alongside the patriots of Zimbabwe who brought down the illegal regime of Ian Smith. These are the traditions we cherish and shall uphold for all South African democrats to emulate.

Comrade chairperson:

No army can survive on the assistance of its friends and allies alone. We have always been of the view that the ingredients for an effective people's army are to be found in the caliber of the men and women who make it up. Umkhonto we Sizwe was founded as an army with a very specific mission, the liberation of the people of South Africa. It is that mission that has always informed and inspired everything that we have done. Unlike a conventional army, MK is made up of committed militants, who have acquired specific military skills in pursuance of the liberation movement's agenda. Ours is not an army of mere soldiers; it is an army of political activists.

We owe the creation, building, and sustaining of this people's army in the first instance to the ANC and its leadership. This has been no mean task. It was a major undertaking whose demand would have daunted and overwhelmed a leadership of lesser capacity. We owe the success that we have achieved also to the commanders and commissars of MK, who have, through their leadership qualities, held before our fighters the vision of what we hope to achieve. We owe it to the combatants of MK, those who are with us here today and those who made the ultimate sacrifice so that our country will be free. I shall request that we all rise and observe a moment's silence in tribute to these noble sons and daughters of our people.

[Moment's silence with flags dipped in tribute; the audience remains on its feet]

We recall the names of the fallen comrades to remind ourselves how much we have lost in the course of the struggle for freedom. Each one of these was a unique, irreplaceable human being. The daughter or the son of some parents. The mother or the father of some child. The beloved of some man or woman. Because they are far too many to recount, we can only enumerate a handful to represent each of the generations of combatants that comprise our army.

From among the founding fighters of MK:

Looksmart Solwandle Ngudle, tortured to death by the South African Security Police in 1964.

Vuyisile Mini, sentenced to death by the South African regime.

Washington Bongco, sentenced to death by the South African regime.

From among the Luthuli Detachment:

Patrick Molaoa, who fell in the Wankie game reserve in 1967.

Andries Morape, who fell in battle in Zimbabwe in 1967.

Basil February, who fell in battle in Zimbabwe in 1967.

Gandhi Hlekani, who fell in battle in Zimbabwe in 1967.

Flag Boshielo, who fell in battle in Zimbabwe in 1970.

Faldeni "Castro" Mziwonke, who fell in battle in Zimbabwe in 1970.

From among the June 16 Detachment:

Solomon Mahlangu, sentenced to death by the South African regime in 1977.

Obadi Mogabudi, killed during the Matola raid in 1981.

Victor Khayiyane, killed in action on the Swaziland border in 1986.

Paul Dikeledi, killed in an ambush in Swaziland in 1987.

Richard "Barney" Molokane, killed in action on the Swaziland border in 1986.

From the Moncada Detachment:
Nomkhosi, the daughter of Vuyisile Mini, killed during the Maseru raid in 1985.

Lucas Bryce Njongwe, killed in battle outside East London in 1983.

Simon Moegoerane, sentenced to death by the South African regime in 1984.

Jerry Mosololi, sentenced to death by the South African regime in 1984.

Marcus Thagbo Motaung, sentenced to death by the South African regime in 1984.

We recall also the names of the combatants who were treacherously murdered during raids by the enemy:

Among those who fell at Matola:[41]
Mduduzeli Guma, also known as Conqueror Ntwana, of the Natal command of MK.

Krishna Rabilal, killed at Matola, of the Natal command of MK.

Among those who fell in Maseru in December 1982:[42]
Zola Nqini, a former political prisoner.

Kentridge Moloisane, from Bloemfontein.

Vuyani Zibi, from Mqanduli in the Transkei.

Patrick Moholo, from Bloemfontein.

Gene Gugushe, from Kroonstad.

Pakamile Mphongoshe, from Port Elizabeth.

Among those who fell during the second Maseru raid in December 1985:
Morris Seabelo, killed in Maseru in December 1985.

Leon Meyer, from East London.

We remember also those who fell at the hands of the enemy and his assassins:
Theo Dlodlo, known as "Viva" of the Transvaal MK machinery, in 1987.

Zwelakhe Nyanda, killed in Swaziland in 1983.

Cassius Make, a member of the NEC and a commander of MK, killed in Swaziland in 1987.

George Phahle, killed in Gaberone in 1985.

Atwell Makaqekeza, killed by the enemy in Lesotho in 1986.

We regret that we cannot give a complete roll call of the fallen. That roll of honor should be forever engraved in the hearts and minds of us all. May we prove worthy of the sacrifice of these fallen combatants by the content and quality of the democracy we build in our country tomorrow!

Please resume your seats, comrades.

In closing, comrade chairperson, I call the attention of you all to the gravity of the issues that this conference has to address. I am certain that you will give a good account of yourselves. Let us emerge from this MK conference a more united and a stronger people's army, determined to take up our tasks with the same measure of dedication and commitment that we have always displayed.

Viva Umkhonto we Sizwe, viva!

Viva Umkhonto we Sizwe, viva!

Comrades, let us commence our work.

Thank you.

Codesa is the fruit of sacrifice and struggle

ADDRESS AT OPENING SESSION OF CODESA, DECEMBER 20, 1991

The speech below was given at the opening of the Convention for a Democratic South Africa (Codesa). Represented at the meeting were nineteen political parties and organizations, including the ANC, National Party, Inkatha, various homeland officials, and the South African government.

Leaders of political parties and movements; distinguished observers from international organizations; members of the diplomatic corps; venerable traditional and religious leaders of our people; comrades and friends:

Today will be indelibly imprinted in the history of our country. If we who are gathered here respond to the challenge before us, today will mark the commencement of the transition from apartheid to democracy. Our people, from every corner of our country, have expressed their yearning for democracy and peace. Codesa represents the historical opportunity to translate that yearning into reality.

For eighty years, the ANC has led the struggle for democracy in South Africa. Along the route traversed during this period, many sacrifices were made by thousands upon thousands of our people. In the arduous battle between freedom and oppression, positions hardened and polarization developed between the people and the state. Even when, in the absence of any other recourse, the ANC took up arms, our objective was to secure a political settlement in South Africa. In the past few years an environment more conducive to establishing mutual trust has been established.

South Africans of many persuasions recognize that this environment, and its institutional product, Codesa, is the fruit of their sacrifices and struggle. They have a justifiable expectation that Codesa will set our country on the road to democracy.

Inasmuch as apartheid has been declared a crime against humanity and the problems of our country have engaged so much of the attention of the international community over decades, the presence of esteemed observers from key international organizations as guests of Codesa is most appropriate.

We welcome the guests from the United Nations Organization, the Organization of African Unity, the Commonwealth, the European Economic Community, and the Nonaligned Movement. We trust that they will avail to the process now unfolding their wisdom, insights, and experience gained in many similar initiatives across the world.

All South Africans share the hope and vision of a land free of apartheid, where internal strife will have no place.

The ANC initiated the search for peace in our country. Since 1987 the ANC has intensively campaigned for a negotiated transfer of power. This campaign reached new heights in 1989 when the OAU, the Nonaligned Movement, and the UN General Assembly all adopted declarations supporting this position. All three declarations stated "that where colonial, racial, and apartheid domination exists, there can be neither peace nor justice."

In keeping with this spirit, Codesa must therefore lay the basis for the elimination of racial and apartheid domination.

It is only by decisive action in this regard that South Africa will be granted entry to the community of nations as a full member.

The strength of the Codesa initiative lies in the range of political parties and persuasions represented here. The presence of so many parties augurs well for the future. The diverse interests represented speak of the capacity to develop consensus across the spectrum and of the desire to maximize common purpose amongst South Africans. Many parties here have already invested so much by way of preparing their constituencies for transformation. Above all else, the investment already made must spur us on to total commitment for the successful outcome of this convention.

[*The following three paragraphs were given in Afrikaans:*]

We regret the fact that there are still parties who exclude themselves from this important process.[43] After Codesa the situation in our country is irreversible. Threats about civil war are irresponsible and totally unacceptable. The time for such talk is long past. If they execute these threats the world will see that they are prolonging the suffering of all South Africans and poisoning the search for peace in our country.

But one thing stands fast: the process of moving towards democracy is unstoppable. History grants all of us a unique opportunity. To exchange this opportunity for a bowl of lentil soup of the past, and negative bravado, is to deny the future. We continue to call on such parties to join Codesa now, even at this late stage.

The message of the ANC through Codesa is straightforward, clear, and for all South Africans: the time for one South Africa, one nation, one vote, one future is here.

The national convention in 1909 was a gathering of whites representing the four British colonies. It was also a betrayal of black people and a denial of democracy. The act of Union entrenched colonial practices and institutions constitutionally. In its wake, our country has lived through eight decades of wasted opportunity. Codesa provides the first opportunity since to attempt to establish democracy in our country.

It is imperative that we also reach consensus on the definition of democracy. From the ANC's perspective, democracy entails:

- that all governments must derive their authority from the consent of the governed;

- no persons or groups of persons shall be subjected to oppression, domination, or discrimination by virtue of their race, gender, ethnic origin, color, or creed;

- all persons should enjoy the right to life;

- all persons should enjoy security in their persons and should be entitled to the peaceful enjoyment of their possessions, including the right to acquire, own, or dispose of property, without distinction based on race, color, language, gender, or creed;

- all persons should have the right to hold and express whatever opinions they wish to subscribe to, provided that in the exercise of that right they do not infringe on the rights of others.

This quality of democracy will indeed only be possible when those who have borne the brunt of apartheid oppression exercise their right to vote in a free and fair election on the basis of universal suffrage. We can see no reason why an election for a constituent assembly should not be possible during 1992.

[*The following three paragraphs were given in Zulu:*]

When oppression necessitated a struggle in South Africa the ANC never retreated but was in the vanguard. Now that the situation is conducive, it is the ANC again that leads the way in the effort to bring peace to the land of our ancestors.

If there are people who need freedom in South Africa it is the black people. They need it now because their economic situation and welfare deteriorate daily.

The right to vote is the essence of the struggle for freedom. Nineteen ninety-two is the year that must bring the first democratic elections in South Africa.

Codesa, on its own, will not deliver democracy. In recording this fact, there is no attempt to demean Codesa. Even absolute consensus during the life of Codesa will still leave an apartheid constitution in place. We need to be reminded that this very constitution was declared null and void by the UN Security Council in 1983.

The invalidation of the prevailing constitution is the most persuasive argument in support of the view that the incumbent government is unsuited to the task of overseeing the transition to democracy. Its oft-stated commitment to democracy must now compel it to make way for an interim government of national unity to supervise the transition.

This is the only cogent outflow from our deliberations at Codesa. The consensus which we arrive at will certainly have far-reaching implications for the birth of a new nationhood. None of us could be satisfied with circumstances where the consensus struck at this meeting is not translated into full legal force.

An interim government, important as it may be, is but the product of agreement between ourselves as political parties and organizations. It will not be the outcome of full participation by the people of our country. Negotiations, to be successful, must be owned and supported by the majority of South Africans.

In the absence of full participation, we must commit ourselves to open negotiations to ensure that notions of secret deals do not arise. This process will also hinge on the confidence by each participating party that the communication of developments be absolutely nonpartisan. Consideration therefore needs to be given to the immediate establishment of the necessary mechanisms to ensure that the state-controlled media accurately and fairly represents the views of all participants. The means of establishing an interim government will not be participatory. Therefore, the consensus at Codesa should curtail both its mandate and its life span.

The ANC remains fully committed to the installation of a government which can justly claim authority because it is based on the will of the people. This reality will have to be underpinned by a constitution which both engenders respect and enjoys legitimacy. There is a compelling urgency about this task. It is inconceivable that such a democratic constitution could be reached in any way but through the portals of an elected constitution-making body, namely a constituent assembly.

It is tragic that our country, so well endowed with natural resources, has been reduced to an economic wasteland by the system of apartheid, based on greed and mismanagement. It is also distressing to note that the deplorable violence has reached such alarming proportions, and others threaten still more. These features are a direct consequence of the determination of a minority to maintain the power and privilege accrued by apartheid. There are large parts of our country where free political activity is still not possible, where law and order is still rule by the jackboot and a large number of political prisoners remain incarcerated. In the spirit of our convention, we call upon the government to proclaim an immediate Codesa amnesty, to take effect before Christmas, for all political prisoners throughout the country.

Nothing could be more irresponsible than for those of us gathered here to deny our people the right to peace and freedom of association and to deny our country its due economic growth.

We can only reverse the current situation if we set our sights on establishing true democracy. The national interest is far, far more important than the sectional interests represented by any party here. Everybody wants a place in the sun of a postapartheid South Africa. No delegation here could possibly have been mandated by its constituency, however small, to attend Codesa in order to annihilate itself.

Recognizing this, however, we want to make a strong appeal to everybody present to place the compelling national concerns above narrow sectional interests.

History will judge us extremely harshly if we fail to turn the opportunity, which it now presents us with, into common good. The risks of further pain and affliction arising from violence, homelessness, unemployment, or gutter education, are immense. No country or people can afford the extension of this anguish, even for a day. The approach which we adopt at Codesa must be fundamentally inclusive. The price of Codesa's failure will be far too great.

We must not trample on the confidence which our people have placed in the successful conclusion to these negotiations. It would be foolhardy to spurn the world for its efforts in assisting to secure peace and prosperity for South Africa. Our people and the world expect a nonracial, nonsexist democracy to emerge from the negotiations on which we are about to embark.

Failure of Codesa is inconceivable; so too is consensus without legal force. There is absolutely no room for error or obstinacy. The challenge which Codesa places before each one of us is to unshackle ourselves from the past and to build anew.

Codesa can be the beginning of reconstruction. Let our common commitment to the future of our country inspire us to build a South Africa of which we can all be truly proud.

The National Party and the government talk peace while conducting a war

SPEECH IN REPLY TO DE KLERK, DECEMBER 20, 1991

The first day of the Codesa meeting was taken up with speeches by representatives of the political forces present. President de Klerk, who spoke last, launched an attack on the ANC for its maintenance of Umkhonto we Sizwe. "An organization which remains committed to an armed struggle cannot be trusted completely," he stated. After de Klerk's speech the convention signed a Declaration of Intent.[44] Then Mandela requested the floor, delivering these remarks.

I am gravely concerned about the behavior of Mr. de Klerk today. He has launched an attack on the ANC and in doing so he has been less than frank. Even the head of an illegitimate, discredited minority regime, as his is, has certain moral standards to uphold. He has no excuse because he is the head of a discredited regime not to uphold moral standards. It is no wonder that the Conservative Party has made such serious inroads into his power base. You can understand why. If a man can come to a conference of this nature and play the type of politics as is in his paper—very few people would like to deal with such a man.

We have had bilateral discussions, but although I was discussing with him until about twenty minutes past eight last night, he never even hinted that he was going to make this attack.

The members of the government persuaded us to allow them to speak last. They were very keen to say the last word here. It is now clear why they did so. He has abused his position, because he hoped that I would not respond. He was completely mistaken. I respond now.

We are still convinced to have discussions with him if he wants. But he must forget that he can impose positions on the African National Congress, as I daresay on any one of the political organizations here.

I have tried very hard in discussions to persuade him that firstly, his witness is to look at matters from the point of view of the National Party and the white minority in this country, not from the point of view of the population of South Africa.

I have also had to say to him that no useful purpose would be served by the ANC trying to undermine the National Party, because we want the National Party to carry the whites in this initiative. I have also said on countless occasions that no useful purpose will be served by the National Party trying to undermine the African National Congress. He clearly continues to do exactly that and we are going to stop it.

I say he is less than frank, because he has not told you that it is the African National Congress, not the National Party, nor P.W. [Botha], that started this initiative. I have been discussing with top government officials since July 1986 when I was still in prison, asking that the ANC and the government sit down to explore a peaceful solution.

As a result of the pressure of the people inside the country and of the international community, and as a result of persuasion from us, they eventually agreed to sit down to discuss with us. We have gone along with the creation of an atmosphere whereby these negotiations can succeed. As part of that process we suspended the armed struggle.

What has been happening on the side of the government? We suspended the armed struggle in spite of the fact that our people were being killed. And the government—with all its capacity to put an end to violence—was doing nothing to stop the slaughter of innocent people. I said to him: "You have got a strong, well-equipped, efficient police force and defense force. Why are you not using that capacity to stop this violence?"

I have pointed out to him that the perception that exists amongst our people is that in the forefront of this violence are elements of the security forces. It is common knowledge that the main task of formations like the CCB is to eliminate freedom fighters in this country.

So many activists have been killed without a trace. The killers have hardly ever been traced. And in all those massacres not a single member of the National Party was even grazed by a spear. It is all activists who are in the opposition, who are fighting apartheid.

Nevertheless, we have told you and done things to show our commitment to the peace process. I have indicated that only last night I had a discussion with him about this very Declaration of Intent. There were certain loopholes which, when it was reported to us, we found unacceptable. I was instructed to make sure that those loopholes were closed.

I discussed the matter with him. He then persuaded me, saying that these had already gone through the relevant committees. We must not amend them at this moment. I agreed with him. I went back to my committee, to say it was too late for us to do anything. They accepted that because of our commitment to the peace process and our desire that this peace process should succeed.

Now he is attacking us because we have not dissolved MK. We had discussions in Cape Town and Pretoria on Umkhonto we Sizwe. We had an agreement in terms of which we had to hand over our weapons for joint patrol by the government and ourselves.

But we linked this to the development of the political process. We said that when the process reached a certain stage which would ensure that we would have an effective control and say in government, then it would be easy because that would be our government. The army would be our army.

I met with him about this before the signing of the peace accords, when he was threatening to do there what he has just done now. I said to him: "You are asking us to commit suicide. When your government is unprepared to intervene and stop the violence; when the perception amongst our people is that it is elements in the security forces that are killing our people; when our people are demanding to be armed—then what political organization would hand over its weapons to the same man who is regarded by the people as killing innocent people? Then I ask you not to insist on this because we will never agree."

I told him that we should discuss the matter and see whether we could reach a solution. I met him Thursday, last week. He raised the same point. I again emphasized to him that he is asking us to do something that is absolutely ridiculous and we wouldn't do so. We could never give our arms to a government which we are sure either has no control over the security forces, or the security forces are doing precisely what you want them to do. I can't see any head of government who would allow such a culture of violence to take root without interfering.

We have discussed certain mechanisms and agreed that these mechanisms should be applied in terms of setting up the peace accord.

Nevertheless, in spite of those mechanisms, violence still continues in this country. He has presented many new statistics to show how many new policemen have been employed, what agencies have been created. He does not relate that to what has happened, because in spite of what you have done the incidents of violence are increasing.

I regret very much that he should try to take advantage of this meeting for petty political gains. It concerns what we have been saying all along: that the National Party and the government have a double agenda.

They are talking peace while at the same time conducting a war against us. They are busy doing certain things that are unacceptable, using taxpayers' money. They are funding certain organizations through the police, and he comes forward and says he doesn't know about it. If the head of the government does not know when as much as seven million rand is spent,[45] he doesn't know about it, then he is not fit to be head of the government.

He is calling on us to disband Umkhonto we Sizwe, yet the hit squads are operating freely in this country. When we had a funeral of a prominent activist, Sam Ntuli, who was gunned down by the same hit squads, eighteen people were killed in broad daylight as the mourners were dispersing, and the police were in the vicinity.[46]

It was clear that these were killers who were carrying out their job in the knowledge that the law enforcement agencies would not interfere with them. They walked away freely, without fear of any detection. You can make your own inferences from that.

If Mr. de Klerk promises to do his duty as the head of government—to put an end to the violence, to restrain his security services, to clean the country of hit squads and other elements who are responsible for killing innocent people—then he can come to us and say: "I want you to hand over your weapons to us for joint control." But as long as he is playing this double game he must be clear that we are not going to cooperate with him on this matter. He can do what he wants. We are not going to disband Umkhonto we Sizwe.

We are not a political party. We are a political organization, perhaps with more support worldwide than he has. We have used Umkhonto we Sizwe to help in the exertion of pressure on the government to change its policies. We have no illusions. It was not the operations of Umkhonto alone which have brought about this development. But Umkhonto has had a very significant contribution. We cannot hand over that instrument to the National Party.

I must appeal to him to work harmoniously and seriously with the African National Congress. This is our initiative. He has tried to undo what his brothers have done to us. Through the policy of apartheid they have created misery beyond words. Nevertheless we are prepared to forget. He has made a contribution towards normalizing the situation, because without him we would not have been this close.

I ask him to place his cards on the table face upwards. Let's work together openly. Let there be no secret agendas. Let him not persuade us that he would be the last speaker because he wants to abuse that privilege and attack us in the hope that we won't respond. I am prepared to work with him in spite of all his mistakes.

I am prepared to make allowances because he is a product of apartheid. Although he wants these democratic changes, he has sometimes very little idea what democracy means. Many people regard his statement here where he threatened us, where he says this cannot be done, as very harsh.

He is forgetting that he cannot speak like a representative of a government which has both legitimacy and which represents the majority of the population. These are statements that can only be used by somebody who represents the majority of the population of the country. He doesn't represent us. He can't talk to us in that language.

Nevertheless I am prepared to work with him, to pursue the democratic changes I introduced in the country. We can only succeed if we are candid and open with one another. This type of thing, of trying to take advantage of the cooperation which we have given him willingly, is something that is very dangerous and I hope that this is the last time he will do so.

Thank you.

We must all march together

MESSAGE TO THE JEWISH COMMUNITY, APRIL 13, 1992

The following message to the South African Jewish community was presented on the occasion of the Passover holiday.

Dear fellow compatriots:

On this most auspicious occasion, on behalf of the leadership of the African National Congress, I would like to convey our best wishes for the Passover.

The Passover festival, commemorating the emancipation from slavery of the children of Israel in ancient times, carries a message of universal human significance that has moved millions throughout history, transcending all boundaries of geography, race, or creed. The figure of Moses, the liberator, has served as an inspiration to every people who have been compelled to struggle for their liberation. The immortal words he spoke to Pharaoh, "Let my people go!" reverberate through the corridors of time. They continue to inspire us in our quest for democracy and justice in South Africa today.

Our country today stands on the very threshold of a momentous transformation which must culminate in the attainment of freedom for all South Africans. We are all required to march together to complete this last mile to freedom.

Despite its relatively small numbers, the Jewish community in this country has made a contribution second to none to the development of South Africa. South African Jews have excelled in the arts, in the sciences, in scholarship, in the law, and as employers and employees in the economy of our country. As a movement, the ANC recognizes the particularly outstanding contribution that the South African Jewish community has made to the struggle for freedom and social justice. We have not, nor shall the ANC ever call into question the right of Jews, or any other community that has made South Africa its home, to live, work, and worship as their faith commands them in our common home.

During these testing times in our country's bitter history, there are forces, fanatically devoted to a discredited past, who wish to destroy all hope of a peaceful future. Through our collective commitment to peace and justice we must deny them success. Those who are responsible for the unleashing of violence and mayhem are clearly bent on thwarting the shared aspirations of black and white South Africans for democracy.

May your special prayers for an end to all violence and oppression touch the hearts of all South Africans and bring you through this festive occasion spiritually enriched.

Shalom aleichem. [Peace unto you]

Peace be with you all during the Passover.

An interim government is essential

SPEECH AT INSTITUTE OF FOREIGN POLICY, SWEDEN, MAY 20, 1992

The second session of the Convention for a Democratic South Africa (Codesa) was held May 15-16, 1992. The meeting ended in a deadlock, as the National Party sought to ensure for itself effective veto power in any future government. After the meeting Mandela made a trip to Norway, Sweden, and Finland, during which he delivered this address.

Ladies and gentlemen:

At the outset let me thank you for the opportunity to meet the distinguished members of the Institute of Foreign Policy. This moment in our history is of critical importance to our nation. Our deliberations have an added urgency because of the events at Codesa 2. What we, as South African politicians, do or fail to do will have very serious consequences for South Africa, for the region, for the whole of Africa, and can have implications for many parts of the world.

It is my firm conviction that we must all act quickly and decisively to defeat all attempts to stall, subvert, or derail the negotiation process under way in South Africa.

The two years since our release and the unbanning of the

ANC have been difficult and demanding. Violence of an unprecedented ferocity and scale has been unleashed against
the democratic forces. This has been coupled with secret
funding of political organizations willing to serve the interests of the regime. The result has been a serious destabilization of the whole process.

Because of this, and in recognition of the fact that it was
in fact the government itself that was the major obstacle to
progress, in April 1991 the ANC suspended all constitutional talks. We concluded that the only solution lay with the
installation of an interim government of national unity.

This is what we concentrated on trying to achieve, holding extensive consultations and discussions with the government and all other political organizations in the country.

Despite the government's initial rejection of our call for
an all-party congress, an interim government, and a democratically elected constitution-making body, these proposals
have now been agreed upon in principle. This was largely
due to extensive mass campaigns and thoroughgoing public
debate on these issues, which found expression in fora such
as the Patriotic Front conference of October 1991.

The process culminated in the historic Convention for a
Democratic South Africa (Codesa), which was held on December 20-21, 1991.

Codesa established five working groups, each of which
had representation from the nineteen organizations participating in Codesa. Their task was to deal with:

1. The creation of a climate for free political activity and
the role of the international community.

2. General constitutional principles and the constitution-
making body.

3. Interim government or transitional arrangements.

4. The future of the Transkei, Bophuthatswana, Venda,
and Ciskei—those Bantustans that became "independent"
from South Africa.

5. Time frames and implementation of the whole process.

These working groups have been in regular session from

February 1992 until their report back to Codesa 2 on May 15 and 16. Broad agreement was reached by all parties on many issues. But the central question was the need for an interim government of national unity to oversee the transition. This would be done in two phases.

The first phase would see the appointment of a transitional executive council to oversee the process leading to free and fair elections to a national assembly which would be charged with the task of drawing up a new constitution.

The second phase would come into being after such democratic elections, the first in the history of our country. The elected national assembly would have two functions: to sit as a constitution-making body, where decisions would be taken by a two-thirds majority, and to serve as a legislature for the purpose of government, where matters would be decided by a simple majority.

And this is where difficulties arose, as there are serious differences between the democratic forces and those of the regime on the constitution-making body.

Despite all our efforts, and extensive compromise on our part in an effort to reach an understanding on the way forward, Codesa 2 stalled. The Pretoria government remains intransigent, acting in narrow self-interest as opposed to the national interest of our country. We are deeply disappointed that Codesa 2 has failed to deliver the breakthrough so many worked so tirelessly to achieve.

The government has placed four major obstacles in the way of forward movement, namely:

1. Unacceptably high percentages to draft a constitution, in essence a veto through the back door.

2. Entrenched regional and local boundaries and powers to be determined in the interim and to be binding on the future democratic constitution.

3. An undemocratic and unelected senate with veto powers.

4. A determination that the interim constitution, a mechanism to ensure continuity during the transition, has wide

veto powers and so becomes a permanent feature remaining in force indefinitely.

It is our view that agreements reached at Codesa can only be treated as a whole package; therefore breakdown over the constitution-making body affects the entire process. The essence of the problem is not one of percentages or arithmetic. It is that the National Party is trying to hold on to power at all costs, introducing minority veto powers in a variety of ways that can only result in a paralysis of decision making, strife, and great instability.

The National Party is creating obstacles in an effort to prevent it suffering any loss of power. This is what lies at the heart of the problem, and fundamentally affects the very process of democratization of the country.

Such intransigence and lack of will to compromise from a government wracked by scandals of such magnitude that should bring any government down is not surprising, but is nevertheless most disturbing. The question is not which minister is responsible for the death squads, the instructions to kill activists, the running of covert police operations, or the squandering of millions of taxpayers' money. Rather it is that the whole government is part of this corruption and abuse of power. The only solution lies with the installation of an interim government of national unity immediately.

We reject the arguments of those who claim that the process is moving too fast and must be slowed down.

We express our grave concern about President de Klerk's recent statement that he is against majority rule. Given all these uncertainties, we can only consider the process irreversible when the oppressed are themselves part of the power structures in a meaningful way.

How does all of this affect our relations with a staunch supporter like Sweden?

Despite the obvious setbacks, we are very optimistic about the future. Knowing our past and where we have come from, developments over the past two years have been rapid, even if they have not achieved as much as we would have liked. We are convinced that an interim government is merely months away. And we are counting on friends like you to make that interim government successful, ensuring it marks a real turning point in the life of our people. Sanctions are clearly a burning issue. We certainly do not want a situation where our friends, because they support our positions, are disadvantaged in the future. We are convinced this will not happen if sanctions are maintained until the installation of an interim government. Let all the groundwork be done now; send exploratory teams out, do all the surveys and investigations that are necessary for investment and trade in the near future. Signing agreements and contracts with this white minority government that cannot last much longer is not a solution. Sustaining economic pressure, however, is a sure way to guarantee the establishment of an interim government.

Furthermore, we look to extending all-round ties well into the future. South Africans have benefited greatly from the developmental assistance Sweden has provided while we were in exile. We want the democratic perspectives you brought to us throughout these years to be part of what renewed links with the international community brings to our country and our people.

We hope that the ending of people-to-people sanctions has already resulted in a flourishing of links between our countries. Tourism, air links, sporting and cultural contacts should be expanded rapidly. This would help create the climate and contact necessary for future trade and investment, to the benefit of both our people.

We know you are impatient, but we ask you to exercise restraint for just a little longer. Installation of an interim government is essential for a secure and stable base from which to proceed. Our victory will be your victory too.

Thank you once again for your attention and the opportunity to speak to you today.

We are prepared to take responsibility for governing and reconstructing South Africa

ADDRESS TO ANC POLICY CONFERENCE, MAY 28, 1992

On May 28-31, 1992, the ANC held a policy conference in Johannesburg, attended by eight hundred delegates. Below is the main section of Mandela's keynote address. In the opening part he reviewed the government's responsibility for the deadlock at Codesa 2 and repeated the ANC's proposals for moving negotiations forward.

This conference is essentially about preparing to govern. We are here to say to ourselves and to the world that we understand and that we are ready and capable of taking responsibility for the process of reconstruction in our land.

We are here because we are mindful of the fact that we have yet to win our freedom. We are here because we understand the link between clear policies and victory.

The ANC must emerge from this conference with clear policy proposals for a future democratic government. So let us be spurred on to even greater levels of seriousness at this conference.

The policies with which we emerge must inspire the broadest possible cross section of South Africans. Most importantly, our policies must provide hope for the most poor, the most downtrodden, those who have borne the brunt of apartheid oppression and exploitation.

Our conference needs to address the demands which are made by the organizations of our people. Let us listen to the cries of our people in the civics, the trade union movement, the sports organizations, the religious bodies, and the many other bodies which have been formed by our people.

Let our conference speak to even those who have benefited from apartheid. Let us provide them with a vision of the future—a vision of a single nation, a vision of an ANC government which will be able to govern competently and inclusively.

Let us inspire all South Africans with a belief in our capacity to create stability and to generate wealth for the benefit of all in our country. Let us also be mindful of the fact that the processes and the outcome of this conference is eagerly awaited throughout the world. On the one hand, our struggle, and the leadership of the ANC within it, represents hope to democrats and struggling people throughout the world who are perturbed by the so-called new world order—this new approach which seems to be so opposed to development and which will result in an ever-widening gap between rich and poor. There are great expectations that our conference will reassert that the role of government is to protect and advance the interests of the most vulnerable. There are also those who are keen to see the ANC abandoning precisely this developmental perspective which we hold so dear. They will be disappointed.

There are also investors who are waiting to get the first tentative signals about the capacity of the ANC to create a stable economic climate where they can invest with confidence. Our policies will establish social justice and democracy. Democracy is our best investment for stability.

Some have asked whether the approach of the ANC is ideological. There is a measure of curiosity in certain quarters about whether we are social democrats, Marxist-Leninist, liberal, or whatever. We are unconcerned about labels. We are concerned about developing a program which will systematically eradicate the ravages of apartheid. Obviously this tilts our policies in favor of the most disadvantaged.

We are also committed to putting into place policies which are sustainable, policies which will ensure systematic growth. To meet these important goals.

The fact that we are a national liberation movement which brings together people across the political spectrum is a strength which we cannot abandon. The very fact that we manage to bring together such a diverse group of South Africans on the basis of their commitment to their country has laid an invaluable basis for a new patriotism.

The fact that we can defend the right of every person to articulate their views, is a lesson in political tolerance which is rarely found in South African politics. The fact that such a wide range of South Africans see the ANC in its current form as the most viable vehicle to realize their hopes and aspirations, is a tribute to our organization and to those who have constantly sought to make the ANC even more broadly based. Our conference must contribute more to this.

The basic objectives of ANC policy are:

• to strive for the right of all South Africans, as a whole, to political and economic self-determination in a united South Africa;

• to overcome the legacy of inequality and injustice created by colonialism and apartheid, in a swift, progressive, and principled way;

• to develop an economy and state infrastructure that will progressively improve the quality of life of all South Africans; and

• to encourage the flourishing of the feeling that South Africa belongs to all who live in it, to promote a common loyalty to and pride in the country, and to create a universal sense of freedom and security within its borders.

The mission of the ANC, as set out in the Freedom Charter, is about creating the conditions which will improve on the quality of life of all South Africans.

In respect of the majority of people, those living in the squalor of the informal settlements without access to sanitation, water, and electricity, who have been denied formal education and who now find themselves virtually unemployable in a failed economy, the import of a major improvement in the quality of life is beyond question.

Even those who have benefited from apartheid live in great fear and insecurity. Undoubtedly, they too are in need of a significant improvement in life quality and also stand to benefit from the policies of a democratic government in South Africa. The significance of the conference, therefore, is that the policy guidelines which we will adopt at this conference are for the entire nation and not only for the ANC.

We must emphasize the fact that we will not be adopting a rigid blueprint for the future South Africa.

These guidelines will describe the framework which will later be filled by detailed policies in respect of each sector. This conference brings together the views of the membership of the ANC, many of whom have only just been exposed to the technical detail of policy formulation.

Our method of policy formulation is important because it creates clarity in the policy environment. A much greater percentage of our membership now understand the resource constraints that an ANC government will face and that there will therefore be no quick fix to decades of apartheid destruction.

Important as this part of the process is, it does not substitute for the technical detail which will have to be worked at after this conference. We can say with pride that the ANC has the capacity within each department to develop the necessary detail to support the mandate which the policy departments will be assigned by this conference. We are also inspired by the many offers from outside our ranks from throughout the world, to provide whatever backup we may request.

The guidelines which we will adopt will describe the legislative, economic, and institutional framework necessary to transform society into one which will serve the interests of the majority. The institutions thus created will have to be staffed by persons who are trained and competent, by civil servants committed to democracy, accountability, and a people-centered approach, and by staff committed to clean and efficient administration.

This part of our preparations to govern cannot be left until we are already in government. The creation of a diligent and professional civil service is a task which is already long overdue.

There will have to be changes in the existing civil service in line with our commitment to affirmative action and our commitment to the establishment of a slim state. We accept that there are fears amongst those currently within the civil service. Changes in the civil service are unavoidable and those who are qualified, competent, and diligent obviously have far less to fear. We repeat that changes will be made in the most humane fashion possible.

An essential element of our democratic policies must be geared towards transforming society, with a special emphasis on transforming the power relations in policy-making structures, in the implementation of those policies, in the workplace, and in the residential areas. The policy guidelines which we adopt must be able to withstand the rigor of scientific test and they must be able to be defended by every ANC member. Above all, the guidelines we adopt must be sustainable.

The Third World is littered with the relics of liberation movements which have successfully liberated their countries from the yoke of colonial oppression, only to be defeated at the polls in the first postcolonial elections.

These unfortunate defeats are not a consequence of the personalities in those movements. The defeats have more often than not been a consequence of unfulfilled promises, a lack of openness in policy making, and the direct consequence of the adoption of policies which could not be sustained by the economies of those countries. These experiences have many valuable lessons for us in South Africa.

There are understandably high expectations that democracy will put the changes in place rapidly.

These expectations are not about luxury. Our people's expectations are about acquiring basic essentials like housing, electrification, water, sanitation, decent education, and jobs. These are the very issues which are set out in our bill of rights, and in the Freedom Charter. One of the threads that runs through all of our policy documents is the unshakable commitment of the ANC to direct resources towards precisely those ends.

We remain totally convinced that these objectives are attainable. What we will need to clarify is the time frames within which we shall be able to deliver these basic goods and services to those most in need thereof. We are challenged to avoid unrealistic expectations and to define a sober set of priorities. Moreover, we are challenged to involve our people in democratic processes to be part of the process to set priorities. This is fundamentally what our gathering over the next four days is charged with.

We must leave this conference with a clear idea of the needs, the prospects, and the constraints. This understanding cannot however be the exclusive property of those delegates who would have had the privilege of attending this conference. It must be reported back in detail to the structures which mandated the delegates. This conference would have been wasted if the information remains in the confines of ANC structures. The task of every branch is to develop creative outreach programs, and to redefine the roles, duties, and responsibilities of each member.

We must leave this conference with an unambiguous commitment to proudly spread the decisions taken here to all South Africans—black or white, rich or poor, urban or rural, young or old.

It is in this assignment that we begin to see the direct interconnection between the future and the present.

The guidelines which we will adopt relate primarily to a future democracy; simultaneously it is on the strength of these guidelines that we will be able to win the struggle for democracy in our country.

The ANC remains unequivocally committed to both growth and redistribution. A failure to secure these in the shortest space of time will result in the further degradation of the social fabric in our country. The costs of this are far too high. The growth path which our country needs is impossible to achieve without the democratic institutions of governance in place. It is imperative, therefore, that Codesa delivers soonest—within the deadlines which we set out on January 8 this year.

Our country cannot be held to ransom by the National Party's stubbornness, selfishness, and greed for power. These have, in fact, been the hallmarks of the National Party since 1948. Even today, their determination to hang on to minority rule is proven through the introduction of the Defence Amendment Bill in order to entrench a racist system of conscription.[47]

The ANC has never allowed itself to be intimidated by this regime; we have no intention of doing so now! The process now under way is one that we initiated; the regime does not own Codesa. We must forge ahead to secure agreements on constitutional principles, on a democratically elected constitution-making body, and on time frames.

In the interests of all the people of our country and of struggling people across the world who are looking to the ANC to redefine the practice of democracy, we must break the deadlock. We know that the masses of our people is one most reliable deadlock-breaking mechanism.

We have said that negotiations are a site of struggle. Consequently, the negotiations under way at Codesa must be supported by other means of struggle. A draft alliance program of action will be discussed in this conference.

A special commission will seek to link the negotiations process with the policies of this conference. This conference will consider activities to break the intransigence of the regime. The draft proposal has earmarked July as the deadline.

The policies which we will adopt will only assume life if we secure democracy soonest. We may not fail the many patriots who have sacrificed so much to bring our country to this point. Nor may we ever fail our people. We bear their hopes and aspirations.

We are the future!

Amandla ngawethu! [Power to the people]

Maatla! [Power]

The National Party regime is killing our people

SPEECH TO RESIDENTS OF BOIPATONG, JUNE 21, 1992

On June 17, 1992, over forty-five people were killed when armed gangs attacked the black township of Boipatong, south of Johannesburg, and the nearby squatter settlement of Slovo Park. The attackers came from a nearby hostel that was a stronghold of the Inkatha Freedom Party; some residents reported seeing white policemen supervising the attack. Mandela visited the township several days later and delivered this speech.

I am here to express my deepest sympathies to the people of Boipatong and Slovo Park for one of the most brutal slaughters of human beings in the history of this country. Innocent and defenseless men, women, and children—pregnant women and unsuspecting babies were not exempted from the bullets and spears of the faceless murderers who work closely with the regime and its security services.

Early in 1960, sixty-seven bodies of unarmed men, women, and children were strewn over the veld in Sharpeville, with four hundred people injured. I come back today to Boipatong, where Sharpeville has been repeated with a ferocity that may completely put an end to negotiations.

Mr. de Klerk and his regime bear full responsibility for the violence in the country, and in these townships in particular. According to the press, Mr. de Klerk expressed shock and concern over the slaughter. Strange that he should be shocked and now suddenly express concern. Why is he shocked now? While these latest killings are horrific, the reality is that there are a number of massacres that have taken place, where deaths turn into double figures. For example, Sebokeng, July 1990, where 32 people died in broad daylight; Swanieville, Krugersdorp, 27 died; Sam Ntuli's funeral, 18 died.[48]

Heads of state throughout the world express their sympathies to families in case of disaster. Mr. de Klerk has been strangely silent on this matter, when black deaths are involved. We welcome his sympathy message, but it comes with crocodile tears.

He and his cabinet colleagues have been making provocative statements, that could only worsen the situation. In Tokyo Mr. de Klerk condemned mass action and said that he had contingency plans to deal with such actions. Mr. Hernus Kriel made it clear that people who marched would not be protected against attackers.

We have said on many occasions before that the regime has the capacity to stop the violence, but has not used that capacity to stop it. For years in the Transvaal the carrying in public of dangerous weapons was a criminal offense. He legalized them after the unbanning of the ANC. By then thousands of our people had been killed or injured with these same weapons. Why would a head of government pass laws to give capacity to murderers to slaughter innocent people?

In May 1991, at a meeting between the ANC and the regime, it was agreed that hostels would be phased out and transformed into family units. It was further agreed that in the meantime fences would be erected to prevent armed hostel dwellers coming out, and armed residents attacking hostels. This has not been done.

In 1990 human rights lawyer Peter Harris warned Mr.

Vlok, General Van der Merwe, and General Erasmus in two
letters of impending attacks in Sebokeng by members of a
well-known black organization. Yet armed people were allowed to enter the township and to massacre innocent residents.

About October 1990 at a meeting with Messrs. de Klerk
and Vlok, I drew attention to the fact that residents in Zank-
iziziwe had been evicted from their homes by members of the
same black organizations, supported by the South African Police, and their homes and property taken. The homes and
property were now being used by those who attacked them.
De Klerk said he would investigate. Nearly two years later the
situation remains the same. I have been given no information
on what the investigations revealed.

I repeat that just as the Nazis in Germany killed people
not because they were a threat to the security of the state,
but because they were Jews, the National Party regime is killing our people simply because they are black. They are killing
our people in an effort to stop the ANC getting into power.

Mr. de Klerk showed his insensitivity and contempt for
the feelings of blacks by what he did and said on June 16,
1992. June 16 is the sacred day where we mourn the killing
of our youth sixteen years ago. He chose that same day to go
to Ulundi to launch an attack on the democratic movement.[49]

With his involvement and that of his party in the violence,
he had the temerity to visit an area where people's feelings
have been inflamed because their beloved ones were massacred with the same weapons of death which he had legalized.
That was a clear provocation. But we must still ask the question: Why did de Klerk now choose to visit these killing fields
when he never cared to do so before? You are all free to make
your guesses. But one thing is certain. The National Party
has already started its election campaign among blacks. May
it be that he chose to shed crocodile tears and to visit this bereaved town in order to win votes? If so, he badly miscalcu-
lated.

An officer, in his presence, gave an order to shoot people without any provocation.[50] It is not likely that an officer would give such an order in his presence without getting his permission. We are back to the Sharpeville days and the gulf between the oppressed and oppressor has overnight become unbridgeable. Mr. de Klerk owes loyalty not to the people of South Africa, but to the National Party. He wants to keep it in power forever by brute force. He sees that as his duty. We have our own duty to do. We are committed to the principle of democracy as understood throughout the world, and we are going to assert that principle through peaceful mass action.

Mr. de Klerk addressed a press conference at the end of his visit. He talked about his regime taking tough action, clearly against the democratic movement. He sounded incoherent, presumably because of the rough time he experienced. I hope when he recovers from his shock, he will weigh the issues soberly. The introduction of antidemocratic measures will result in a defiance campaign of major dimensions in this country. We will resist such measures to the bitter end.

As we brace ourselves for whatever lies ahead, we must call for the strictest discipline in our ranks. Do not allow yourselves to be provoked into violence. Be careful of agents provocateurs. We have won many freedom battles precisely because of that discipline. When conflict looms on the horizon, that discipline becomes the lifeblood of the democratic movement.

What is our response to this challenge? The negotiation process is clearly in disarray. I am calling an emergency meeting of the National Executive Committee of the ANC on June 23, 1992, to examine options. I can no longer explain to our people why we keep on talking peace to men who are conducting a war against us, men of corruption who kill innocent people.

There is a bilateral meeting between the ANC and the National Party scheduled to meet Tuesday. I have instructed the secretary-general [Cyril Ramaphosa] to cancel that meeting. The voice of our people is coming out strong and clear. Their demand is: no more contact with the regime. I will be guided in this regard by the NEC and other democratic formations.[51]

We call on all our people to observe a day of mourning, to stay in their homes and to close business on August 3.

We call on Iscor to close KwaMadala Hostel, which has become a haven for those who spread death, destruction, and fear.[52]

We urge Mr. de Klerk and his minister of police to stop inciting violent attacks on the ANC because of mass action. Nothing they can do will stop mass action, other than encourage the slaughter of innocent people.

We urge the South African Police to clean the force of those elements who foment murder in order to save the National Party. We make a special appeal to black members of the SAP not to be party to killing their own kith and kin. The freedom we are fighting for is for them as well. Only under a fully democratic government will they rise to the highest positions in their profession.

We also urge whites to join the ANC in its effort to win the struggle for a nonracial democracy in our country. The future of South Africa lies in moving away from the sectarian policies of the National Party.

Members of Inkatha should not allow themselves to be pawns of the National Party in its crusade to destroy the democratic movement. There is enough room for you in the struggle for the immediate transfer of power to the people.

All covert police houses and operations in the Vaal must be exposed. The command structure of the SAP in this region is rotten through and through, and this violence cannot be stopped until the whole of that structure is totally dismantled and every officer transferred from this area.

One of the most controversial figures in the South African Police is Capt. Craig Kotze, who is tarnishing whatever reputation and credibility the SAP might still have. He is a propaganda agent of the National Party in police uniform.[53]

We urge business to take a clear stand in this conflict. They must commit themselves clearly to the demand for the immediate installation of democracy.

As far as the international community is concerned, I am going to request the secretary-general of the UN to call a special session of the Security Council on the massacres committed by Mr. de Klerk and his regime. I will address that session.

We call on the antiapartheid movement to intensify the struggle against apartheid South Africa, and to pressurize their respective governments not to hurry to lift sanctions against South Africa. De Klerk should not be rewarded for waging violence against unarmed people.

In this connection it is a disturbing fact that the international community is so quiet about the ongoing massacres. Our people are making serious allegations about the cooperation between certain Western governments and Mr. de Klerk. Why would he pose as a reformer and democrat, and at the same time allow indiscriminate murder of innocent people?

In conclusion, I want to announce that the ANC is proposing the establishment of a disaster fund for all the victims of this violence throughout the country; such a fund to be administered by the International Committee of the Red Cross. In this regard the ANC has made an initial donation of R100,000. We urge Mr. de Klerk and the National Party to join us in this effort. We hope they will contribute more than the R8,250,000 they gave to the Inkatha Freedom Party. We appeal to black and white business and to all organizations—religious, sports, and political—to give freely to this worthy initiative.

Close your ranks and do not weaken the democratic forces by quarreling among yourselves. Those people, no matter who they are, who create tensions, are not freedom fighters, they have no vision, and they do not love you. We must speak with one voice.

For a democratically elected and sovereign constituent assembly

LETTER TO PRESIDENT DE KLERK, JULY 9, 1992

Below is the major part of an open letter sent to state president F.W. de Klerk. It followed an exchange of letters between Mandela and de Klerk over the political deadlock and the steps to overcome it. The questions dealt with in Secton 2, on "Violence," are addressed in the earlier speech at Boipatong and at the United Nations Security Council, which follows.

Dear Mr. de Klerk:

I acknowledge receipt of your reply dated 2 July 1992.

It is unfortunate that your reply has not addressed the issues I raised in my memorandum of 26 June 1992. Instead, you deliberately obscure matters.

It appears that we are all agreed that South Africa faces a serious crisis. When it comes to charting a way out of the crisis, however, it is clear that there are hardly any points of convergence.

This is particularly so because you have chosen to elevate a number of peripheral issues to the status of "fundamental" ones, while relegating those of critical significance to a secondary place. The matter is made worse by the factual inaccuracies, distortions, and blatant party political propaganda involved in the manner in which you raised these so-called fundamental issues. To call for face-to-face talks in such a situation is entirely unacceptable. We would sit down to do no more than haggle about what should constitute the agenda of such talks, rather than the serious business of taking our country to a democracy and developing firm foundations for curbing and eliminating violence.

Reaffirmations about your commitment to a negotiated resolution to the South African conflict need to be supported by stating positions which offer the potential to break the deadlock.

1. Negotiations

1.1. You state that "the fundamental difference between the approach of the ANC and that of the government regarding *the purpose of negotiations* lies, on the one hand, in our commitment to constitutionality and a transitional government as soon as possible; and on the other hand, on the ANC's insistence on an unstructured and immediate transfer of power before a proper transitional constitution is negotiated."

1.2. This is indeed a novel description of the purpose of negotiations, to say nothing about its gross distortion and patent party political propaganda. The characterization of your own position as "commitment to constitutionality and a transitional government as soon as possible" bears very little relationship to the purpose of negotiations, as set out in the Declaration of Intent we adopted together at Codesa 1, namely;

"5. To set in motion the process of drawing up and establishing a constitution that will ensure, inter alia:

"*a*. that South Africa will be a united, democratic, nonracial, and nonsexist state in which sovereign authority is exercised over the whole of its territory;

"*b*. that the constitution will be the supreme law and

that it will be guarded over by an independent, nonracial, and impartial judiciary;

"*c.* that there will be a multiparty democracy with the right to form and join political parties and with regular elections on the basis of universal adult suffrage on a common voters' roll; in general the basic electoral system shall be that of proportional representation;

"*d.* that there shall be a separation of powers between the legislature, executive, and judiciary with appropriate checks and balances;

"*e.* that the diversity of languages, cultures, and religions of the people of South Africa shall be acknowledged;

"*f.* that all shall enjoy universally accepted human rights, freedoms, and civil liberties including freedom of religion, speech, and assembly protected by an entrenched and justiciable bill of rights and a legal system that guarantees equality of all before the law."

Working Group 2 was specifically charged with determining the set of general constitutional principles consistent with and including those in the declaration, as well as the form and content of the constitution-making body/processes.

1.3. The question of a transitional government was the subject matter of one of the five working groups created at Codesa 1. Unless the question of the constitution-making body is dealt with as the primary focus of negotiations, issues relating to transitional arrangements are deprived of their proper relevance. Your insistence on elevating this to the central focus of negotiations betrays the positions your government has been taking and which lie at the heart of the crisis.

1.4. If there is to be a way out of this impasse then it is imperative that we isolate the question of transitional arrangements from that of the constitution-making body. With regard to the constitution-making body (constituent assembly), it is necessary that you pronounce yourselves in keeping with basic democratic principles. A democratic constitution will be fatally flawed if the body charged with drafting and adopting it is itself undemocratic—be it in its composition or the way in which it is to function. Your response to our positions is therefore critical. It is the authority of the people, through their elected representatives, that gives a constitution its fundamental legitimacy. Our position is founded on the basic features of any democratic structure charged with the task of constitution making:

1.4.1. The constitution-making body shall be sovereign.

1.4.2. The constitution-making body shall be bound by the general constitutional principles agreed upon at Codesa, with the necessary checks to ensure that these are adhered to.

1.4.3. It shall be democratically elected on the basis of one person, one vote in the context of multiparty democracy where each party would be represented in proportion to the votes gained.

1.4.4. It shall be single-chambered and shall not be subject to the veto or overseeing powers of any other body.

1.4.5. In the South African context there is the additional requirement that such a constitution-making body constitute a unifying and legitimizing process which must however not thwart the will of the overwhelming majority. Therefore, the constitution-making body shall arrive at decisions by a two-thirds majority.

1.4.6. In order to ensure that regional differences, irrespective of whether they arise from ethnic factors or vested interests nurtured by the apartheid fragmentation of our country, are fully accommodated, the constituent assembly shall:

• be composed of 50 percent delegates elected by means of a national list, and 50 percent elected on the basis of a regional list, both on proportional representation and one person, one vote;

• in deciding on those aspects of the constitution which deal with regional structures, their powers and duties, the constituent assembly would take decisions first by means of a two-thirds majority of the entire assembly and, further, that such a decision would require the endorsement of a two-thirds majority of that half of the constituent assembly delegates who have been elected through the regional list.

1.4.7. So as to ensure that the transition is as expeditious as possible, there should be effective and timeous deadlock-breaking mechanisms in the functioning of the constitution-making body. The depth of the crisis facing our country is such that it is essential that there is a speedy transition to democracy. We cannot accept three years as a time frame for the constituent assembly to discharge its duties.

1.5. Your reply evades these questions. To the extent that it deals with any of them, what emerges is your opposition to such a sovereign and democratically elected constitution-making body. The composition and function of this sovereign body is the acid test of your commitment to democracy.

You deliberately distort our proposals to constitute "simple majoritarianism." You falsely accuse us of wanting the constituent assembly to function in a constitutional void. At the same time you seek to preempt the work of the constituent assembly by the Codesa process.

Besides subjecting the work of the constituent assembly to the veto of a regionally elected senate, you seek to entrench federalism by subterfuge. This becomes clear by your requirement that the boundaries, powers, functions, and form of regional government will have to be approved by the majority of the representatives from *each electoral region* that will be affected in *each* case.

It is necessary that there should be a clear understanding that all interim arrangements relating to the administration and governance of regions shall be such as not to preempt the decisions of the constitution-making body. The question of the form of government, be it federal or unitary or whatever, is a matter that should be left to a democratically elected constitution-making body.

1.6. The manner in which you have elevated the transitional arrangements to the central focus of negotiations betrays your preoccupation with obtaining guarantees of a constitutionally entrenched role for the National Party, which you recognize will remain a minority party in the event of a democratic constitution.

1.7. You are more than aware that your allegation that the ANC insists on "an unstructured and an immediate transfer of power" bears no relation to the truth. Long before Codesa was established, the ANC proposed that there should be an interim government of national unity so as to ensure that no party occupies the position of player and referee. This demand was first put in the Harare Declaration of 1989. It was not put forward as an end in itself. It was proposed as a means by which a democratically elected and sovereign constituent assembly would be brought into being for the purposes of drafting and adopting a democratic constitution for a united, nonracial, and nonsexist South Africa.

1.8. In the agreements reached at Codesa with regards to transitional arrangements, it is clearly stated in paragraph 1.12 of the report of Working Group 3 that "the following agreements were reached with regard to the first stage of the transition. These agreements and their implementation are dependent upon agreement being reached by Codesa in respect of the second stage of the transition, including an interim constitution, and general constitutional principles."

1.9. Indeed we were all parties to the insertion of this clause. That is to say, there appears to be agreement that none of us could walk blindfolded into the first stage of the transition if we could not define for ourselves and for the citizens of our country the central question as to the nature and functioning of a constitution-making body. At the same time it is evidenced in the records of Working Group 3 that the ANC fully supports constitutional and legislative measures to ensure that there is no constitutional void.

1.10. And yet at the same time you have sought, by one means or another, to get an unconditional commitment from us to transitional arrangements without a clear agreement on the constitution-making body. That is why we insist that the deadlock with regard to the constitution-making body needs to be addressed by you.

1.11. It is a matter of public record that with regards to the interim government arrangements, it is the ANC which insisted on the idea of an interim government of national unity in order to stress the need for an interim period that would be broadly inclusive. In pursuance of such inclusivity we proposed that all parties elected would be represented in the interim executive in proportion to their proven electoral support.

1.12. In the light of these proposals we cannot understand why your party persists in seeking to impose undemocratic solutions. All parties, including yours, are assured of a place in the future on the basis of proven electoral support. All parties have been offered a place in the executive in the interim period. To carry such interim arrangements into a future constitution to be adopted by the constituent assembly is to deny the principle of majority rule and vest minority political parties with veto powers. Furthermore, this would place minority parties in a conflictual situation with the majority and undermine the security minority parties seek. . . .

3. Other issues raised in your letter

3.1. In the face of the two critical issues which stand in the way of the transition to democracy, you have chosen to raise other issues as matters requiring urgent negotiations. Instead of addressing the critical issues with the statesmanship they require, your entire letter takes the form of a party political reply. Perhaps this confusion on your side is understandable in the context of your being the head of the NP government. But it is inexcusable in the context of your persistent claims based on the right to govern and your position as state president.

3.2. Your charges against the ANC and its allies are part of the baggage of apartheid ideology. We reject with contempt your propagandistic version of what is supposed to be happening inside the ANC and the alliance. It has been the tradition of successive National Party regimes to try to discredit our movement on the basis that you know black people better than black people know themselves.

3.3. With the right to peaceful demonstration goes our inherent right to determine its nature and aims. The dangers of further violence must be laid at the doors of those who are resisting change. Successive NP regimes have always sought to crush our mass campaigns by raising the specter of violence and disruption as being inherent in our campaigns. This was so in the case of the Defiance Campaign of 1952, the Freedom Charter campaign of 1955, the Alexandra bus boycott of 1957, the numerous national stayaways, etc., including those of the recent period.[54]

But the record is clear; wherever and whenever violence raised its head, it has been initiated and provoked by the government side. And in the more recent cases they include your surrogates.

4. Conclusion

4.1. Given the party political nature of your reply, we would urge you to desist from this course in addressing our demands. Find a way within yourself to recognize the gravity of the crisis. The starting point for this is that you stop deluding yourself that it is the ANC and its allies' program of mass action which is the cause of the crisis. It would be a grave mistake if your government thinks that resorting to repression and the use of the military and police power that it commands can be a means of resolving the conflict. Find a way to address the demands we have placed before you with regards to the negotiations deadlock and those relating to the violence, so that negotiations can become meaningful and be vested with the urgency that the situation requires. Failure to respond in this way can only exacerbate the crisis. You may succeed in delaying, but never in preventing, the transition of South Africa to a democracy.

Yours sincerely,
Nelson R. Mandela

A cold-blooded strategy of state terrorism

ADDRESS TO UNITED NATIONS SECURITY COUNCIL, JULY 15, 1992

The remarks below were delivered in New York at a special session of the UN Security Council requested by the ANC. Also participating in the debate were South African foreign minister Roelof F. (Pik) Botha and Inkatha leader Mangosuthu Buthelezi.

Mr. President; distinguished members of the Security Council; Your Excellency, Dr. Boutros Boutros-Ghali, secretary-general of the United Nations; ministers and ambassadors; ladies and gentlemen:

First of all, we would like to express our appreciation to the Security Council for agreeing to convene on the question of South Africa. We would also like to thank you most sincerely for giving us the opportunity to address you.

The United Nations has been seized with the question of South Africa for the past forty-five years. The reason for this is that our people have been subjected to the policy of apartheid, which the United Nations has determined is a crime against humanity. The decisions which have been taken by the Security Council and the General Assembly on the question of South Africa have been directed at ending this apartheid crime against humanity and helping to transform our country into a nonracial democracy.

This objective has not yet been achieved. South Africa continues to be governed by a white minority regime. The overwhelming majority of our people are still denied the vote. They remain deprived of the right to determine their destiny.

Representatives of the South African government will also address you today. However sweet-sounding the words they may utter, they represent the system of white minority rule to which the United Nations is opposed. They continue to govern our country under a constitution which the Security Council has declared null and void.

Precisely because its purposes have not yet been achieved, the United Nations must remain seized with the question of South Africa. It must continue to look for ways and means by which it can help to expedite the process leading to the democratic transformation of our country.

In the meantime, an extremely critical situation has arisen.

Whereas in the Declaration of Intent adopted at the Convention for a Democratic South Africa on December 21, 1991, we all committed ourselves to set in motion the process whereby a democratic constitution would be drafted and adopted for a united, nonracial, and nonsexist South Africa, the process is deadlocked.

The problem is that the ruling white minority government continues to look for ways and means by which it can guarantee itself the continued exercise of power, regardless of its electoral support. The regime insists that the political majority, no matter how large, should be subjected to veto by minority political parties. Unless government is forthcoming with a firm commitment to full democracy based on internationally accepted principles, and an acceptance of a sovereign and democratic constitution-making body, the process will not move forward.

But the council meets today because this process has been brought to a halt by the carnage in the black townships.

Over the last five to six years, at least 11,000 people have died as a result of this violence. During the month of June 1992 there have been 373 deaths and 395 injuries; 1,806 have been killed and 2,931 injured during the period January 1992 to June 1992.

Control of state power by the National Party regime allows it the space to deny and cover up the role of the regime, its surrogates, the state security forces and the police, in fostering and fomenting the violence. Our memorandum of July 9, 1992, to Mr. F.W. de Klerk sets out the evidence of numerous instances, both of acts of omission and commission, which bear out government involvement in the violence. In particular, we draw your attention to the annexure entitled "Involvement of the Security Forces in the Fomenting and Escalation of Violence," and Annexure 3 entitled "South African Government Support for the Inkatha Freedom Party."

Mr. President:

Many years of struggle both inside and outside of South Africa brought us to the point in 1989 when, in its consensus "Declaration on Apartheid and its Destructive Consequences in Southern Africa," the General Assembly concluded that circumstances existed for a negotiated resolution of the South Africa question.

In that declaration the General Assembly said that such negotiations should, as a result of agreements that would be entered into by the liberation movement and the government, be conducted in an atmosphere free of violence.

We were and are in full agreement with these positions. They were adopted by the General Assembly precisely because it was correctly foreseen that the process of negotiations could not succeed while a virtual civil war raged in the country.

Pursuant to this objective, in August 1990 the ANC decided to suspend all armed actions. We did this unilaterally as a demonstration of our good faith and to help create an atmosphere free of violence.

At the same time it was expected that, for its part, the

regime would carry out various measures which would remove obstacles to negotiations, and that it would ensure that a proper climate for negotiations did in fact exist. Instead we have been confronted with an escalating spiral of violence.

An independent sociopolitical and development agency known as Community Agency for Social Enquiry (CASE) has prepared five reports with regard to the pattern of violence. One of these reports comes to the conclusion that "The violence appears to be switched on and off at strategic moments."

It continues: "Behind the scale of brutality . . . is the clear evidence that the violence erupts at points when it most weakens the ANC and its allies and dies down dramatically when it would most harm the government of F.W. de Klerk."

It then goes on to say: "Two political parties have clearly benefited from the Reef violence. The first is the National Party government. . . . The second major beneficiary has been Inkatha."

Another report deals with thirteen attacks on funerals or funeral vigils which took place on the Reef between July 1990 and July 1991. This study concludes that there is "an overwhelming predominance of acts of aggression carried out by supporters of the Inkatha Freedom Party. Those attacks, moreover, are carried out with the active or passive support of the South African Police."

It is more than clear to us that this violence is both organized and orchestrated. It is specifically directed at the democratic movement, whose activists, members, and supporters make up the overwhelming majority of its victims.

It constitutes a cold-blooded strategy of state terrorism intended to create the conditions under which the forces responsible for the introduction and entrenchment of the system of apartheid would have the possibility of imposing their will on a weakened democratic movement at the negotiations table.

However, as had been foreseen by this organization, this

violence also has the effect of making negotiations impossible. Already in April 1991, when this campaign of terror grew to new heights, we were left with no choice but to suspend the bilateral negotiations with the regime until it took various measures to address the question of violence.

It is now common cause that the agreements that the government reached with the ANC in May 1991 aimed at the curbing of violence have not been carried out by the regime.

Faced with the horrendous escalation of the violence, as evidenced in the Boipatong massacre, occurring in the context of the negotiations deadlock, the ANC has been forced to withdraw from the multilateral process of negotiations which had been taking place in the Convention for a Democratic South Africa.

The blame for this lies squarely at the door of the regime. It, and nobody else, has the law enforcement personnel and the legal authority to stop this violence and to act against the perpetrators.

As the governing authority, it has the obligation to protect the lives and property of all the people. It has failed dismally to do this.

The regime's actions, including its persistent efforts to shift the blame for the violence and the responsibility to act against it to political organizations, have served to ensure the escalation of the carnage.

Though the causes of the violence are many and complex, it is important that we should all have a clear perspective. It is the regime which controls state power, with the capacity to bring the violence to an end. Complicity of state security forces is established by the evidence which emerged in numerous court trials, inquests, and commissions and is recognized in the Goldstone commission as well as reports of international fact-finding missions.

It is also clear that the central thrust of the violence is to weaken the ANC and the democratic movement of the country.

In the face of this situation, it is also true that there are instances of counterviolence by members of the democratic movement. At the same time, it is a matter of public record that the ANC policy stands opposed to the promotion of violence. We remain firmly committed to this position. But our task of ensuring that this policy position is fully and completely adhered to is made more than difficult because of the practice of the state security forces, its surrogates, and the fact that it is the police controlled by the regime who remain in charge of investigating the violence, in which the state security forces are implicated, and bringing the perpetrators to book.

The ANC maintains that government culpability for the violence extends to acts of commission as well as omission.

The International Commission of Jurists and Amnesty International have blamed the government for failure to act against the violence. Amnesty International notes government's "failure to bring to justice all but a tiny proportion of those involved in human rights violations."

Judge Goldstone in his report dated July 6, 1992, complains of several instances where the authorities have ignored the recommendations of his commission.

Not a single person has been convicted in connection with the forty-nine massacres that claimed the lives of at least ten people in each of the incidents that have occurred in the past two years.

Where there have been proper investigations and vigorous prosecution, as resulted from the Trust Feed massacre of December 1988, convictions have been secured. Those convicted were policemen.[55]

In 1985 Matthew Goniwe and three other Eastern Cape leaders were murdered. In May this year a document whose authenticity has not been challenged [came to light], a message from the SADF military intelligence chief, [in which] General C.P. Van der Westhuizen (then a brigadier) proposed to the State Security Council that the four authorize "the urgent removal from society" of Goniwe and the others. No move has been made to suspend Van der Westhuizen from his position.[56]

No action has been taken to suspend the head of the SAP forensic laboratories, General Lothar Neethling, after a Supreme Court civil case finding in January 1991 that his involvement in the poisoning of activists was on the balance of probabilities, true.

Despite a judicial commission finding implicating several Civil Cooperation Bureau members in political violence, none has been charged. At least twenty CCB members, and probably many more, remain on the SADF payroll. Others have been offered or received huge pensions. Several have demanded immunity from prosecution.

In February 1992 it came to light that local white policemen based at the Ermelo police station encouraged and actively helped a gang of vigilantes in Wesselton. No policemen concerned have been suspended.

In an official operation in 1986, the SADF gave military training in Namibia to two hundred Inkatha members who were later absorbed into the KwaZulu Police. Several trainees, in sworn affidavits, claimed to have been trained in offensive warfare. The regime has dismissed this incident on the grounds that they received VIP-protection training. Some of the trainees have subsequently been implicated in the violence in Natal.

No action has been taken to control and limit the powers of the KwaZulu Police. Extensive evidence exists of Kwa-Zulu partiality and involvement in the violence in the Natal province.

However, as recently as July 1, 1992, the powers of the KZP have in fact been strengthened. From that date the South African Police's Internal Stability Unit will only act on unrest in KwaZulu if called on to do so by the KZP district commissioner.

In 1990 the Pretoria regime issued specific proclamations legalizing the carrying of dangerous weapons in public. This repealed a prohibition which had been in force since 1891.

In other words, after the ANC and other organizations

were unbanned in 1990, the Pretoria regime has created a situation in which hordes of men would spill out into the streets and enter public places with the most dangerous weapons. The government is unable to explain why it virtually gave people the license to kill and maim. It has never explained why its police and army regularly accompanied these killers after many murderous rampages and arrested nobody.

We charge, without equivocation, that there is a rational basis for these acts of omission on the part of the South African government. The hard facts of the matter are the South African government has never relented in its war against the democratic movement in our country.

Recently a covert police unit, operating in the area around Boipatong, came to public attention. It, and ten others operating in other regions of the country, exist for the purpose of suppressing the democratic movement, which the government still regards as the enemy and a threat to so-called national security. Former officers and personnel of the security police have been redeployed into these clandestine networks.

There are persistent allegations that members of these units, as well as those in special forces units composed of foreign nationals, such as Angolans, Mozambicans, and Namibians, are engaged in covert operations that include the assassination of leaders and activists of the democratic movement. They are also implicated in carrying out acts of terror against the population at large.

In order to confuse the issue and evade its responsibilities, the government insists that the source of the violence is rivalry between the ANC and the Inkatha Freedom Party. The fact of the matter, however, is that the IFP has permitted itself to become an extension of the Pretoria regime, its instrument and surrogate.

Its activities have been financed by the South African government. Its members have been armed and trained by the South African government. There is an abundance of evidence that it continues to benefit from covert cooperation with the South African government.

It therefore becomes unclear whether its members act as an independent force or as an agency on behalf of the South African government. However, it is not an independent force with whom the ANC must enter into an agreement to end the violence, as the Pretoria regime asserts.

The documentation we have given to members of the council details all the points we have raised, all of which confirm the criminal failure of the government to properly address the question of political violence, which has claimed too many lives already, is tearing our country apart, and making the process of negotiations impossible.

We would like to recall earlier decisions of this council to help the people of South Africa to transform their country into a nonracial democracy. We believe that commitment places an urgent obligation on the council to intervene in the South African situation to end the carnage.

The very interest of the council to see the negotiations resumed so that a peaceful solution can be found, in keeping with the democratic principles contained in the General Assembly declaration on southern Africa of 1989 and the resolutions of the Security Council, itself requires of the council that it act on this matter of violence in South Africa firmly and with the necessary speed.

We believe that this violence, like the system of apartheid itself, is a direct challenge to the authority of the council and a subversion of its global tasks of furthering peace and promoting the objectives contained in both the UN Charter and the Declaration on Human Rights.

Failure on the part of the council to act firmly and decisively cannot but undermine its prestige and authority at a time when the council and the United Nations as a whole are called upon to play an even more active role in the ordering of world affairs.

We would therefore urge that the council should request the secretary-general to appoint a special representative on South Africa.

This representative should move speedily to investigate

the situation in South Africa with a view to helping the council to decide on the measures it should take to help us end the violence. The council should then take the necessary decisions to implement such measures, including the continuous monitoring of the situation, to ensure the effectiveness of such measures as it would have undertaken.

We would also like to bring it to the notice of the council, for the purpose of its information, that we have required of the government that it also completes the process of the release of political prisoners as well as the repeal of repressive legislation.

Again, these are concrete steps visualized in the UN declaration to create a climate conducive to negotiations. That these matters remain on the agenda more than two years after we entered into a formal agreement with the South African government that they would be attended to, demonstrates the problem we face of the reliability of the government in terms of implementing agreements it has entered into.

We would also like to take advantage of this opportunity to reaffirm our own commitment both to the process of negotiations and to a genuinely democratic outcome.

In this regard, we would again like to inform you that we have still to convince the government that it also should be committed to such a democratic outcome, accepting such ordinary concepts of a democratic system as majority rule and the absence of vetoes by minority parties.

We therefore still have to overcome these obstacles so that the process of negotiations itself, as conducted within the Convention for a Democratic South Africa, can succeed.

We would further like to assure the council that we, who are after all the victims of the evil system of apartheid, are determined that the process of negotiations should lead to a democratic outcome as soon as possible.

We therefore need no urging regarding this matter. What we do need is the assistance of this august body to help us reopen the door to bona fide negotiations.

Mr. President, distinguished members of the council:

We thank you for the opportunity you have given us to address the council, and hope that you will respond to our appeal to help us end the carnage in South Africa with the understanding of the gravity of the situation which we know you share. Our people look forward to your decisions with great expectation.[57]

Thank you.

A decisive blow for peace and democracy

SPEECH TO DEMONSTRATION AT UNION BUILDINGS, PRETORIA, AUGUST 5, 1992

On August 3-4, 1992, the ANC-led alliance called a general strike in support of its demands for meaningful negotiations and a halt to government-organized attacks on the democratic movement. The strike, observed by four million workers and involving 90 percent of the black work force, was part of a weeklong series of mass actions that included twenty-eight rallies, seventy-four marches, and hundreds of other actions throughout the country. The largest demonstration was a peaceful march of over a hundred thousand to the Union Buildings in Pretoria, the seat of the South African government, from which Mandela delivered the following remarks.

Our country is passing through the most important phase in its history. The passing of the old order of apartheid rule and the birth of a new era of peace, democracy, and justice is marked with trials, tribulations, and immense sacrifice.

The general strike on Monday and Tuesday is unquestionably one of the greatest events in our history. More than four million workers stayed away. Millions more of youth and students, housewives, business people, and civil servants participated. It is time for all of us to read the lessons correctly.

What makes four million workers stay away from work, forgo their wages in the midst of rampant unemployment, poverty, and when fear stalks their lives in the townships? A sacrifice of such immense magnitude by the most downtrodden sections of our people, who have acted in the name of peace and democracy, requires an answer that measures up to the responsibility that this places on our shoulders.

Let us congratulate the people for the disciplined and peaceful way in which they have conducted the general strike. That is why it succeeded. They did not allow themselves to be intimidated by the government and all those forces who did everything in their power to defeat the action of the people. Nor did they allow themselves to be misled by the barrage of misinformation and false propaganda.

Nothing can detract from the fact that this general strike was peaceful. Those who still cling to the idea that the success of this mass action was based on intimidation do themselves an injustice. Because this could only be true if they believed that the ANC and its allies have the power to intimidate so many millions of people.

Let us congratulate all those employers, big and small, who responded to the call for peace and democracy, who closed their enterprises, and who committed themselves not to victimize their employees for staying away from work. They aligned themselves with the forces of democracy at great sacrifice. We say this advisedly because we know that they have to survive in an economy which is stagnating because of decades of apartheid rule, mismanagement, and corruption.

The success of the general strike is also due to the way in which all the structures of the alliance, of COSATU, the South African Communist Party, and the ANC, persevered with the formidable task of organizing the strike. In this regard, we congratulate all the democratic formations including the civics, the religious, students', teachers', women's, youth, and cultural organizations. It is of special significance that the Coloured and Indian communities overwhelmingly participated in the stayaway. They all acted with a unity of purpose which made the general strike a decisive blow for peace and democracy.

We congratulate the international community for rallying to our cause. The presence of the small United Nations monitoring force played no small role in ensuring that the democratic right of our people to engage in mass action was realized in practice.

This is not a victory for the ANC or COSATU or the SACP. It is a victory of the people of South Africa. It is a victory for peace and democracy. All South Africans, black and white, want peace, economic stability, and a happy future for their children.

The ANC and its allies, in embarking on mass action, did not act in order to score points for our organizations. The objectives behind the mass action are too serious to allow anyone to play party politics with the future of our people and the country.

Together all have struck a blow for peace and democracy.

It is in this spirit that we are all obliged to see the period ahead. We have not come here to gloat. We are here to take South Africa along the road to peace and democracy.

If the government of the day responds in this same spirit, our action will have been the best thing that could have happened for the negotiations process. All the people of our country and the entire international community await the response of the government.

It should now be clear to all that an interim government of national unity is an urgent and critical step to take our country forward. Such a government can only be based on the political realities which reflect the sentiments of all South African citizens. Unless our country decisively moves forward to the establishment of an interim government, there will be no progress.

The creation of an interim government of national unity has to be linked to a vision which ensures that our entire people will have a direct say in the drafting and adoption of a constitution which embodies democracy. This means that there must be a commitment to a sovereign, democratically elected constituent assembly.

It is critical that practical steps are taken by the government to curb the violence which is ravaging the lives of our people in the townships. These three categories of demands constitute the fourteen we have made to the government. Unless they are met satisfactorily by the government, negotiations cannot be resumed.

It is time for the government to abandon the path that it has been following. While pursuing negotiations, it simultaneously sought to weaken the ANC and the democratic forces. Along this direction it also sought to build alliances with all sorts of dubious political formations in the hope that this will add to the process of weakening the ANC. This has been one of the gravest mistakes it committed in the current period. The time has arrived for it to abandon this path.

The ANC and its allies remain committed to the search for a negotiated resolution of the crisis facing our country. We have engaged in mass action with the clear objective of ensuring that the outcome of the negotiations is a democratic future for our country. What happens next, and what form the campaign for peace and democracy takes, depends on how the government responds to our demands which address the crucial obstacles in the path of negotiations.

History will not forgive any of us if the search for face-saving formulae prevents us from finding the correct responses which facilitate negotiations to be resumed and to be successful.

The outcome of the mass action campaign must not allow any of us to become dizzy with success. Our people have shown that in the midst of poverty, unemployment, and economic crisis, they remain firmly committed to act for peace and democracy. The millions who have shown this commitment need to be organized.

The campaign for peace and democracy must become a tidal wave which will thrust our country into a future where justice prevails, peace is assured, and democracy becomes a way of life.

Let unity, discipline, and peaceful action become the hallmark of everything we do.

Viva peace! Viva democracy!

We must pull South Africa out from the morass

INTERVIEW WITH 'JOHANNESBURG STAR,' PUBLISHED SEPTEMBER 15, 1992

The following is the major part of an interview conducted by Richard Steyn and Shaun Johnson.

On the prospects of the summit:

I think that in spite of the fact that we came very near to a disaster (after the Bisho massacre), the move that we have now jointly made—myself and Mr. de Klerk—has saved the country from that disaster.[58] We welcome Mr. de Klerk's move, because whatever has been said by Pik Botha, this move of Mr. de Klerk's is nevertheless calculated to break the deadlock.

Our concentration is on the installation of democracy in the country, and for this, compromises become absolutely essential. That is why I decided to respond as I did. I first had doubts as to whether I should act, because Mr. de Klerk's invitation had its propagandistic elements, but people have died. The biggest question is how we are going to avoid a repetition of Bisho.

Of course there are certain preconditions, and I hope you will regard these as reasonable. The government agreed to act on the hostels, political prisoners, and dangerous weapons. This they can do without meeting us.

On our part we are going to cooperate, and hope Mr. de Klerk is going to cooperate. My message to the government is: make good on the undertakings you have given to us and Mr. Cyrus Vance. We are not challenging here, not demanding. It is our deep concerns we have put forward.

What has happened now is that the negotiations process has lost credibility, has become discredited. You must realize it was a heated debate within the ANC when we decided to suspend armed struggle and to negotiate. But we convinced one another then. Now my people are beginning to say to me: "What was the value? Let's abandon negotiations; they will never be able to take us to our goal."

I am saying, therefore, it is urgent that the government makes some visible, practical move to restore the credibility of negotiations. And once the government does that, by moving just on these three points, we are prepared to reconsider the whole question of having pulled out of negotiations. . . .

On why the ANC insists on mass action:

One of the mistakes that has been made by both the ANC and the National Party is that we have embarked on an electioneering campaign while we are negotiating. One party is talking to the other while at the same time trying to undermine that party. Now that destroys the whole atmosphere of negotiations.

But I have explained that we must have free political activity, and the efforts we have made to ensure that. In addition, it is quite clear that the government is now fighting an electoral campaign, and that they are using these homelands as areas where they can start with maximum votes, where they have no competition.

Look at our situation. We have done everything in our power. We are left with two years (before elections). We must make sure that all political parties can operate throughout the country. If we can't make progress as far as negotiations are concerned, if we can't make progress in discussions with the Bantustan leaders affected, what are we expected to do? We can't sit down and fold our arms. The ordinary people in these particular areas want action.

On the limits of acceptable mass action:

We are very concerned about the situation, but as I've said, we cannot just fold our arms. However, while the regions can take decisions, they must always keep in mind the national perspective.

Nothing should be done by the organization which suggests that we now want to violate the parameters of the National Peace Accord[59] or the guidelines of the Goldstone commission. And in the last meeting of the NEC I stressed this point, as I did in King William's Town the day after the massacre. We must be seen to respect the structures that have been created, and the guidelines.

We do not feel that the mere launching of mass action in itself is anything which needs to worsen the position—no. The masses of the people, the overwhelming majority, want the right to operate in their own area. And they have been prevented by Gqozo. I am saying, therefore, that as far as we are concerned, we will make sure that in this volatile atmosphere we will not do anything that is likely to worsen the situation. But we must do something when people are being persecuted in these areas, when there is no democracy there. Can we be expected to do anything else?

On whether the Bisho march crossed the line between protest and insurrection:

Regional leaders must always consider what effect their actions will have on the country as a whole. Now our image has been affected to some extent by what happened in Bisho. Even some of our loyal friends locally and internationally have got reservations about what we did in that demonstration.

But you must understand that what happened in Bisho has not been the pattern of mass action. On August 5 I led the march on Pretoria. It was disciplined and the police said the crowd behaved magnificently. That was the position throughout the country generally, although there were exceptions where there was intimidation and looting. When this was drawn to my attention I actually went to these areas to see businessmen, to apologize. But generally speaking, we are able to control our people.

Now we said we were going to occupy Bisho. Remember that we occupied the Union Buildings, actually hoisted our flag. There was no interference from Mr. de Klerk or his police. He was completely relaxed. After I had left he came out and addressed the press, complimented me for my conciliatory speech.

On Ronnie Kasrils's actions:

Our concern is not primarily the actions of individuals. What we are concerned with is: What can we do to prevent a repetition of what happened at Bisho? And in that context we are discussing, therefore, what individuals have done.

But you must also remember that I actually asked the secretary-general, Cyril Ramaphosa, the head of the Women's League, Gertrude Shope, Steve Tshwete, the man who has normalized sport, to go down and lead that demonstration. Now the concentration is on Ronnie Kasrils, which is not really the proper perspective.

You must also remember that the idea of the march, to which we all agreed, was that just as we did in Pretoria, we would do the same in Bisho.

That was not the decision of Ronnie Kasrils, it was ours. Therefore, his judgment may not have been a correct one, to go beyond the stadium once the magistrate had said we should not, but the idea of us going to Bisho was a decision of the organization which he was merely carrying out.

But I can assure you that this is a matter that we are going to examine very carefully. Ronnie Kasrils and Chris Hani are very loyal members of the ANC who have made tremendous sacrifices. Secondly, they are disciplined. If I were to say there should be no further (independent) statements by anybody (on behalf of the ANC), and this was the decision taken regarding future demonstrations, I will get their maximum support.

On who was to blame at Bisho:

There have been accusations and counteraccusations, some correct and others incorrect, from both sides. But leaving this aside, we still have to answer the question: Has the ANC any strategy to pull South Africa out from the morass in which decades of apartheid generally, and this massacre in Bisho particularly, have plunged it?

Now it seems to me that we should not worry very much at this stage with what mistakes individuals have made. The crucial question is how to mobilize the democratic forces in the country to concentrate on the task of saving South Africa. I am talking about neither the ANC nor the government, but we, the people of South Africa, black and white.

Our problem is that Brigadier Gqozo ignored the guidelines for demonstrations. The guidelines say that even if one party deviated from an agreement on the course of a march, the other party is not entitled to use force unless it is threatened. They must meet during the march. Gqozo was not prepared to talk to us right from the beginning. He violated the peace accord right from the beginning. The marching out of the stadium towards Bisho was not actually a violation of the peace accord itself. But even if it was, then the task of the other party was to have called us and discussed it—just as has happened in other areas.

On 'radicals' and 'moderates' within the ANC:

It is not correct to say that there is a conflict between radicals and moderates in the ANC, although I fear it could develop (in circumstances like those at Bisho).

But you can be assured that we will be addressing any

statements which were made which might have been harmful to the cause of democracy in the country generally, and that of the ANC in particular. We will not be seen to be doing anything which is a violation of the National Peace Accord or the Goldstone guidelines.

On pressure within the ANC:

(If we cannot secure free political activity) I am going to face a situation in which it becomes increasingly difficult to resist the demands of my own people to arm and defend themselves. You know, when I went to Boipatong, I was met with placards, "Mandela, give us guns." And these were not coming from the youth, but elderly people, members of the branch.

Then I went to the rally, and I went round as I normally do to greet people. And the song they were singing was, "Mandela, you behave like a lamb while we are being killed." I had to make a speech there to say I had noted what they were saying.

Now if we don't do something visible to show that we are fighting against oppression, those who are demanding the resumption of the armed struggle are going to prevail. Mass action is actually a peaceful form of channeling the anger of the people—for us to say we don't need armed struggle, we can make progress through mass action.

You must understand that mass action is being used today throughout the democratic world, and by people who have the vote. We haven't got the vote. What else can we do?

On political control of the security forces:

As you know, very late on May 15 at Codesa 2, I went to see Mr. de Klerk. I said to him: "The whole of South Africa and the world is looking upon you and I. Let us save the peace process. Let us reach some agreement. Let us leave the door open and say we have made progress. We need to fix a date."

On that day he was adamant, he wouldn't listen to me. I was with Cyril Ramaphosa and he was with Roelf Meyer. (I complained that the police had not taken action against an armed Inkatha demonstration) and he answered: "Mr. Mandela, when you join me, you will realize I do not have the power which you think I have." That was his answer.

I was raising a serious question about people using violence in the presence of the police and that was his answer. This is the kind of problem we are dealing with. If there is anything that has cooled relations between me and Mr. de Klerk, it is his paralysis as far as violence is concerned. Because I believe he has got the capacity to put an end to the violence. That is the issue for me, and we need to resolve it.

1993 can be a year of decisive achievements

INTERVIEW WITH 'MAYIBUYE,' PUBLISHED FEBRUARY 1993

Following discussions between Mandela and de Klerk, a Record of Understanding was signed on September 26, 1992. In it the government and ANC agreed to an elected constituent assembly to draft the new constitution, installation of an interim government, release of all political prisoners within two months, banning the public display of dangerous weapons, and building fences around migrant worker hostels. The following interview summing up the year's events and reviewing prospects for 1993 was conducted by Brian Hoga and published in *Mayibuye,* the monthly magazine of the ANC.

MAYIBUYE: Last year was described by many as a horrible one. Is this your assessment?

MANDELA: We had a lot of problems throughout last year. The ANC was compelled to suspend talks with the government because of its intransigence, and the whole negotiations process was slowed down. But I don't share the view that, merely because there were serious problems, and the targets that we had set for ourselves were not reached, 1992 was a year of disaster.

On the contrary, it was a year in which some significant progress was made. That was the year in which we agreed that elections should be held towards the end of 1993. It was the year in which we agreed on the installation of an interim government. It was the year in which we agreed on a Record of Understanding. Therefore, in spite of the slow progress we made, I think it was not a year without achievement.

MAYIBUYE: The sense of despondency arises partly from the fact that, since 1990, negotiations have proceeded at a snail's pace. Does the ANC lack the capacity to speed up the process?

MANDELA: It may well be. But some people and organizations were too optimistic about the pace that the talks would take. If you look at the matter from the point of view of the conditions under which these negotiations occurred, I think we have made reasonable progress.

Who would have thought that, as a result of these discussions, the state of emergency would be lifted, political prisoners released, exiles allowed to return, a climate of free political activity in the greater part of South Africa would prevail, and repressive legislation would either be amended or repealed?

We have signed a Declaration of Intent, which provides a basis for movement towards a united, nonracial, democratic, and nonsexist South Africa. These achievements have been made within a period of three years.

Having regard to the history of the country, especially the history of apartheid, we have made very good progress. Therefore, the ANC had and still has the capacity to see to it that the peace process moves forward.

MAYIBUYE: So what are the prospects this year?

MANDELA: I think it is reasonable to accept that almost all political parties have realized the need for a peaceful settlement in the near future, and I think that we are likely to turn 1993 into a year of decisive achievements.

MAYIBUYE: What impact has the ANC's new strategic perspective on negotiations had on the process? What exactly does it entail?

MANDELA: I think it has had a very healthy impact. We must remember that the essence of the "Strategic Perspective" document is to ensure the transfer of political power from a minority government to the people as a whole.[60] It is based on the acceptance of the principle of majority rule and the total elimination of all forms of apartheid and minority rule.

At the same time the document takes into account the realities of our situation. We totally reject a forced coalition as the government demands. At the same time we realize the importance of a government of national unity, both during the interim period and when a democratic government has been installed.

We would like to forestall the possibility of a counterrevolutionary onslaught on the democratic government which will be established. We think we have a very good chance of achieving that objective if we are able to form a government of national unity as a result of a decision of any majority party which will emerge after the general election.

So this document, therefore, stands for the principle of majority rule, which is observed in all democratic countries.

The party that emerges strongest in the election, especially if it has the overall majority, should be called upon to form the government. That party is then free to invite other political parties with a significant following to join the government. We therefore think that the democratic government which will be installed in that way will be in a position to have a firm hold on the levers of power.

We also hold the firm view that the army, police, and civil service should be restructured to serve the interests of democracy and reflect, in their composition, South African society as a whole.

But we are also saying that individuals currently serving in these machineries will not simply be thrown out into the streets. Some retrenchment packages might have to be considered.

All these proposals of the ANC should help allay fears of

some sections among whites. The proposals can contribute to breaking their resistance to the transition.

But the essence of our approach remains the achievement of democratic majority rule.

MAYIBUYE: Concretely, what specific steps do you envisage in negotiations and the transition this year?

MANDELA: We envisage the installation of a transitional executive council, and elections for a constituent assembly towards the end of the year. The CA will then draw up a new constitution for the country. That might take some time and might go beyond 1993.

MAYIBUYE: Other organizations are calling for the reopening of Codesa decisions and the setting up of a new forum altogether. Is this not reasonable, in view of the fact that Codesa 2 failed, and new forces might be coming in?

MANDELA: No, that we totally reject. It has taken a long time to establish Codesa. For us now to try and set up another multiparty forum may take as long, and we are not prepared for that. Codesa is an effective organization for any future multiparty talks. All that is necessary is that parties which want to make a contribution to the process can come and join. We will listen to any suggestions they make which can improve the effectiveness of the existing Codesa. But we are not prepared to waste time by setting up a new forum.

MAYIBUYE: Do the ANC, the regime, and any other parties see eye to eye on this issue?

MANDELA: The ANC and its allies, as well as the government, do. In the last December three-day bilateral between the government and the ANC, we agreed that the forum for multiparty talks is the existing Codesa. It might be restructured though, in the sense that parties which are not members will be allowed to come in and to canvass their point of view. We have agreed that Codesa will be the forum for multiparty discussions.

MAYIBUYE: If this issue and perhaps others lead to a deadlock, will those who agree proceed?

MANDELA: We don't think that any political party will be

Left, with African heads of state, Lusaka, Zambia, March 1990. Below, with Fidel Castro, July 1991.

"Due to the enormous sacrifices of our people and the solidarity and support of the international community, apartheid is nearing its end."

TOP: RUTH HASWELL/MILITANT; BOTTOM: GREG McCARTAN/MILITANT

Left top: ANC rally in Durban, June 1991. Left bottom: December 1991 rally in Soweto for Umkhonto we Sizwe.

Right: ANC banner over street in East London. Below: March 1990 rally in Lenasia, a suburb of Johannesburg.

"It is in actual struggle that the masses will acquire the political experience to mould themselves into an effective and victorious political force."

"We see negotiations as a continuation of the struggle leading to our central objective: the transfer of power to the people."

Above: President F. W. de Klerk and Nelson Mandela.
Left, top to bottom: Mandela greeting delegates at Convention for a Democratic South Africa (Codesa), December 20, 1991; ANC delegation to Codesa meeting holds press conference (seated next to Mandela are Cyril Ramaphosa and Jacob Zuma); Conservative Party delegation at multiparty planning conference, March 5-6, 1993. Right: delegates' table at March 1993 meeting.

Mandela addresses UN Security Council July 15, 1992. The two-day meeting was called following June 17 massacre at Boipatong. Bottom right, families of some of the victims are overcome by grief. Above right, Mandela visits Boipatong, June 21, 1992.

"This violence is both organized and orchestrated. It constitutes a cold-blooded strategy of state terrorism intended to create the conditions under which the forces responsible for apartheid would have the possibility of imposing their will on a weakened democratic movement."

"The campaign for peace and democracy must become a tidal wave which will thrust our country into a future where justice prevails, peace is assured, and democracy becomes a way of life."

ANC leads more than 100,000 in march on Union Buildings in Pretoria, seat of South Africa's government, August 5, 1992.

NIGEL DENNIS / ANC DIP

"We would like to appeal to all political leaders to join us in the search for peace."

Mandela visits violence-torn Natal Midlands region, March 12-14, 1993. Top left, University of Natal at Pietermaritzburg; bottom left, Indian community in Northdale; right-hand page, Kwa-Ximba.

"We take very seriously the repeated reports that a good number of our leaders and activists have been put on death lists by white right-wing groups, within or outside the state security force."

ANNA ZIEMINSKI / IMPACT VISUALS

RICH STUART / MILITANT

Top: Eugene TerreBlanche addresses rally of Afrikaner Resistance Movement (AWB) in Pretoria, February 1990. Bottom: AWB members march in Durban, November 1991.

"Now is the time for all South Africans to stand together against those who wish to destroy what Chris Hani gave his life for—the freedom of all of us."

Right: Chris Hani, assassinated April 10, 1993.
Above: rally protesting assassination outside Pretoria.

"The struggle is far from over. Go back to your homes, your regions, and organize as never before."

Across page, Mandela addresses rally in Port Elizabeth, June 23, 1992. Top right, speaking to meeting in Cape Town, March 19, 1992; bottom right, being greeted in Wembezi in Natal Midlands, March 12, 1993.

PHOTOS: NIGEL DENNIS/ANC DIP

"To attend a convention of the NAACP is for us a homecoming. We are here not as guests, not as people from another land, but as part of the historic coalition of organizations that has fought for the emancipation of black people everywhere."

Mandela at convention of NAACP in Indianapolis, Indiana, July 10, 1993. At left, Benjamin Chavis, NAACP executive director; at right, NAACP board chairman William Gibson.

justified in refusing to join Codesa, and we will try and avoid that. But if, in spite of all our efforts, we are unable to persuade other political parties to join Codesa, we will have no alternative but to proceed without them.

MAYIBUYE: But won't those spurned unleash violence and derail the whole process?

MANDELA: We hope not. We hope all political parties will use nonviolent means of expressing their point of view. We will find the resort to violence unacceptable, and it will be the duty of the democratic government to address that question.

MAYIBUYE: What is your assessment of the armed attacks against whites in E. Cape and OFS [Orange Free State]?[61]

MANDELA: It is difficult to know who exactly is responsible for these attacks. I had occasion to talk to a high-ranking government official, dealing with the allegation that a particular black political organization is responsible for these attacks. I asked whether they had evidence to this effect, and he said they had none.

There are views that there are other sinister forces behind these attacks, which want to achieve exactly the aim of justifying destabilization in certain regions, targeting ANC and MK members for elimination, and derailing negotiations. We will have to wait for further evidence to decide exactly who is behind these attacks. But whoever is behind them, their effect is to destabilize the negotiations process.

MAYIBUYE: Is there any hope of eliminating violence?

MANDELA: The National Peace Committee is addressing this question. We are hoping that the installation of an interim government of national unity, which will then control the security forces, will have a better chance of addressing the question of violence. It is quite clear that the present government alone is unable to address this issue. Let us hope that an interim government will have the resources and capacity to put an end to the violence.

MAYIBUYE: And elections: Is the ANC prepared, given

the overwhelming experience and resources of the NP and other parties?

MANDELA: We can perhaps deal with this question by referring to opinion polls. They have been consistent in the view that, if an election were held today, the ANC would have an outright victory over all parties put together.

But we, as the ANC, would be committing a serious mistake if we rested on our laurels because this is the trend of the opinion polls.

We have to go out to the country areas and see to it that the massive support which we undoubtedly enjoy is turned into organized and disciplined membership. That is the task facing us. I think we are tackling it and are in a position to achieve that objective.

MAYIBUYE: What alliances does the ANC envisage, and will those who have all along worked within the system not undermine the ANC's thrust?

MANDELA: We have the ANC/SACP/COSATU tripartite alliance. That is a very powerful alliance and we think it is capable of winning an election. But we have a broader alliance between the tripartite and the Patriotic Front inside Codesa. It is our view that we can build a solid alliance, not only within the tripartite, but with the PF as well.

Whether these parties in the PF will be able to go along with us the full hog will have to be seen. But up to now the PF inside Codesa is working very well, raising the hope that we will be able to come even closer in the future.

We are on the eve of great changes

SPEECH AT INTERNATIONAL SOLIDARITY CONFERENCE, FEBRUARY 20, 1993

On February 19-21, 1993, an International Solidarity Conference organized by the ANC and held in Johannesburg was attended by nine hundred participants from almost seventy countries. Mandela, who had fallen ill, spoke briefly to the delegates before beginning two weeks of recuperation on doctor's orders.

Dear friends and colleagues:

Allow me to apologize for not being with you yesterday. However, it was fitting that our national chairperson, Oliver Tambo, spoke in my place. He is the one who spearheaded international mobilization for all those years, and to whom all South Africa is deeply indebted for making it possible for us to reach this stage in our struggle.

There are certain moments that capture the essence of life itself. Today is such a moment for me. For you are the friends from five continents who kept hope alive. You took the plight of our people, our hopes, our dreams, and our struggle, to your hearts and made it your own. You have forged bonds of friendship that are unbreakable. You refused to let the world ignore the tragedy wreaked by apartheid.

And today you are here with us, many of you for the first time. While you are here you will see what I saw coming out of prison after twenty-seven years:

• that our people are still the hewers of wood and the drawers of water;

• that our people know only hunger, disease, poverty, and violence;

• that in the decades of apartheid rule, we were reduced to beggars in our own land.

You are here to help us transform all this, to help us move from antiapartheid to democracy. We are on the eve of great changes that place enormous responsibilities on all our shoulders.

These are complicated and difficult times, for which there are no pat answers. Before we have even attained our freedom we are experiencing an incipient counterrevolution. After so much sacrifice by so many, we have the obligation to prevent disintegration into a Yugoslavia.

And one of the ways to do this is to hold free and fair elections, where every South African will vote, for the first time, for a government of their choice.

We know that you will march this last mile with us, will work with us to win a resounding victory in these elections. We know you will help us reconstruct South Africa in the vision of the Freedom Charter, as a country that belongs to all its people, black and white.

We know you will go back to your countries and begin work on the enormous tasks that lie ahead. Together we cannot fail.

My doctors have given me a clean bill of health. In order to prepare for the strenuous tasks that lie ahead, I will now begin my two weeks of complete rest. Your love sustained me throughout my prison years. Your concern for my well-being now overwhelms me. I thank you all from the bottom of my heart.

We have come to this region to start a peace campaign

VISIT TO NATAL, MARCH 12-14, 1993

In mid-March 1993 Mandela made a three-day visit to the Midlands region of Natal province. The trip was organized in response to three incidents earlier in the month in the Table Mountain area, where twenty people—including six schoolchildren—had been killed in armed ambushes of vans and buses. Several ANC members were arrested and charged with the attack on the school van. ANC supporters traveling to the arraignment of these accused members were targets in another of the shootings. Included in Mandela's delegation were Chris Hani, chairperson of the South African Communist Party; John Gomomo, president of COSATU; Harry Gwala, chairperson of the ANC Regional Executive Committee in the Midlands; Peter Mokaba, president of the ANC Youth League; and others. Below are excerpts from several of Mandela's appearances during the trip.

Remarks to community residents

BRUNTVILLE, MARCH 12, 1993

In condemning this slaughter [of the six schoolchildren], we say that the people who are responsible for such a slaughter—whether they are members of the ANC, members of the IFP, or members of the state security services—they are no longer human beings. They are animals. And they should be treated as such if we find them guilty. The law must take its course, and if they are responsible for this massacre they must be punished.

But the principle of our laws is that a man is innocent until he is proved guilty. Therefore, if there are members of the African National Congress who are involved in this massacre, we will find attorneys to defend them, because they are innocent until they are found guilty by the court.

It is possible that the court may find sufficient evidence to convict them. It is possible that the court may find no evidence and discharge them. But whatever the court does, we are going to start our own investigation, and if we find them guilty, even if there is no legal evidence before the court and they are discharged, if we find them guilty we will take the strongest disciplinary action, because they will have violated the code of conduct of the ANC.

We started the peace process, and we are not going to allow anybody, whether he is a member of the ANC, Inkatha Freedom Party, or the security services, to interfere with the peace process in this country. We are also confident that the peace forces in this country will eventually put an end to this violence and win a victory for democracy. There is no doubt in our mind as far as that is concerned.

One of the mistakes which we have all made—the ANC, the National Party, the government, Azapo, the PAC, the IFP—is to concentrate in criticizing other organizations and other leaders. All of us have made that mistake. It is time we move away from that. When leaders have the courage and the honesty to criticize their mistakes, and once they have done so, they can then criticize other leaders, other organizations, as well. That is what we must do.

But subject to that, I want to say, there is massive corruption in this country, corruption caused by senior state officials. Millions of rands, of the monies we pay as taxpayers, have been stolen by senior state officials. Freedom fighters have been murdered by senior state officials. There are a number of inquiries that are taking place today involving senior state officials. And of course, as in all countries, leaders of government take decisions and get their juniors to carry out those decisions. And when the crunch comes, they say, "We are not responsible," and they put the blame on the juniors, whom they themselves asked to commit these crimes.

What therefore is required today is a commission of inquiry, not appointed by the National Party or the government of de Klerk. We want a commission of inquiry which has legitimacy, which has credibility, to investigate the whole question of corruption in this country, the question of senior state officials killing innocent individuals, simply because they are condemning apartheid and they want a nonracial society in their own country.[62] In the appointment of that commission, the government, the National Party, the ANC, Azapo, the PAC, the IFP, the Democratic Party, the Conservative Party if they want to join us—even TerreBlanche can join if he wants to—let us have a commission which is representative of the people of South Africa, which we can trust, because it has people who are acceptable to the entire community. That is the only way in which we'll be able to stop this corruption.

I have already discussed the question of the setting up of an internal national peace force to address the question of violence. I'm not going to repeat that. And I've asked for a commander which is appointed by the United Nations, after consultation with other world bodies. This command structure of this internal national peace force, which is composed solely of South Africans, it must be accountable to a commander who is properly trained, experienced, and appointed by the United Nations. I will be seeing the secretary-general of the United Nations to ask for his support insofar as this project is concerned. It is one step which would be a breakthrough and which would save many lives.

And of course those political parties which are responsible for this violence, who wanted to use the corpses of innocent individuals for the purpose of keeping themselves in power, will oppose this proposal. We will wait and see, but this is a proposal we must carry out.

Finally, to demonstrate how corrupt this government is, they are now contemplating in breaking the Patriotic Front around the African National Congress. They have started investigations in those homelands who are part of the Patriotic Front—KaNgwene, Lebowa, KwaNdebele—they have come up with evidence which shows gross irregularity on the part of the governments of these homelands. And indeed there is a lot of corruption in all the homelands.

But what they are doing is to investigate only those homelands which are democratic, which are now trying to work with the democratic forces, like these three that I mentioned. And yet the greatest corruption is to be found in other Bantustans, but the government does not want to touch them, because they have permitted this corruption together and they fear that if they investigate these other homelands there will be revelations which involve the government itself. Because the corruption in the homelands is a reflection of the corruption of the government itself. And it is therefore for that reason that we are demanding that all the homelands should be investigated. Just as we should investigate the corruption of the government and the type of crimes which they have committed. And these are the steps which I think, if they are taken, there will be a breakthrough.

Speech to members of the Indian community
NORTHDALE, PIETERMARITZBURG, MARCH 12, 1993

This is a special occasion, I'm sure, for many of us here. We have been reading the results of surveys which have been conducted by a number of research companies in this country, some with a very good reputation. And the results of those surveys show that the support for the National Party from the Indian community ranges about 64 percent, whereas that of the ANC is less than 10 percent. Many of my comrades, especially comrades from the Indian community, have challenged these conclusions, and my view has always been that it would be a delusion for us to challenge those so-called scientific surveys without producing equally scientific surveys, and that in all of the organizational work we should accept the results of those surveys. But tonight I doubt if the National Party in this place could ever rally even a tenth of the crowd that is here.

Whatever the position may be in other areas of the country, it is certainly not true insofar as Pietermaritzburg is concerned, and this is the matter that has given most of us a lot of strength and hope for the future.

It is fitting on an occasion like this to review in very brief outline the role that has been played by the Indian community in this country. It is particularly important at a time when this region is in the grip of the most shattering violence in the history of this country. We have had schoolchildren who were massacred only the other day. And the violence that is raging and the way it has been portrayed by the mass media, the government, and some black organizations, who have allowed themselves to be used as tools by sinister forces in this country, it is necessary for us at such a stage in our political development, to sketch out, within the time at our disposal, the contribution that has been made by the Indian community in the struggle for democratic changes in this country, precisely because this violence tends to offend the good senses of the Indian community, who have been brought up in the tradition of nonviolence and peace.

The first organized and disciplined political organization in this country was the Natal Indian Congress, which was established in 1894 by Mahatma Gandhi. His weapon was none other than nonviolence. And one of the most important campaigns which he staged was in 1913, when he led the Indian community to challenge the immigration laws which did not allow members of the Indian community from one province to cross the boundaries and enter another province. They challenged those laws, that law. Almost every Indian family took part in that campaign and was jailed.

Then the next very important landmark in the struggle of the Indian community was the passive resistance campaign in 1946.[63] Again almost every Indian family throughout the country went to jail, some families twice. . . .

That is the tradition in the struggle for democratic changes in this country that has been established by the Indian community. The National Party has been ruthless in applying the policy, which is the most brutal form of racial oppression this country has ever seen, and they were particularly merciless on the Indian community. They uprooted them from the areas in which they invested in property and buildings and moved them into open tracts. And it says a lot for the Indian community that nevertheless they were able in those tracts to establish a city which compares with any in South Africa.

The support of the Indian community is very crucial to us and I hope that they will never forget what the Nats did to them. They have come now to cheat the community and suddenly became friends: "Join our political party." What they actually say is: "We are a white party, we are a party of a particular white tribe in this country. Democratic changes are coming. We want you—whom we oppressed, denied basic human rights—we want you to join our party and help us to continue in other forms the principle, the policy of white minority rule." And unfortunately, some of our friends, some of our Indian comrades, have fallen for that trap. Because it means to them as Indians some material gains, and they have placed their personal interests above those of the community to which they belong. . . .

We also have been informed by these opinion polls that the Coloured community supports the National Party more than it supports the African National Congress. And of course I accepted this as I already indicated. But some time after, I went to Cape Town and I went to address the Coloured community. I was amazed by the crowd I saw. It was supposed to be an indoor meeting. But the crowd outside—it was difficult for me to enter the hall, and they were forced to bring a mike and to address the people outside. After I had addressed them I went inside, and I referred to these opinion polls, and I said we must take them seriously. And the chairperson of this meeting said, "I don't care what happens in other areas, but here in Cape Town one of the biggest branches is the branch in the Coloured community. And here there is no National Party among Coloureds."

That was refreshing, because we appreciate the concerns of the Indian and the Coloured communities, precisely because of the mistakes made by the African National Congress itself, because the African National Congress, in spite of its policies, realistically it is still an organization of Africans. Singing "Nkosi Sikelel'i"[64]—no reference to the culture, the history, the contribution of the Indian and the Coloured communities, purely based on the history and the aspirations of the African people.

In some of our power structures, you cannot find any member of the Indian community, any member of the Coloured community. That is a serious mistake. And as long as that is the image we are projecting, it is going to be difficult for us to mobilize to the maximum the support of the Indian and Coloured communities.[65]

Speech at the University of Natal
PIETERMARITZBURG, MARCH 13, 1993

There has been a great deal of concern about the very principle which has now been adopted as the strategy of the African National Congress. Voices have been heard to the effect that the African National Congress has betrayed the liberation movement by adopting this strategy. Some people have even accused us of having decided to share power with the National Party and its government. Almost without exception, the people who have said this have no alternative to put, either in relation to the strategy, the general strategy of negotiations, or the government of national unity. Many of those who criticize us have either not read our policy document or, if they have, they have not understood either the ideas or the language in which those ideas are expressed.

We started negotiations as far back as July 1986—our motivation being that the African National Congress has, from its inception, adopted a nonviolent, peaceful, and disciplined struggle. We maintained that over the years, until the sixties, when the Nationalist government, with the most brutal form of repression this country has seen, tightened all the screws of repression, closed all channels of political agitation, and even when we called strikes and asked our people to stay inside doors, they called the military, they went from house to house, especially in places like Soweto. They often drove people back to work. Any form of demonstration, no matter how peaceful and disciplined, was regarded as a declaration of war on white minority rule.

We had therefore no alternative but to resort to armed struggle. But we have never been under any misconception that we would be able to achieve a military victory against this regime. We knew we had the advantage of numbers, and therefore the potential to defeat this government in due course. But what we were determined to do was for the oppressed people in this country to be able to stand on their feet and to strike back. We did so, and in that process we produced the Chris Hanis, the Joe Modises, who commanded that liberation army, and made quite an impact, a psychological impact, for blacks who had been deprived of everything which could be a source of pride to them. To see a white man running away from a black soldier was something unheard of in this country, and which gave us a lot of strength, a great deal of pride, and hope in our future.

But we thought that we had made our point, and in 1986 I was instructed by the leadership to see the government and to raise the question: Why slaughter one another, when we could sit down and talk, and try and resolve our problems peacefully? We have, as a result of those discussions, achieved a great deal.

Some people say: You can't achieve anything without that black organization—you all know what organization it is. We say: all the achievements that have been made as a result of negotiations have been due to the discussions between the African National Congress and the National Party, or government, on the other side. The unbanning of the ANC and other political organizations, the lifting of the state of emergency which was enforced for no less than three years, the release of political prisoners, the return of political exiles, the repeal of repressive legislation, the introduction of a climate of free political activity in the greater part of South Africa— all these are the achievements of only two organizations in this country: the ANC on the one hand, and the National Party and the government on the other. No contribution whatsoever by those black organizations where people tell us: You can't go forward without this organization.

But in the course of these negotiations, we have said: We want an elected and sovereign constituent assembly. The government has said, "We agree to an elected constituent assembly." But having said that, they go on now to try and undermine the sovereignty of the constituent assembly. They are demanding that today Codesa, which is an unelected body with no credibility, no legitimacy, must today take a decision on the powers, the functions, the duties, and the boundaries of regions, and that that decision, taken by an unelected body, will then bind the decision of an elected body, the constituent assembly. We say: that will never happen. No elected body can be bound by decisions taken, amongst others, by people coming from Bantustans. It will never have legitimacy and credibility.

Then there is the question of the duration by which the constituent assembly is meant to draw up a new constitution for South Africa. And there is a conflict between us and the government. We say the task of drawing up a constitution must last only for nine months, not more than nine months. The government says, "No, this task must not be rushed, it should take anything up to three years." We know why they are saying so. It is because they are in government, they are in power. No government anywhere in the world will surrender power without a tremendous amount of pressure.

So we understand when de Klerk says, "No, let them take three years, let's not be in a hurry." What we can't understand is black organizations—where people are oppressed, where there is no decent housing, no educational facilities, where there is poverty and unemployment, where there are no medical facilities, where there is gross disparity in pensions—we can't understand any black leader who says, "Let's not be in a hurry. Let's take anywhere from three to five years before we can have a solution." There are such black leaders—some of them are your fellows in this province. We are not going to agree to that. . . .

We have never put forward as a solution the idea of power sharing, never. We have resisted it right from the beginning. In our policy document, "Negotiations: A Strategic Perspective," which has been misunderstood by many people, we mention the term "power sharing" once, and we mention it in the context of rejecting it. We say we don't agree with the concept of power sharing. That's the only time it's mentioned.

And yet, many of our critics say the African National Congress has agreed to power sharing. The government means by power sharing a type of dispensation where the party that loses an election, instead of going into opposition, as happens in democratic countries, will remain in government and be able to block legislation by the majority party. If for example Gqozo's party gets 75 percent in the coming election and the National Party gets the balance, in the view of the National Party, if Gqozo's party decides to take a particular policy decision, with its 75 percent majority in parliament, and the National Party has 25, the National Party can block that decision. It won't be carried out, it won't be implemented as law as long as the National Party does not agree. That is power sharing, as understood by the government. We have totally rejected that.

Our policy is a government of national unity, which is totally different from power sharing. What we say is that the coming election must be fought like all democratic elections; the principle of majority rule must be respected. The party that has an outright majority is entitled to form the government singlehandedly. But that party may invite all political parties which get more than 5 percent of the vote to join the government. It's not something that is required; it is the discretion of the majority party.

But we have gone beyond that. We say: the problems of our country demand that we should address them collectively. We are having problems now. We are having the beginnings of a counterrevolution, in which certain elements are slaughtering innocent people in order to destroy, to prevent the democratic process. We haven't got the power—in spite of the fact that we are drawing unprecedented crowds in our regions—we have not got the power to stop the violence.

When a democratic government is installed, you are going to see a different situation. They will even launch a civil war to destroy that government.

It is comparatively easy to gain political power, to win an election. But when you do so, you merely hold political office. You don't have political power. Because to gain political power means you have to control the civil service, you have to control the army, the police. You have to go out and get the support of business, of technicians, academicians. That is a process which is going to last for years. We will start to reorganize the civil service and the security services, but to do so is going to take some years. What happens in the meantime? It is easy to win an election. But to hold political power is something extremely more difficult than winning an election. . . .

We want a government where every one of us can say, "I am represented in that government." You must also think in terms of the minorities—the whites, the so-called Coloureds, the Indians. During the transition, minorities everywhere will say: "If this change comes, what is going to happen to me, to my spouse, to my children, to the national group to which I belong, to the values in which I believe, to my possessions?" There are always these concerns and doubts. It is our duty as the architects of negotiations to succeed in bringing about unity, uniformity of thought, in this country; that all of us should speak with one voice. And the only way in which we can do that is through a government of national unity, which we say should last anything up to three to five years. Because to address these crucial problems facing the country is something extremely serious. . . .

Now, however, we have called for this government of national unity. We challenge everybody. We say: give us an alternative to address this particular problem. What people tell us is that we have power. Last year we brought into the street through mass action no less than four million people. We have the power. We say we have the power, that is true. Why can't you stop the violence that is raging today if you have the power? Why can't you reduce the unemployment which is facing our people? What do you say about Angola, where the MPLA won an election and an outright majority; Savimbi has refused to recognize that result, took up arms. He almost over-ran the whole country.[66] In our view, the only solution is a government of national unity.

Remarks to community residents
NDALENI, MARCH 14, 1993

The Inkatha Freedom Party has issued a constitution declaring Natal as a separate region. Some people say that that constitution amounts to secession, is the first step toward secession; I am not saying so myself. I am prepared to accept that they want to be part of a region of South Africa. But what they are saying is that its boundaries, its powers and functions, must be determined now by Codesa or the multiparty conference by decision. We totally rejected that without reservations; and it is not going to happen. There is a history in this country, and that history is not going to be changed simply because the democratic forces are about to gain power.

When this country adopted a constitution in 1910, that

constitution was drawn up by authorized people. It was in that constitution that the powers of the central government on the regions, with the provinces and with local government, should be based within that constitution. It was not the other way around. The provinces were not created before that constitution was adopted. It is true that the provinces were there as independent countries, but in 1910 they all joined and the constitution was then drawn up, and the new powers were then given to the provinces, to the regions. We are not going to do anything different.

But if the Inkatha Freedom Party and any other political party comes into the negotiation forum with a view of persuading us to consider its demands, we want peace, we want compromise, and we will discuss the issue with them in a friendly and peaceful manner intended to create a mutual confidence amongst all of us, and in particular between the African National Congress and the Inkatha Freedom Party. But any threat to force conclusions down our throats, that we will reject without any reservation.

There is no organization in this country that can force solutions on us. The National Party—with its successive prime ministers, with its formidable army and police force, with its prisons—they were unable to smash the ANC. They are now talking to us. And no other body in this country is going to force solutions which have not been properly discussed. And I want you therefore to know our attitude on this question. We are prepared to examine their demand, if it is brought to a multiparty forum, and to examine it on merits and in the light of our history. We are prepared to compromise. Because we want peace in this country.

But you have a duty to go to members of Inkatha in this region, persuade them that we should abandon weapons of death, we should sit down and try to resolve our problems peacefully. That is how people who think, who are decent, handle their problems. And you yourselves must avoid violence. I don't say you should not defend yourself when you are attacked. But it is no defense, if innocent people are killed, for us to go and kill innocent people, even if they are members of Inkatha. You defend yourself against people who are carrying weapons of death and killing people, defend yourself against those people, but don't go and kill innocent people. I know that you will bear this in mind, because you will follow good advice.

Statement to the press
PIETERMARITZBURG AIRPORT, MARCH 14, 1993

I and my colleagues have come to this region to start the peace campaign, in an effort to save lives. Thousands of innocent people have perished. And the fact that since 1984, when this violence started, we have not been able to bring it to an end is a serious indictment against the entire African leadership. This is not a question of finger pointing. It is a question of a critical self-examination of each organization, to address the question honestly whether we have been able to get our own followers to follow the code of conduct which will help to save lives. We have tended to blame one another. And it is possible that this wrong approach will continue even for the future. But we do hope that there are men and women in all organizations that are involved that appreciate the importance of peace and who are making efforts to save lives. And this campaign is about saving lives.

And of course, the massacres that have taken place in Table Mountain involving the slaughter of innocent children has given further momentum to the campaign itself. In this regard, we would like to appeal to all political leaders generally, and to the leadership of Inkatha, to join us in the search for peace. We also, in all these meetings, have appealed to our members to engage members of Inkatha in their regions and to discuss the whole question of violence and the importance of peace. I have urged our members and supporters in all the meetings that I've attended, that members of Inkatha are our flesh and blood and there is no reason why we should slaughter one another, for whatever reason. And that peace is a more effective way of gaining a new South Africa than the use of violence.

I would like to appeal to our traditional leaders, the chiefs, who have played an important role in the formation of a disciplined and organized political struggle in this country, because the African National Congress in its foundation was composed of a house of chiefs, and a house of commons. In fact, a famous monarch, King Dinizulu, was honorary president of the ANC, and he died holding that position. And we said to the chiefs that they must play a role in the search for peace. They do not have to be members of the ANC or any other organization in order to play this role. It is their people who are being slaughtered in this violence. And unless they themselves take it upon themselves to preach peace in their respective areas, people are going to continue to die.

And I repeat, that we don't want them to be members of the ANC or to be members of a Congress-aligned organization. They serve a purpose when they are independent, not aligned to any political body, because I have gone round South Africa greeting and paying my respects to all the traditional leaders—except the king of the Zulus and the chiefs of that area, because he has not cooperated in my desire to visit him in his palace, so that I can pay my respects to him. And I appeal to the chiefs to play this role.

I also appeal to the church leaders, not only the Christian church, but the Muslims, people of the Muslim faith, Hindus, and members of the Jewish faith, because the church can play a very important role in the fight for peace. In fact, when freedom fighters had to flee the country and seek political asylum outside the country, when others inside the country were gagged and could not speak and could not travel, and others were thrown into jail, it was the church that kept the fire burning, and kept the ideas for which they were suffering alive. And leaders like Archbishop Tutu, Dr. Allan Boesak, Frank Chikane, and others became prominent in the fight against apartheid.

We also appeal to students, both black and white. We owe

students in this country a debt, which we cannot fully repay. It must be understood that it was the English-speaking universities, through NUSAS [National Union of South African Students] and other bodies, who led the fight against section 6 of the Terrorism Act at a time when the repression was so severe that black students themselves could not take that initiative. They challenged the most repressive clause in the Terrorism Act, and held demonstrations, were arrested. And they raised funds and bought books for those who were studying in jail. And it was after that impressive demonstration that a black student organization was formed—and of course that's SASO [South African Students' Organisation]. They also played an impressive role. And we think that, if all these constituencies could make a determined effort to save lives in this country, and to promote the cause of peace, we will be on the way to solving the question of violence and saving lives.

When we act together, with discipline and determination, nothing can stop us

ADDRESS TO THE NATION FOLLOWING CHRIS HANI'S ASSASSINATION, APRIL 13, 1993

On April 10, 1993, ANC leader Chris Hani, who was also general secretary of the South African Communist Party, was assassinated at his home in a Johannesburg suburb. Police arrested Janusz Walus, a member of the ultra-right Afrikaner Resistance Movement (AWB) and a native of Poland, after a neighbor of Hani reported the license plate of a car leaving the scene. Subsequently Clive Derby-Lewis, a leading Conservative Party member of Parliament, and his wife were also arrested and charged.

The following address was delivered to a nationwide audience over South African television.

Tonight I am reaching out to every single South African, black and white, from the very depths of my being.

A white man, full of prejudice and hate, came to our country and committed a deed so foul that our whole nation now teeters on the brink of disaster. A white woman, of Afrikaner origin, risked her life so that we may know, and bring to justice, this assassin.

The cold-blooded murder of Chris Hani has sent shock waves throughout the country and the world. Our grief and

235

anger is tearing us apart. What has happened is a national tragedy that has touched millions of people, across the political and color divide.

Our shared grief and legitimate anger will find expression in nationwide commemorations that coincide with the funeral service. Tomorrow, in many towns and villages, there will be memorial services to pay homage to one of the greatest revolutionaries this country has ever known. Every service will open a Memorial Book for Freedom, in which all who want peace and democracy pledge their commitment.

Now is the time for all South Africans to stand together against those who, from any quarter, wish to destroy what Chris Hani gave his life for—the freedom of all of us.

Now is the time for our white compatriots, from whom messages of condolence continue to pour in, to reach out with an understanding of the grievous loss to our nation, to join in the memorial services and the funeral commemorations.

Now is the time for the police to act with sensitivity and restraint, to be real community policemen and -women who serve the population as a whole. There must be no further loss of life at this tragic time.

This is a watershed moment for all of us. Our decisions and actions will determine whether we use our pain, our grief, and our outrage to move forward to what is the only lasting solution for our country—an elected government of the people, by the people, and for the people.

We must not let the men who worship war, and who lust after blood, precipitate actions that will plunge our country into another Angola.

Chris Hani was a soldier. He believed in iron discipline. He carried out instructions to the letter. He practiced what he preached.

Any lack of discipline is trampling on the values that Chris Hani stood for. Those who commit such acts serve only the interests of the assassins, and desecrate his memory. When we, as one people, act together decisively, with discipline and determination, nothing can stop us.

Let us honor this soldier for peace in a fitting manner. Let us rededicate ourselves to bringing about the democracy he fought for all his life; democracy that will bring real, tangible changes in the lives of the working people, the poor, the jobless, the landless.

Chris Hani is irreplaceable in the heart of our nation and people. When he first returned to South Africa after three decades in exile, he said, "I have lived with death most of my life. I want to live in a free South Africa even if I have to lay down my life for it."

The body of Chris Hani will lie in state at the FNB Stadium, Soweto, from 12:00 noon on Sunday April 18, until the start of the vigil at 6:00 p.m. The funeral service will commence at 9:00 a.m. on Monday, April 19. The cortege will leave for Boksburg Cemetery, where the burial is scheduled for 1:00 p.m.

These funeral services and rallies must be conducted with dignity. We will give disciplined expression to our emotions at our pickets, prayer meetings, and gatherings, in our homes, our churches, and our schools. We will not be provoked into any rash actions. We are a nation in mourning.

To the youth of South Africa we have a special message: You have lost a great hero. You have repeatedly shown that your love of freedom is greater than that most precious gift, life itself. But you are the leaders of tomorrow. Your country, your people, your organization need you to act with wisdom. A particular responsibility rests on your shoulders.

We pay tribute to all our people for the courage and restraint they have shown in the face of such extreme provocation. We are sure this same indomitable spirit will carry us through the difficult days ahead.

Chris Hani has made the supreme sacrifice. The greatest tribute we can pay to his life's work is to ensure we win that freedom for all our people.

Apartheid must not be reformed; it must be uprooted in its entirety

SPEECH AT FUNERAL OF CHRIS HANI, APRIL 19, 1993

On April 14, 1993, a one-day national strike was held to protest the Hani assassination, observed by up to 90 percent of the country's black workers. An estimated 1.5 million people participated in demonstrations and rallies around the country that day.

Mandela delivered the main speech at the funeral ceremony for Hani, held several days later at the FNB Stadium in Soweto before a crowd of eighty thousand.

Comrade chairpersons;

To the family; our daughter-in-law, Limpho; and grandchildren Neo, Nomakwezi, and Lindiwe; Gilbert and Mary Hani, parents of Chris; Dushe and Nkosana, Chris's older and younger brothers;

Distinguished participants at this solemn occasion;

To the tens of thousands of you, both here in the stadium, those gathered already at the graveside, and all participating in memorial services throughout the country:

We have all come together to pay our last respects to one of the greatest revolutionaries this country has ever known.

238

I ask you all to rise for a moment's silence in tribute to his memory. Even as we do so, let us also remember those who have died in the last few days and hours here at FNB, at Sebokeng, Vanderbijlpark, and elsewhere during these days of mourning.[67]

Thank you.

Sabalele, in Cofimvaba district, is a place well known to me. Not for its beauty, but for its harshness. No running water. No electricity. No decent housing. Inadequate health care. Little formal education. Yet this small, virtually unknown village produced a Chris Hani, whose life shook the whole country and impacted on the world's stage. Chris Hani's passion for justice, for addressing the problems that plague the rural poor, were rooted in his childhood in Sabalele. His roots were so deep, so true, that he never lost them.

Through three decades of exile Chris Hani remained steadfast in his commitment to free our people from bondage. Feted in many capitals of the world, he never succumbed to the glamor and glitter that was offered him.

He was taken to our hearts, as a people, as a nation, because he lived so that we may be free. Chris Hani touched the very heart of millions of us because he knew our pain, and eased it by giving us hope, giving us courage, giving us a way forward.

Chris Hani loved life, and lived it to the full. But he loved freedom more.

Chris Hani loved our people, our organizations, our South African nation, and for that love he was brutally murdered.

Yesterday, thousands of you filed past his coffin to pay your last respects. Like me, I am sure that upon leaving you had difficulty holding back the tears.

Chris Hani's murder was no aberration. It was consistent with the patterns of the past. Scores of assassinations remain "unsolved." Rick Turner, Matthew Goniwe, Sparrow Mkhonto, David Webster, Ruth First, and Dulcie September are but a few.[68] Their killers remain unnamed because the criminals investigate themselves.

By killing Chris Hani the murderers made a fatal error, for he will not become just another statistic.

The regime has announced the arrest of a leading member of the Conservative Party, Clive Derby-Lewis, in connection with this murder. We insist he be brought before the courts without delay. We demand to know what he did, who he worked with, and above all we demand justice. We do not want to see a situation where those arrested for such heinous crimes simply go free once the hue and cry dies down, as has happened in the past.

In 1991, when we spoke of a "third force" being responsible for the violence, we were ridiculed and criticized by everyone. Now both South Africa and the world recognize not only the existence of that same third force, but also the extent of its activities.

That is why de Klerk retired army and police generals with golden handshakes, but neither we nor the country know what activities they were dismissed for.[69]

When Chris Hani criticized the theft of weapons from the air force base, and said those weapons were not stolen, but were taken to be used in covert operations, he too was ridiculed. Guns from those same stolen weapons were used to kill him.[70]

This secret web of hit men and covert operations is funded by our taxes. While we remain without homes, without food, without education, almost nine billion rand was spent in the last two years on these secret operations. But we, the taxpayer, do not know what it was spent on. We only know that our people continue to die in violence on the trains, in massacres, and by assassination.

The killing must stop!

A major initiative that Chris Hani proposed shortly before his death was that peace brigades be established under the National Peace Accord. Let us pay tribute to his memory by forming such peace brigades throughout the country. Let them be part of the reconstruction of our country, ravaged by the war waged against us over forty-five years of apartheid rule.

There has been a deliberate and massive propaganda offensive against Umkhonto we Sizwe, its cadres and leadership. No effort has been spared to criminalize both MK and Chris Hani. This has deliberately created a climate of acceptance when an MK cadre is assassinated, as dozens have been over the past months.

To criminalize is to outlaw, and the hunting down of an outlaw is regarded as legitimate. That is why, although millions of people have been outraged at the murder of Chris Hani, few were really surprised.

Those who have deliberately created this climate that legitimates political assassinations are as much responsible for the death of Chris Hani as the man who pulled the trigger, and the conspiracy that plotted his murder.

In this regard, the minister of law and order and the chief of the army both have a great deal to answer for.

But culpability does not stop there. The indecent haste with which Minister Kobie Coetsee pushed the Indemnity Bill through the President's Council granted a licence to kill to the men who wish to plunge this country into a racial war.[71] Through this legislation, they were told that they could murder without fear of punishment. We say to them, loud and clear, that we do not recognize such indemnity. We will not accept that a murder can be committed and the assassin pleads political indemnity. Justice must be carried out to the full extent of the law.

We want a police force that is there to serve our communities, to protect our lives and property, to respect us as citizens. That is our right. We want an army that is professional, that does not regard us as the enemy.

The only way to get this is by bringing all security forces and armed formations under multiparty control with immediate effect. This should include the SADF, the South African Police, Umkhonto we Sizwe, the KwaZulu Police, the Transkei Defence Force, the Bophuthatswana police force, and any other such formations. Only then will we be able to begin the task of training, upgrading, and developing a South African army and police force that serves all South Africans. Only then can we begin to change the culture so prevalent in the police force and army that the people are the enemy. And nowhere has this attitude of seeing us as the enemy been more clearly demonstrated than in President de Klerk's actions since the assassination of Chris Hani.

His first response was to call a meeting of the State Security Council. His second response was to deploy 23,000 more troops, telling white South Africans that they had enough troops for them to feel secure. But why deploy troops against mourners?

They say we cannot control our forces. We are not cattle to be controlled. And we say to de Klerk: It is your forces that lost control and, completely unprovoked, shot innocent marchers in Protea. It is you who have allowed the bully-boy tactics of the AWB to go unchallenged. We, the victims of violence, have been blamed for the very acts that take our lives. Yet you treat the far right with kid gloves, allowing them to publish hit lists when it is a crime to do so. Your police do not protect marchers from gunmen who mow them down, as in Vanderbijlpark.

Black lives are cheap, and will remain so as long as apartheid continues to exist. And let there be no mistake: there have been many changes, and negotiations have started, but for the ordinary black person of this country, apartheid is alive and well.

Thousands of us die from TB every year, our children still play in open sewers and die from preventable diseases. Education is still a privilege. Our homes remain the tin shacks and overcrowded townships. And no black South African has the vote.

They talk of peace as if wanting peace is pacifism. They paint a picture of us as militant youth, or mindless radicals. They want to present the ANC as the other half of the National Party.

We want peace, but we are not pacifists. We are all militants. We are all radicals. That is the very essence of the ANC, for it is a liberation movement fighting for freedom for all our people.

It is our unceasing struggles—in the prisons, in mass campaigns, through the armed struggle—that has brought the regime to the negotiating table. And those negotiations are themselves a site of struggle. It is not a question of armed struggle or negotiations. Armed struggle brought about negotiations. It is precisely because negotiations will force them to relinquish power that certain elements are resorting to the cowardly tactics of assassinations.

This government is illegitimate, unrepresentative, corrupt, and unfit to govern. We want the immediate installation of a transitional executive council with one purpose: to ensure that free and fair elections are held in the shortest possible time.

This TEC must put in place multiparty control of such areas as the security forces, the budget, foreign relations, local government. An independent electoral commission must be established. We also want an independent media commission. We have the right to know what is going on, to receive accurate information, and to put our views across without manipulation and distortion. Above all, we want an agreed election date to be announced.

What does an election mean for us? A one person, one vote election, throughout South Africa—and that includes the TBVC states [Transkei, Bophuthatswana, Venda, Ciskei]—is, at this point in time and given the gains we have made, the shortest route to a real transfer of power. Such an election will produce a government that, for the first time in our long and arduous struggle, will be a government that represents the democratic wishes of all South Africans. For the first time in our history an elected government will be answerable to all the people.

That government will face tremendous challenges.

South Africa will then, through radical opposition to

apartheid, be transformed into a united, nonracial, democratic, and nonsexist country.

Of the highest priority will be the issues that were closest to the heart of Chris Hani: the reconstruction of South Africa so as to ensure that apartheid is not reformed, but uprooted in its entirety. In the interests of all our people we will build national unity, drawing on the wealth of our human resources, the courage and strength of all our people.

We want to build a nation free from hunger, disease, and poverty; free from ignorance, homelessness, and humiliation; a country in which there is peace, security, and jobs.

These achievements will be living monuments to the heroes like Chris Hani who died fighting for such a vision.

Speed is of the essence. We want an end to white minority rule now. We want an election date now. We want to know when we will have a government of our choice, that follows a program that is in the interests of all the people of this country.

Forward movement can no longer be held hostage to narrow party political or even individual interests. Freedom, peace, and stability can no longer be postponed because of selfish and sectarian goals. We warn all who seek to impose endless negotiations that any further delay will discredit the negotiation process itself and place on the national agenda the need for change by other means. We take this solemn occasion to make an earnest appeal to all political leaders and organizations in our country to recognize the urgency and gravity of the situation.

It demands of all of us that we act with real respect for human life. It demands that those who still occupy government office end their ideas of reverting to repression against our people. It demands new initiatives to move our country forward to freedom as quickly as possible. We will be consulting leaders of civil society, religious leaders, community organizations, business, cultural, and other leaders on such initiatives.

The leadership of the ANC draws its strength from you,

our people. Over the death of Chris Hani you have shown your determination, your courage, your love of freedom.

We will be leaving here shortly to go to the cemetery and the Hani home, to place the mortal remains of this great son of our soil in its last resting place. Before we go, I wish to address a few words to all of you.

Minister Kriel blusters on and says that today's proceedings are a test of our political leadership. We say to him: He has tested our patience too long. Where were the police during the four hours when gunmen rampaged through Sebokeng last night leaving over fifteen people dead? Where was his political leadership exercised in decisive action against those who opened fire in Protea?

In this situation, it is the government and its ministers who have been found to be sadly lacking in both leadership, vision, and ability. Chris Hani has a very special place in our hearts. But each and every one of you is precious to us. You are our people, our pride and joy, our future. We love you all.

And we want all of you to reach home safely. When we leave here, let us do so with the pride and dignity of our nation. Let us not be provoked.

The struggle is far from over. You are our soldiers of peace, our army for the elections that will transform this country. Go back to your homes, your regions, and organize as never before. Together, we are invincible.

That is how we will pay the greatest tribute we can to Chris Hani: freedom in South Africa. Let Chris Hani live on through all of us.

To the Hani family, you have suffered a loss that no amount of tears can replace. The ANC and SACP have lost a giant of struggle. But perhaps the greatest loss is to South Africa as a whole, now and in the future, for our country has been deprived of the wisdom, courage, and insight that was unique to Chris Hani.

I would also like to address a final word to Chris himself—comrade, friend, and confidant.

We worked together in the National Executive Committee of the ANC. We had vigorous debates and an intense exchange of ideas. You were completely unafraid. No task was too small for you to perform. Your ready smile and warm friendship was a source of strength and companionship. You lived in my home, and I loved you like the true son you were.

In our heart, as in the heart of all our people, you are irreplaceable. We have been struck a blow that wounds so deeply that the scars will remain forever. You laid down your life so that we may know freedom. No greater sacrifice is possible.

We lay you to rest with the pledge that the day of freedom you lived and died for will dawn. We all owe you a debt that can only be repaid through the achievement of the liberation of our people, which was the passion of your life.

Fighter, revolutionary, soldier for peace, we mourn deeply for you. You will remain in our hearts forever.

Amandla!

We must act together to give birth to a new South Africa

SPEECH TO MEMBERS OF BRITISH PARLIAMENT, MAY 5, 1993

The following address was given to members of Parliament inside London's House of Commons.

Chairperson; my lords, distinguished members of Parliament; ladies and gentlemen:

I would like to thank the Conservative Party and Labour Party's Foreign Affairs Committee for the honor they extended to us by inviting us to be with you today. We are conscious of the fact that the buildings where we are today represent a political history which reaches back through many centuries.

They symbolize past heroic struggles against tyranny and autocracy. They have meaning because, long before today, there was a determined striving to ensure that the people shall govern.

These houses of Parliament remain today living structures, because whatever the imperfections of your political system—and there must be many—these structures continue to provide a seat for the furtherance of the humane perspective that the natural conflict of interests, ideas, and instincts among any people, can and should be expressed through peaceful struggle rather than through actions which are predicated on violence and death.

I say these things because our own country and people are striving to create a social order, as well as establish the institutions, that will ensure that we, too, resolve the natural conflict of interests, ideas, and instincts among ourselves through a peaceful contest rather than through the pursuit of policies whose success is measured by the success of terror.

But I also speak thus, within this historic enclave, because, hidden by the dim mists of history, there is also the reality that, from here, there issued decisions which imposed on my own country and people a condition of existence which condemned us, as South Africans, to seek to resolve our conflicts not through peaceful means but by other than peaceful means.

Your right to determine your own destiny was used to deny us to determine our own.

Thus history brought our peoples together in its own peculiar ways.

That history demands of us that we should strive to achieve, what you, through the rediscovery of the practice of democracy, achieved for yourselves.

It demands of you that you should assist us, and therefore yourselves as well, to rediscover for ourselves, as a people, the practice of democracy.

And I say "demands" not because I want to entrust to you the role of a guardian and impose on ourselves the condition of an innocent ward.

I say history demands of you that you help us achieve a speedy transition to a nonracial and nonsexist democracy because your very national interest requires that you do so.

This, history has decreed, and not the sentimental heart of an old man.

My lords, ladies and gentlemen:

The universe we inhabit as human beings is becoming a common home that shows growing disrespect for the rigidities imposed on humanity by national boundaries.

These much-used words of one of your great poets, John Donne, speak to what we are trying to say:
"No man is an island, entire of itself;
"Every man is a piece of the continent,
"A part of the main."

South Africa and the former Yugoslavia, Somalia and Angola, Liberia and Nagorno-Karabakh, the Sudan and Northern Ireland are all part of the main.

The evil that occurs in any of these places diminishes us all and the good elevates all humanity.

Many peoples across the globe are hurt, and their rights to independence and sovereignty undermined, when you who are relatively wealthy, attach certain conditionalities to any economic assistance to those who are poor, such as the establishment of democratic systems, respect for human rights, reduction of military expenditures, and resolution of disputes by peaceful means.

But as Africans, we too believe that we should, together, transform our continent into one that is governed according to these precepts.

Therefore, between us, there is no difference as to the objectives that must be achieved. There may however be differences about the means that must be used and the route to travel to arrive at these common goals.

But once more, these processes emphasize precisely the point about the ever-growing interdependence among the peoples.

South Africa has been on your national agenda in various ways since the seventeenth century, when the ships of the English East India Company sailed around the Cape.

In more recent times, and with regard to South Africa, the great preoccupation of members of these houses of Parliament, the British government, and the public at large has been with the issue of apartheid.

This country has produced men and women whose names are well known in South Africa, because they, together with thousands of others of your citizens, stood up to oppose this evil system and helped to bring us to where we are today, when we can say: at last, freedom is in sight.

These Britons acted in the way they did because they realized that they and their country had as much a moral obligation and a strategic imperative to uproot the pernicious system of racism in South Africa, as they had to destroy a similar system in Nazi Germany.

We firmly believe that, through their struggles, these, your compatriots, have established the fundamental point that you and the people you represent have an obligation to act together with us as we strive to give birth to a new South Africa.

The agenda for that process of transforming South Africa has a number of items that stand out in bold relief. These are:

- the determination of an election date;
- the creation of a climate conducive to free and fair elections, including the establishment of a multiparty transitional executive council, an independent electoral commission, and an independent media commission;
- the holding of the first-ever general elections in our country, based on the principle of one person, one vote, and thus ending the system of white minority rule;
- as a consequence of these elections, the formation of an elected constituent assembly to draft a democratic constitution;
- as a second consequence of these elections, the formation of an interim government of national unity that will include all the political organizations that will have demonstrated that they have significant support;
- the implementation of programs aimed at dismantling the system of apartheid and reconstructing South Africa into a truly united, democratic, nonracial, and nonsexist country;
- the rebuilding and the restructuring of its economy to

ensure rapid growth; more equitable distribution of income, wealth, and opportunities; and an end to poverty as well as racial and gender inequalities; and

• the normalization of South Africa's relations with the rest of the world.

We would like you to play a role with regard to all these processes.

First among them is your contribution to ensuring that all political actors in South Africa understand that the situation in the country demands a speedy transition to a nonracial democracy. There should be no further delay in agreeing on an election date.

We request that you use such contact as you have with political actors to persuade them to abandon their selfish and sectarian positions and stop blocking movement forward.

We would further urge you to use your influence to ensure the earliest possible establishment of the transitional executive council and the related commissions so that all the political parties and organizations in our country can, inter alia, begin to attend jointly to such matters as ending political violence and implementing poverty-alleviation programs.

As you are aware, political violence in South Africa continues to be a matter of grave concern. If anybody had any doubt about how serious the issue is, the recent brutal assassination of one of our outstanding leaders, Chris Hani, should have put paid to these doubts.

We take very seriously the repeated reports we get that a good number of our leaders and activists have been put on death lists by white right-wing groups, whether they are within or outside the state security force, who are opposed to change and are prepared to take lives to ensure the perpetuation of the apartheid system.

We ourselves are doing everything in our power to address this matter. It is nevertheless incontestable that the government of the day has to do a lot more to deal with this matter and so must other parties. As we have said, we are also convinced that the establishment of the transitional executive council with its structures for multiparty control of all armed formations and the police would make a decisive contribution in helping us to contain and reduce the level of violence.

Accordingly, we urge that you put pressure on those concerned within South Africa to carry out their obligations with regard to this matter of violence.

We would like to take this opportunity to express our appreciation for the role that this country has already played with regard to this matter, by sending police officers and other experts into South Africa and by the contributions it has made through the United Nations, the Commonwealth, and the European Community.

When the elections are held, it will be important that the international community place observers in South Africa to help us ensure that the elections are free and fair and therefore that their outcome is recognized by everybody as being legitimate and acceptable.

We are certain that you will play your part in helping us benefit from such international assistance.

Three years ago we emerged from thirty years of illegality, during which much of our leadership was imprisoned or exiled and the members inside the country forced to operate as clandestine units.

In addition to this, precisely because the majority had been denied the right to vote, we suffer from the added disadvantage that we have no experience of elections, of parliamentary practice, and of state administration.

And yet I daresay that stability cannot be achieved in South Africa unless the ANC, which represents the overwhelming majority of our people, plays a central role in bringing these masses into the peace process, organizing that they go to the polls in their millions, and ensuring that any constitution and government that result from these processes are accepted as being expressive of the will of the people.

The fact that we, like other political formations, will participate in the elections, does not therefore remove the obligation on the international community to assist us and the rest of the democratic movement of our country, both materially and politically.

Indeed, I would venture to say that the process of change enhances the need to strengthen this democratic movement and not the other way round.

I am certain that many of you in this room will recognize the relevance and correctness of what I am saying from your experiences here in Europe.

The processes of democratic transformation in such countries as Spain, Portugal, and Greece could not have been as relatively smooth as they were without relatively strong democratic political organizations.

The same lesson is now being confirmed in other parts of Europe, again demonstrating that democratic change requires democratic organizations.

We trust that you will respond to these observations as they affect South Africa positively, and open yourselves to persuasion that, in the common interest, you should extend all-round assistance to us.

As you know, in 1989 the United Nations General Assembly adopted a consensus declaration on southern Africa, with the active participation of the British government. That declaration has provided the broad framework for the process of negotiations in South Africa.

It includes within it a set of principles which the international community thought had to be implemented to provide the basis for an internationally acceptable solution of the South African question.

Accordingly, we would urge that you should maintain such pressure as is necessary until we do indeed arrive at this internationally acceptable solution.

There can be no gainsaying the point that the very survival of the democratic settlement towards which we strive cannot be guaranteed unless we address speedily and successfully the socioeconomic upliftment of the majority of our people.

Central to this is the achievement of a relatively high rate of growth of the South African economy. We hope that British companies will participate in this process, to the mutual benefit by investing directly to raise the level of capital formation, help modernize our economy through the transfer of technology, open the way to new markets, and create new jobs to absorb the millions of the unemployed.

We also hope that both your public and private sectors will help us to address the urgent issues of education and training, in particular to raise the levels of productivity without which it would be impossible to have a modern and an internationally competitive economy.

Together, we have to confront another particular matter, which has to do with a false perception of what South Africa is.

This has to do with our classification as a middle-income country. This impacts on the issue whether we can receive overseas development assistance or not.

The actual reality of South Africa is that beyond the aggregate statistics, the majority of our population, which happens to be black, lives in conditions of dire poverty.

The situation which these millions face is not only catastrophic in quantitative terms, but also of a crisis nature in a qualitative and structural sense.

In reality, we face a situation of the coexistence within one country of a First World and a Third World economy.

The aggregate statistics disguise the reality of structural poverty and endemic underdevelopment to which the majority of the population is condemned.

This is possible because so rich are the few that are rich that it becomes impossible to see that the poor exist at all.

We raise this matter because it will be necessary that we get your support to persuade the OECD [Organization for Economic Cooperation and Development], GATT [General Agreement on Tariffs and Trade], the UNDP [United Nations Development Program], and similar organizations, that in dealing with South Africa we are dealing with a developing country.

As you know, this is critically relevant to the issue of how you and other developed countries will handle such issues as development assistance, soft loans, and market access as they relate to a democratic South Africa.

Related to this is the challenge to define the relationship between democratic South Africa and the European Community, our largest international economic partner.

To arrive at the correct framework with regard to this matter will require that you, as parliamentarians who understand what needs to be done really to end the system of apartheid, should use your influence and the influence of your parties to get the European Community to enter into a mutually beneficial agreement with the new South Africa, as soon as is practicable and feasible.

With regard to these socioeconomic matters, we are also convinced that it is important that the mass antiapartheid movement of this country should, in addition to opposing the apartheid system and maintaining the pressure for speedy movement forward to democratic change, also look for ways and means by which it could assist with regard to the developmental issues that face us.

We are therefore very keen that there should be established person-to-person relations between our peoples, so that those who spent their lives fighting the apartheid system should, at the nongovernmental level, use their considerable energies to generate the resources which will enable the ordinary people of this country to remain engaged in the struggle to make South Africa into the country which all of us would like it to be.

We are convinced that a genuinely democratic South Africa will be your reliable partner as the international community continue to grapple with such critical matters as a democratic world order, human rights, development, peace, and the protection of the environment.

We therefore believe that it is as much in your interest as ours to ensure that we move forward as speedily as possible to arrive at the point where we do indeed become a democratic country.

A few days ago we bade farewell to a man very dear to me, our former president, Oliver Tambo, who many of you knew.[72]

I was very pleased and moved by the presence of very high-level international delegations at Oliver's funeral. Their participation in this dignified and solemn occasion was both befitting the status of Oliver Tambo and also said to us that the peoples of the world remain true to their pledge that they will stand with us until the apartheid crime against humanity is a thing of the past.

We count you among these millions who are true friends and dependable allies.

A landmark decision

INTERVIEW WITH 'TIME' MAGAZINE, PUBLISHED JUNE 14, 1993

In March 1993 multiparty negotiations got under way again, this time involving twenty-six political parties and organizations. On June 4 the negotiating forum voted to set April 27, 1994, as a tentative date for South Africa's first nonracial elections. The decision was taken over the objections of the Conservative Party and Inkatha, whose delegations walked out of the talks. The election date was subsequently ratified at another multiparty meeting on July 2.

TIME: How important a milestone is the setting of the election date?

MANDELA: This decision to have an election by April 27 introduces an element of irreversibility. It is a landmark.

TIME: Is it a safe assumption that you will be the next president of South Africa?

MANDELA: [*Chuckling*] Some of the young men would not agree with you, because they all want to be president. The opinion polls say that if elections were held today, the ANC would probably win by an outright majority. It is then for the ANC to decide who should be president. We have many dynamic people, and I would be prepared to serve under them.

TIME: Do you believe de Klerk's National Party will abide by the results of the election?

MANDELA: I have no reason to doubt they are negotiating in good faith. But of course their concept of democracy is different from yours and mine. We have already encountered this problem in their concept of power sharing, which to them means the party that loses the election should continue to govern. Now we have moved them away from that, and they are coming to accept our concept of a government of national unity which is based on majority rule. We are saying all political parties with a substantial following should be included in government, so we can face problems together.

TIME: But in the end, won't their bottom line be permanent power sharing?

MANDELA: My view is that they are moving away from that bottom line.

TIME: Can you deliver on people's expectations, or is the damage of apartheid too deep?

MANDELA: Forty years of apartheid have been like forty years of war. Our economy and our social life have been completely devastated, in some respects beyond repair. That was the situation in Europe after the last world war. What the Western world did was to mobilize their resources and introduce Marshall Plan aid to ensure that the countries of Europe devastated by the war recovered. What we expect—and this is a matter which I'm going to raise with President Clinton—is that the Western world, led by the U.S., should ensure that massive measures of assistance are given to the people of South Africa so we can address their expectations.

TIME: What do you say to your supporters who don't want to share power with former practitioners of apartheid?

MANDELA: Last week I met the Executive Committee of the African National Congress Youth League, which has been vocal in criticizing the government of national unity. Quite understandably, they say, "These are the people who have been oppressing us since 1948. We are on the verge of overthrowing apartheid and their government, and now you say we must work with these people." That is perfectly reasonable. But we discussed the matter at length, and at the end of that meeting they accepted that the strategy of a government of national unity is a correct one.

TIME: And what about those on the right who fear and might resist black majority rule?

MANDELA: In the referendum last year, the right wing polled no less than 800,000 votes.[73] In addition, they have got a substantial section of the civil service, the police force, the army, which support them. Now they have said if the ANC wins the election and establishes the government, they will take up arms. That is the threat facing us. It's a serious threat, but we aren't overly concerned. We have to reorganize the police force and make sure it is capable of defending democracy.

TIME: Can you think of any precedent for a minority that has held power for centuries and surrendered it peacefully?

MANDELA: We are now making joint decisions with that minority. They said they would never talk with the ANC, and they fought almost every election on that basis. We have made them sit down and talk to us. We are now together planning the future South Africa. They have had to unban the ANC, to lift the state of emergency, to allow a climate of free political activity, which they had not allowed for more than forty years. They have released political prisoners, allowed political exiles to return to the country, amended and even repealed repressive legislation, and agreed on the installation of a transitional executive council. And now they are agreeing with us on a date for an election in the country.

TIME: Why have they cooperated?

MANDELA: I think they realized that not only were the overwhelming majority of South Africans prepared to fight for the right to run their lives, but the whole international community was against South Africa.

TIME: So, did sanctions work?

MANDELA: Oh, there is no doubt.

TIME: Should sanctions now be lifted?

MANDELA: We have come to the verge of calling them off. Our official policy was that until free and fair elections were held, we would maintain sanctions. But the problems facing our country—seven million people unemployed, rocketing crime, the violence, and so on—has made us revise our time frame. If the transitional executive council is installed and if an election date is set, we would call off sanctions.

TIME: Three and a half years ago, you were still under arrest. Now you're engaged in the process of rebuilding the country. Did you ever think this was going to happen in your lifetime?

MANDELA: There were definitely moments when I was not so certain this day would come. But as you know, I did send a message that was read by my daughter at a public meeting attended by Archbishop Tutu, where I said, "I will return." So that perception was always there. But that doesn't mean there were not moments when I doubted whether this moment would come. But the strength of the struggle in the country and the support of the international community has always been powerful, and that kept our morale very high, and it made us feel that the forces of change were too powerful to be ignored by the government.

TIME: Many have commented about your lack of bitterness. How could you put the past behind you?

MANDELA: Perhaps if I was idle and did not have a job to do, I would be as bitter as others. But because I have been given a job to do, I have not had time to think about the cruel experiences I've had. I'm not unique. Others have every reason to be more bitter than I. There are countless people who went to jail and aren't bitter at all, because they can see that their sacrifices were not in vain, and the ideas for which we lived and sacrificed are about to come to fruition. And that removes the bitterness from their hearts.

New tasks on our common agenda

SPEECH TO NAACP CONVENTION, INDIANAPOLIS, JULY 10, 1993

The address below was delivered at a convention of the National Association for the Advancement of Colored People (NAACP), given during a tour of the United States.

Chairperson; distinguished delegates; brothers and sisters:

To attend a convention of the NAACP is for us a homecoming. We are here today not as guests but as comrades-in-arms. We stand here not as people from another land but as part of you, part of the great family of black people that is to be found in many parts of the world.

We have come as a component part of the historic coalition of organizations, to which both the NAACP and the ANC belong, that has fought for the emancipation of black people everywhere. The fact that we are together at this convention is an affirmation of the bonds of solidarity and common purpose that have united our people even before our two organizations were formed.

I am very glad that I have at last been able to be with you in person, to thank you for the honor you bestowed on us when you linked us to a real hero by awarding me the W.E.B. Du Bois Medal in 1986. We heard the powerful message you sent by this act within the prison walls where we were held and within the larger prison that was apartheid South Africa.

A great tribute is due to that outstanding giant of our common struggle for emancipation, W.E.B. Du Bois, who, as early as 1900 at the Races Conference in London, raised the issue of the oppression and exploitation of the black people of South Africa.

We all know the famous text contained in his classic work, *The Souls of Black Folk,* where he writes that: "The problem of the twentieth century is the problem of the color-line—the relation of the darker to the lighter races of men in Asia and Africa, in America and in the islands of the sea."

Because Du Bois and his peers understood that the freedom of the black people was indivisible, the issue of the liquidation of the system of white minority rule in South Africa has been on the agenda of the NAACP since its foundation in 1909.

Time does not allow for a recollection of the inspiring struggle that your organization has waged for the emancipation of your brothers and sisters in South Africa, which includes the denunciation of the South African Act of Union of 1909; opposition to the racist ideas of Jan Smuts, who became a friend of U.S. president Wilson; your granting of a platform to one of our former secretaries-general, Sol Plaatje, who addressed an NAACP convention in Detroit in the 1920s; drought relief in the Eastern Cape in the '40s; your cooperation with the ANC during the various Pan-African congresses; and the work that W.E.B. Du Bois and Paul Robeson did, after 1948, to mobilize opposition to the system of apartheid.

Our own Campaign for the Defiance of Unjust Laws of 1952 later found an echo in your own defiance of unjust laws and practices in this country as you launched the historic civil rights struggle to address the question of the freedom and human dignity of the black folk of the United States of America.

What a great tribute it was both to the ordinary people who have found a home in this organization and to the association itself that it was a simple activist of the NAACP, Rosa Parks, who by her single act of defiance became the David that challenged Goliath, thus setting in train your unforgettable mass offensive for civil rights.

When Thurgood Marshall, acting for the NAACP Legal Defense and Education Fund, convinced your Supreme Court, in the famous *Brown v. Board of Education* case, to determine that "in the field of public education, the doctrine of 'separate but equal' has no place," he struck a mighty blow against the system of apartheid in South Africa which, as Du Bois and Robeson had clearly seen, was but a mere extension of the Jim Crow laws which imposed a new slavery on the black people of this country.

With so much that binds us, which says very clearly that we have a common destiny, it was therefore both timely and most appropriate that your executive director, Dr. Ben Chavis, Jr., should have set himself the task of working further to strengthen the ties between the NAACP and the ANC.

We believe that this is right! We believe that it must be done!

Our common struggle for the termination of the apartheid crime against humanity and the transformation of South Africa into a united, democratic, nonracial, and nonsexist country has reached a decisive point.

The forces of racism in South Africa are on the retreat. The countdown to the democratic transfer of power to the people has begun. The first-ever general election in our country conducted on the basis of one person, one vote, will be held on April 27, 1994.

The historic challenge facing us all is to ensure that as a result of those elections, democracy wins, nonracism emerges triumphant, nonsexism becomes the victor, and the people take power into their hands.

One of the major tasks we face in the struggle to attain

these goals, is to ensure that the forthcoming elections are free and fair.

The results they produce must be a genuine and correct reflection of the feelings and aspirations of the people of our country. They must inspire such confidence that their outcome is accepted by both South Africans and the rest of the world as legitimate.

To address this situation, both of us must make certain that the cross-fertilization which has characterized the relations between our two peoples and organizations must once more express itself in concrete action.

In *The Souls of Black Folk,* Dr. Du Bois called on his black contemporaries to "value the privileges and duty of voting."

Ninety years later, this is the message we must convey to 23 million of your black brothers and sisters.

Strange as it might seem, given that we are approaching the end of the second millennium, it is only next year that these millions will have the right and possibility to vote. It is only now that we can participate in peaceful processes to determine our own destiny and to decide the future of our country.

Late as it may be, this represents a decisive victory over the forces of racism. That victory has put new tasks on our common agenda.

I refer, in particular, to the work we have to do in South Africa concerning voter education, voter identification, and voter mobilization.

As part of the process of the empowerment of the black people of this country, you have been ahead of us in dealing with the same questions. What we now need is your experience. What we need is your input to ensure that we organize those who are now voteless to exercise their democratic and inalienable right.

We need to ensure that these masses, millions of whom are illiterate, do not spoil their ballot papers, that they do not vote for any party by mistake, that they actually go to the polling stations on voting day, and that they understand fully the liberating effect for themselves of a secret ballot.

All of this is going to need substantial financial resources to enable us to carry out our work effectively. We appeal to you to join the campaign to generate these resources, understanding, as you do, that the victory we must obtain in South Africa is one that must address the concerns and aspirations of all oppressed people everywhere.

Let me also say something briefly about the so-called black-on-black violence in our country. We would like to make this matter very clear—that what we are confronted with here is a problem of violent resistance to democratic change, and not a situation of ethnic conflicts that are supposedly inherent in African societies.

South Africa is not Bosnia-Herzegovina. Neither is it Somalia or Beirut.

Behind the political violence in the country stand forces that are unwilling to lose the privileged positions given to them by the apartheid system and do not want us to create a climate favorable to free political activity and conducive to the holding of free and fair elections.

It is these thuggish forces that invaded the seat of the negotiations at the World Trade Centre outside Johannesburg a short while ago, intent on halting the negotiations through the use of brute force.[74]

It is they who carried out the dastardly murder of one of our outstanding leaders, Chris Hani, hoping that they can terrorize the people into submission.

As has happened in other countries, there are also black people who derive some benefit from the oppression of their own kith and kin and are therefore ready to kill to frustrate the process of change.

We want to assure you, dear brothers and sisters, that we shall not allow these conspirators to succeed, including those who are to be found within the structures of the incumbent government.

We will continue to talk to those among our people who are lost and misled. We will continue our efforts to bring into the peace process those whites who are driven to resistance by fear and prejudice.

But surely we have no alternative but to act and to oblige the government to act against those who resort to criminal activity to perpetuate a crime against humanity. Nobody has the right to block the long-overdue transformation of our country into a nonracial and nonsexist democracy! Nobody will be allowed to do so!

In the near future, when the matter of the transitional arrangements leading to the holding of free and fair elections has been settled, we shall be calling on the peoples of the world to end the economic sanctions against South Africa.

Let me take advantage of this important occasion to thank you and all those in this country who have stood by us down the years by imposing and supporting sanctions against the Pretoria regime and its hated apartheid policies and practices.

Today we talk abut democratic elections because those sanctions worked. The democratic movement of our country will be involved in the statutory transitional structures that will take us to democracy because your pressure worked.

The moment is approaching when we shall have to say that given the achievements to which I have referred, the time has come for us to address the burning question of feeding the millions in our country that are hungry, clothing the millions that are naked, accommodating the millions that are homeless, and creating jobs for the millions who are unemployed.

We will then need the investment, the enlightened management, the training capacity, the technology, and the expertise that are to be found in this country, within the public sector, in the private sector, and among our own black people.

We are convinced that you understand this in the same way that we do, that the new South Africa must provide a better quality of life for all its people, especially the black masses, and that the success of the democratic transformation itself depends on the success we will achieve in addressing the material needs of the people.

We invite the business people to get ready to return. Those who have sanctions legislation on their statute books and those institutions which correctly remain bound by sanctions resolutions should position themselves in such a way that they will be able to remove these restrictions as soon as the democratic movement of our country says that the time to end the sanctions has come.

I am informed that with us here today there are, among others, senior executives of Apple Computer. I want to take this opportunity to express our appreciation for the commitment they have made to help us address the issue of the appalling levels of education in our country, that with such technology as they dispose of, they can help us to take a leap into the twenty-first century in our efforts to educate our children, train our workers, start new enterprises, and provide a decent standard of living for our people.

I invite them and other U.S. corporations to take their place in the new South Africa, for the mutual benefit.

History has placed a challenge at both our doors and commands that, acting together for the common good, we must make an outstanding success of the historic processes of transforming South Africa into a democratic, prosperous, and peaceful country.

We must succeed in all this, in the fundamental interest of all who value freedom and human dignity. The poor, the dispossessed, the despised await our common victory with an expectation we dare not disappoint.

Furthermore, we leave it to you to be our own voice to the government of this country itself, to find the resources that would help us to achieve the political and socioeconomic objectives that are on our common agenda.

If the peoples of Eastern Europe deserved of help, so surely do those of Africa whose cause addresses the very core of the issue of the creation of a just and equitable human society.

Let me close with these words from an anthem of liberty:[75]

"Stony the road we trod, bitter the chast'ning rod,
"Felt in the days when hope unborn had died;
"Yet with a steady beat, have not our weary feet,
"Come to the place for which our fathers sighed?"

When the countdown to democracy in South Africa is done, shall we not then:

"Lift ev'ry voice and sing, till earth and heaven ring,
"Ring with the harmonies of liberty;"

we who:

"have come, treading our path thro' the blood of the
　　　slaughtered,
"Out from the gloomy past, till now we stand at last,
"Where the white gleam of our bright star is cast."

Let us march on till victory is won!

1. *Hintsa,* a Gcaleka chief, was killed in 1835 while resisting European colonization. *Sekhukhune* was a Pedi chief who fought the British during his rule from 1861 to 1881.

2. The Frontline States—named because of their proximity to South Africa—include Angola, Botswana, Mozambique, Tanzania, Zambia, and Zimbabwe. They were repeatedly targeted for military attacks and economic pressure by the apartheid regime.

3. The Harare Declaration was issued August 21, 1989, by the Organization of African Unity at a meeting in Harare, Zimbabwe. It denounced apartheid in South Africa and called on the Pretoria regime to negotiate with the ANC and other liberation organizations. It set as preconditions for negotiations the release of all political prisoners and detainees, lifting the state of emergency, removal of troops from the black townships, lifting the bans and restrictions on individuals and organizations, and cessation of political trials and executions.

4. The quote is from Mandela's defense statement during the 1964 Rivonia trial, named after the site of the arrest of his co-defendants. It can be found in *The Struggle Is My Life* (New York: Pathfinder, 1990), p. 181.

5. *W.E.B. Du Bois* (1868-1963) was a noted author, historian, and black rights advocate who helped found the National Association for the Advancement of Colored People (NAACP) in 1909. *Sojourner Truth* (1797?-1883), an escaped slave, became a prominent leader of the abolitionist struggle. *Paul Robeson* (1898-1976) was a prominent singer known internationally as an opponent of racism. *Rosa Parks* (1909-) was arrested in 1955 for refusing to sit at the back of a bus in Montgomery, Alabama; this incident touched off a bus boycott that drew nationwide attention to the growing civil rights movement. *Martin Luther King, Jr.* (1929-1968), a leader of the Montgomery bus boycott, became the most well-known figure in the civil rights movement. *Marcus Garvey* (1887-1940) founded the Universal Negro Improvement Association, which at its height had chapters in the United States, the Caribbean, and elsewhere. *Fannie Lou Hamer* (1917-1977) was a leader of the civil rights movement in Mississippi in the 1960s. *Adam Clayton Powell* (1908-1972), was the representative in Con-

gress from Harlem, 1945-70. *Malcolm X* (1925-1965), who formed the Organization of Afro-American Unity in 1964, was an outstanding revolutionary leader. *Harriet Tubman* (1820?-1913) an ex-slave, helped hundreds of slaves from the South escape before the U.S. Civil War.

6. On June 7, 1990, the South African government lifted the national state of emergency that had been in effect since June 1986, although it remained in place in Natal until October. The Separate Amenities Act, an apartheid law institutionalizing racial segregation of public facilities, was repealed on June 19, 1990. In June 1991, the apartheid parliament repealed a number of laws including the Group Areas Act, which established segregated residential areas for Africans, Coloureds, and Indians; the Population Registration Act, which classified every resident on the basis of apartheid's racial categories; and the Land Acts of 1913 and 1936, which barred Africans from owning land outside the 13.5 percent of the least arable and mineral-poor land set aside for them.

7. Mandela is paraphrasing a line from Shakespeare's *Cymbeline:* "Golden lads and girls all must, as chimney sweepers, come to dust."

8. The U.S. Congress passed the Comprehensive Anti-Apartheid Act in October 1986. Among the sanctions it included were a ban on new loans and investments; on the import of many iron, steel, and agricultural products; on air flights between the two countries; and on accepting bank deposits from South African government agencies. It also called on the ANC to break its ties with the South African Communist Party and suspend "terrorist activities."

9. *John Brown* (1800-1859) organized a group of white and black opponents of chattel slavery in the United States to attack a federal arsenal in Virginia in 1859, trying to spark a slave rebellion; he was captured by government troops and hanged. *Frederick Douglass* (1817-1895), an ex-slave, was a prominent leader of the U.S. antislavery movement. For *W.E.B. Du Bois, Sojourner Truth, Marcus Garvey,* and *Martin Luther King, Jr.,* see note 5.

10. Operation Vulindlela (Vula) was a plan begun by the ANC in the late 1980s to strengthen its political and military underground operations inside South Africa.

11. Umkhonto we Sizwe's Luthuli Detachment fought the white minority regime of Southern Rhodesia (Zimbabwe) along-

side liberation fighters from that country. After a long struggle against the regime of Ian Smith, Zimbabwe won its independence in 1980.

12. Formal talks between the ANC and the government were held at Groote Schuur, in suburban Cape Town, May 2-4, 1990. A joint statement at the conclusion of the meeting, the Groote Schuur Minute, established a framework for further negotiations. A subsequent meeting was held August 6 in Pretoria.

13. The South African Act of Union was passed by the British Parliament in 1909. In it the British settler colonies of the Cape and Natal, as well as the former Afrikaner republics of the Orange Free State and Transvaal—all four under British rule since 1902—were amalgamated into a single state named the Union of South Africa. With the ratification of the Act of Union by the South African Parliament in 1910, the white supremacist state became independent from Britain.

14. Following two rounds of talks in 1990 in which the government agreed to the release of many political prisoners, the return of political refugees, and other preliminary conditions for serious negotiations, the ANC announced on August 7, 1990, that it was suspending its armed struggle against the apartheid regime.

15. "Homelands" (also known as Bantustans) are areas established by the apartheid regime beginning in the 1950s where a majority of the African population were forced to live. The ten homelands comprise 13 percent of the land in South Africa. Pretoria has sought to establish puppet governments in these areas. Four of the ten—Transkei, Bophuthatswana, Venda, and Ciskei—were declared by the regime to be "independent," although no other government in the world recognized them as such.

16. The Anglo-Boer War of 1899-1902 was waged by British imperialism against the Afrikaner colonial-settler states of the Transvaal and Orange Free State. London's aim was to seize the massive gold and diamond deposits and to strengthen its own domination over the indigenous peoples, resting on the super-exploitation of black labor.

17. ANC President Oliver Tambo had suffered a serious stroke in 1989 that sharply restricted his activity.

18. On July 22, 1990, a squad of Inkatha members, protected by heavily armed police and army units, attacked ANC supporters in the township of Sebokeng, killing thirty. Four months

earlier, on March 26, police had fired on a demonstration of fifty thousand in Sebokeng, killing seventeen.

19. The Isitwalandwe Seaperankoe award is the highest formal honor in the ANC.

20. Afrikaners (also called "Boers") are descendants of the Dutch settlers who originally came to South Africa in the seventeenth century. A substantial majority of National Party leaders are Afrikaners.

21. The trial of Winnie Mandela on charges of kidnapping and asssault, stemming from a 1988 incident, began on February 4, 1991. On May 13 she was convicted and sentenced to six years in prison, although her sentence was subsequently suspended. Nelson and Winnie Mandela announced their separation on April 14, 1992.

22. As the government stepped up its repression against the rising mass movement in the mid-1980s, a spate of killings began in Natal province—often initiated by forces from Inkatha. Following 1990 the killings spread to other regions.

23. On January 29, 1991, Mandela met with Inkatha leader Mangosuthu Buthelezi. Together they agreed to work toward putting an end to the violence in the black townships.

24. A reference to Johannesburg and the surrounding townships. The Reef is the ridge along which gold was discovered, around which Johannesburg was built.

25. Councillors were members of Community Councils (formerly Urban Bantu Councils) set up by the apartheid regime in the 1970s to administer and police the segregated townships in which blacks were forced to live. The democratic movement has conducted a boycott of these structures; in the 1983 elections to these bodies fewer than 10 percent voted.

26. The *Askaris* were a secret assassination squad of the South African Police, including ex-members of the ANC and PAC military structures captured and coerced into police service. The *Civil Cooperation Bureau* (CCB), a secret unit of the South African Special Forces, was responsible for infiltrating antiapartheid organizations and assassinating leading antiapartheid figures. *Battalion 32* was formed in 1975 by South African military intelligence out of remnants from Angolan forces that had fought the MPLA regime in that country. It functioned in Namibia and southern Angola, attacking government troops, murdering civilians, and de-

stroying property. It was subsequently used within South Africa itself. *Koevoet* (Crowbar) was a special elite unit used by the South African police during its war against the Namibian liberation struggle and later within South Africa itself.

27. Foreign ministers of the European Community voted on April 15, 1991, to lift their 1986 ban on the import of gold coins, steel, and iron from South Africa. The unanimous decision was taken despite a specific request from the ANC to keep the sanctions in place.

28. The Freedom Charter was adopted in 1955 by the Congress of the People, a gathering of nearly three thousand delegates held in Kliptown, outside of Johannesburg. The meeting was convened by the ANC together with the South African Indian Congress, the Coloured People's Organisation, and the Congress of Democrats. The Freedom Charter has served for decades as a guide to action in the battle to bring down apartheid. It is contained in Nelson Mandela, *The Struggle Is My Life* and *Nelson Mandela: Speeches 1990* (New York: Pathfinder, 1990).

29. In 1989 the UN General Assembly unanimously approved the "Declaration on Apartheid and Its Destructive Consequences in Southern Africa," which endorsed the conclusions of the Harare Declaration and called for stepping up world support for the movement against apartheid. It called for ensuring "that the international community does not relax existing measures aimed at encouraging the South African regime to eradicate apartheid until there is clear evidence of profound and irreversible changes" in the system of racist domination.

30. According to apartheid's racial classification system, the country's population is divided into black (75 percent); Coloured (mixed ancestry—9 percent); Asian (predominantly of Indian ancestry—3 percent); and white (13 percent).

31. Castro's speech, together with Mandela's, is published in *How Far We Slaves Have Come!* (New York: Pathfinder, 1991).

32. Fidel Castro led an attack on the *Moncada* army garrison in Santiago de Cuba on July 26, 1953, marking the beginning of the revolutionary struggle against the U.S.-backed tyranny of Fulgencio Batista. After the attack's failure, Batista's forces massacred more than fifty of the captured revolutionaries. On December 2, 1956, eighty-two revolutionary combatants led by Castro landed in southeastern Cuba on the boat *Granma*, following a seven-day

journey from Mexico. Despite initial setbacks, the guerrilla fighters were able to establish a base for the Rebel Army in the *Sierra Maestra* mountains, from which they led the workers and peasants in the revolutionary war against the dictatorship. On *January 1, 1959,* in the face of the Rebel Army's advances, Batista fled the country and the revolution triumphed amid a general strike and massive popular mobilizations.

33. Ernesto Che Guevara, born in Argentina, was a central leader of the anti-Batista struggle and new revolutionary government in Cuba. In 1965 he resigned his government posts to participate directly in revolutionary struggles in other countries. He spent several months in the Congo (today Zaire), where he aided supporters of murdered prime minister Patrice Lumumba in their battle against the reactionary regime backed by Belgian and U.S. imperialism. Later Guevara led a guerrilla movement against the military dictatorship in Bolivia and was killed by the Bolivian army in a CIA-directed operation in 1967.

34. Shortly before Angola's independence from Portuguese colonial rule on November 11, 1975, the country's new government—led by the Popular Movement for the Liberation of Angola (MPLA)—was attacked by South African and Zairean troops. The invading forces were allied with the Angolan National Liberation Front (FNLA) and the Union for the Total Independence of Angola (UNITA).

35. In early 1988 Cuban, Angolan, and Namibian forces dealt a decisive military defeat to South Africa's invading troops, who were driving to capture the town of Cuito Cuanavale in southeastern Angola. That stand, combined with a determined drive by Cuban and Angolan forces to reinforce the defense of southern Angola, led to an accord signed in December 1988 in which Pretoria agreed to withdraw its troops from Angola and to begin negotiations that culminated in granting independence to Namibia in March 1990.

36. *Dingane,* king of the Zulus from 1828 to 1839, defended their territory against Afrikaner colonists. *Moshoeshoe,* chief of the Sotho, fought the encroachment of the Afrikaners in the 1850s and 1860s. *Bambatha,* a Zulu chief deposed by the British, led a rebellion of Africans in Natal in 1906. For *Hintsa* and *Sekhukhune,* see note 1.

37. The 1913 Natives Land Act reserved for white owner-

ship the vast majority of the land in South Africa. It was used to drive 3.5 million African farmers off the land and effectively deny them the right to farm.

38. On July 19, 1991, it was revealed in the South African press that Pretoria had secretly funneled hundreds of thousands of dollars to Inkatha and its allied organizations as part of the regime's efforts to undermine the ANC. In addition, it subsequently came to light that the South African army had secretly spent more than $1 million to train Inkatha paramilitary units for attacks on the ANC.

39. Young students protesting apartheid education in *Soweto* were massacred by police on June 16, 1976, touching off a new rise of mass struggles by workers and youth in the late 1970s and 1980s. MK commandos exploded bombs at the *Sasol* oil-refining plant in 1980 and the *Koeberg* Nuclear Power Station in 1982, causing millions of dollars in damage.

40. On March 21, 1960, police opened fire on a crowd of black protesters at *Sharpeville,* killing sixty-nine. Following this a state of emergency was declared, and the ANC and other anti-apartheid organizations were banned. That same day police fired on a crowd of ten thousand demonstrators in *Langa,* killing two and wounding forty-nine. On June 6, 1960, government troops fired on a meeting of peasants near *Ngquza Hill* in Pondoland, killing eleven. In response to a planned three-day *general strike in May 1961* inititated by the ANC, the government imposed a law providing for detention without trial, banned meetings throughout the country, and arrested over ten thousand people.

41. On January 30, 1981, South African commandos attacked Matola in Mozambique, outside the capital city of Maputo. Thirteen members and supporters of the ANC were killed in the raid.

42. On December 9, 1982, South African commandos raided ANC refugee houses in Maseru, the capital of Lesotho, murdering thirty South African ANC supporters and twelve Lesotho citizens. A second attack on Maseru was conducted in 1985, killing nine.

43. The Conservative Party, Pan-Africanist Congress, and Azapo did not attend Codesa's first session.

44. The Declaration of Intent was signed by seventeen of the nineteen political organizations attending (the Bophuthatswana

government and the Inkatha Freedom Party did not sign). The document called for setting in motion "the process of drawing up and establishing a constitution" ensuring "that South Africa will be a united, democratic, nonracial, and nonsexist state, in which sovereign authority is exercised over the whole of its territory," with "regular elections on the basis of universal adult suffrage on a common voters' roll." It stated that Codesa would establish a mechanism to help draft legislation to implement the agreements.

45. Seven million rand, at the time, was equal to roughly US$2.5 million.

46. Sam Ntuli, general secretary of the Civic Associations of the Southern Transvaal, was gunned down outside his home on September 29, 1991. On October 7, eighteen mourners were slain by a group of armed attackers.

47. The Defence Amendment Bill was introduced into the South African Parliament on May 20, 1992. Under the guise of guaranteeing the right of conscientious objection, the bill aimed to entrench the whites-only draft and reintroduce compulsory sentences for those not meeting the government's definition of "conscientious objectors."

48. Hostel dwellers belonging to Inkatha attacked the *Swanieville* squatter camp near Krugersdorp on May 12, 1991. For information on the July 1990 *Sebokeng* massacre and the attack on *Sam Ntuli's funeral*, see notes 18 and 46.

49. On June 16, 1992—the anniversary of the 1976 Soweto uprising—de Klerk criticized the democratic movement while speaking to the KwaZulu legislature in Ulundi, which is dominated by the Inkatha Freedom Party. "What we are not prepared to do is to exchange one form of domination with just another form of domination," he stated. "Too many politicans are playing political games around the issue of violence and its underlying causes."

50. De Klerk had gone to Boipatong on June 20, 1992, as a "show of concern." He sped away minutes later when met by a surging crowd of angry residents. After de Klerk left, police opened fire and killed three.

51. The ANC National Executive Committee voted on June 23, 1992, to break off talks with the government. It called on Pretoria to disband the special police units involved in political repression and covert operations, to prosecute state security personnel involved in the violence, to phase out workers' hostels, and to

ban the public display of weapons of death.

52. KwaMadala hostel housed migrant workers at the Iscor steelworks. Controlled by supporters of Inkatha, it became, with the help of the police, a staging ground for numerous attacks on the surrounding communities.

53. Capt. Craig Kotze, a spokesman for the Ministry of Law and Order, had charged that the ANC's mass action campaign had "undoubtedly created a climate in which it is easier for such incidents to take place."

54. The *Defiance Campaign* of 1952, called by the ANC and the South African Indian Congress, was a movement of mass civil disobedience against recently imposed apartheid laws. Thousands were arrested for refusing to abide by apartheid's pass laws, curfew laws, and railway regulations. The mass campaign around the Congress of the People that approved the *Freedom Charter* is described in note 28. The *Alexandra bus boycott* of 1957 defeated the government's efforts to increase fares. Since the 1950s, the antiapartheid movement has called a number of "*stayaways*" ("strikes" by black workers were illegal), with thousands refusing to go to work.

55. On December 3, 1988, gunmen burst into a house in Trust Feed township in Natal—a scene of conflict between ANC and Inkatha supporters—and killed eleven people. A 1990 investigation revealed that the killers were from the police. On April 23, 1992, a court found a white police captain and four black officers guilty of murder. The captain was sentenced to death, and the others received fifteen-year prison terms.

56. Antiapartheid activists Matthew Goniwe, Sicelo Mhlauli, Fort Catala, and Sparrow Mkonto were abducted and murdered in 1985 three weeks after Van der Westhuizen's message. The revelation came on May 8, 1992, when the *New Nation* published minutes of the phone conversation between Van der Westhuizen and a state security official.

57. At the conclusion of the meeting the Security Council voted to send a special envoy to South Africa to investigate conditions and recommend steps to speed negotiations for a transition to majority rule. It also urged the government to take immediate steps to halt the violence.

58. Bisho, the capital of the Ciskei Bantustan, was the scene of a massacre on September 7, 1992, when Ciskei troops opened fire on a peaceful ANC march of seventy thousand protesting the

proapartheid regime of Brigadier Oupa Gqozo. Dozens were killed and nearly two hundred wounded in the incident. The troops began shooting into the crowd after ANC leader Ronnie Kasrils led a section of the marchers through a gap in a razor-wire fence erected by Gqozo's forces and headed toward Bisho's business district. Three days later, the ANC, seeking to curb the escalating violence in the country and break the deadlock in negotiations, agreed to a proposal by de Klerk for an emergency meeting with Mandela.

59. The National Peace Accord was signed September 14, 1991, by twenty-three organizations, including the ANC, the Inkatha Freedom Party, and the South African government. Aimed at ending violence in the townships, the plan included a ban on the carrying of dangerous weapons at demonstrations, the establishment of special courts to deal with the violence, and the formation of special units to investigate police misconduct.

60. "Negotiations: A Strategic Perspective" was adopted by the ANC National Executive Committee on November 25, 1992. It was published in the *New Nation* (Johannesburg), November 13-19, 1992; the *African Communist* (Johannesburg), fourth quarter 1992; and the *Militant* (New York), December 25, 1992.

61. Four whites were killed in King William's Town in the Eastern Cape when a group of gunmen attacked a dining room at a golf clubhouse on November 28, 1992. APLA, the armed wing of the PAC, claimed responsibility, although the PAC itself disclaimed knowledge. On December 19, a girl in Ficksburg, Orange Free State, was killed by a squad armed with rifles and grenades.

62. A number of recent disclosures had revealed a pattern of corruption by top government officials. Twenty-nine government ministers and deputy ministers, for example, had received money for personal use. This included a grant of $42,000 to foreign minister Pik Botha for "maintenance" of his $245,000 home. In addition, $750 million was spent in 1992 to cover budget overdrafts by the so-called independent homelands. For information on the revelations of government-ordered assassinations, see note 56.

63. The South African Indian Congress organized a resistance campaign in June 1946 to protest the government's "Ghetto Bill," limiting where Indians could live and trade, and preventing land transfers between Indians and non-Indians. Several thousand people were arrested.

64. "Nkosi Sikelel' i-Afrika" (God Bless Africa), composed

in 1897 by Enoch Mankayi Sontonga, is the national anthem of the ANC.

65. In his closing speech to the ANC's July 1991 national conference, Mandela had stated, "Some of our structures have been so set up as to exclude the minority groups. That has been a serious weakness, because it indicates that the overwhelming majority of the Africans in this country are not taking into account the minority groups of this country. It is true that our policies are nonracial, but let us be realistic about it. There are different ethnic groups in this country, and ethnicity, especially because of the policies of the government, is still a dangerous threat to us. We have to redouble our efforts to make sure we have the confidence of all the different sections of the people of this country, something which is not there at the present moment."

66. In elections held in Angola in September 1992, the governing MPLA defeated the forces of UNITA, led by Jonas Savimbi and backed for many years by the South African and U.S. governments. The following month, however, UNITA resumed its war against the government, seizing large parts of the country.

67. On April 14, 1993, police fired on a peaceful demonstration of tens of thousands in front of the Protea police station in *Soweto,* killing five and injuring 245. On April 18, nineteen were massacred in *Sebokeng* by unknown black gunmen. That same day, a white man opened fire on a demonstration in *Vanderbijlpark,* killing two. On April 19, three ANC supporters were shot in *Vosloorus* township when shots were fired from a hostel controlled by the Inkatha Freedom Party.

68. *Rick Turner,* a banned lecturer at Natal University, was shot at his Durban home in 1978. *Sparrow Mkhonto* was murdered in June 1985 along with *Matthew Goniwe* and two other antiapartheid activists in the Eastern Cape. *David Webster,* an ANC member and lecturer at Witwatersrand University, was shot and killed in May 1989. *Ruth First,* an ANC activist and noted author, was killed in 1982 by a letter bomb sent by the South African security forces to her office in Maputo, Mozambique. *Dulcie September,* an ANC activist, was assassinated in March 1988 in Paris.

69. President de Klerk announced on December 19, 1992, the dismissal of twenty-three officers, among them six generals, suspected of activities up to and including political assassination.

He did so without disclosing any information concerning what they did.

70. The gun used to kill Hani was identified as a weapon stolen by members of the neofascist AWB when they broke into a South African air force arsenal in Pretoria on April 14, 1990.

71. An Indemnity Bill granting blanket amnesty to state officials involved in crimes was defeated in the apartheid parliament in October 1992, when the chamber reserved for Indians refused to approve it. Nevertheless, de Klerk's Presidential Council overrode the parliament and enacted the bill anyway on October 30.

72. ANC national chairperson Oliver Tambo died on April 24, 1993.

73. A whites-only referendum was held March 17, 1992, in which a two-thirds majority endorsed continued government negotiations on the country's future.

74. On June 25, 1993, 1,500 armed supporters of the Afrikaner Resistance Movement and other ultraright organizations broke into the World Trade Centre in Johannesburg, where multiparty negotiations were taking up the scheduled election date. Police and security forces made no effort to halt the attack, which lasted for several hours, during which the right-wingers spray painted the inside of the building and physically abused some of those inside.

75. The song "Lift Ev'ry Voice and Sing," known for many years as the Negro National Anthem, was written in 1900 by James Weldon Johnson.

GLOSSARY

African National Congress (ANC)—leading organization in antiapartheid struggle in South Africa; formed 1912 to fight for full equality for Africans; legalized 1990 after 30-year ban.

APLA (Azanian People's Liberation Army)—armed wing of Pan-Africanist Congress.

AWB (Afrikaner Weerstandsbeweging—Afrikaner Resistance Movement)—ultraright paramilitary organization.

Azapo (Azanian People's Organisation)—founded 1978 by wing of Black Consciousness Movement that arose in early 1970s; critical of ANC nonracial strategy and perspective summarized in Freedom Charter.

Baard, Frances (1901-)—active in trade union movement and Federation of South African Women during 1950s and 1960s; imprisoned 1963-69.

Boesak, Allan (1945-)—president of World Alliance of Reformed Churches 1982-91; a leader of United Democratic Front 1983-91; currently ANC chairperson in Western Cape region.

Botha, P.W. (1916-)—leader of National Party 1978-89; prime minister 1978-84; state president 1984-89.

Botha, Roelof Frederik (Pik) (1932-)—South African minister of foreign affairs since 1977; a leader of National Party.

Buthelezi, Mangosuthu Gatsha (1928-)—Zulu chief; leader of Inkatha Freedom Party.

Chikane, Frank (1951-)—general secretary, South African Council of Churches since 1987; active in antiapartheid movement.

Civics—organizations of community struggle that emerged during 1980s; South African National Civic Organisation (SANCO) launched March 1992.

Codesa (Convention for a Democratic South Africa)—multiparty negotiations forum established 1991.

Conservative Party—formed 1982 as right-wing split-off from National Party.

COSATU (Congress of South African Trade Unions)—founded 1985 as South Africa's largest union federation; part of tripartite alliance with ANC and South African Communist Party.

Dadoo, Yusuf (1909-1983)—ANC leader; former president of

South African Indian Congress; Communist Party national chairperson at time of death.

de Klerk, Frederik Willem (1936-)—leader of National Party; became state president in September 1989.

Democratic Party—liberal opposition within apartheid Parliament; formed 1989 by merger of Independent Party and Progressive Federal Party, supporting gradual dismantling of apartheid institutions.

Dinizulu (1868-1913)—Zulu king deposed and exiled to Transvaal by British; an honorary president of ANC.

Fischer, Abram (Bram) (1908-1975)—leader of Communist Party and ANC; attorney for Mandela during Rivonia trial; imprisoned 1964 until his death.

Frontline States—grouping of governments bordering South Africa, including Angola, Botswana, Mozambique, Tanzania, Zambia, and Zimbabwe.

Gandhi, Mohandas (Mahatma) (1869-1948)—central leader of India's independence movement; lived in South Africa 1893-1914.

Goldstone, Richard J. (1938-)—South African appeals judge; chairman of Commission Concerning the Prevention of Public Violence and Intimidation formed 1991.

Gqozo, Oupa Josh (1952-)—military leader of Ciskei since March 1990; founded African Democratic Movement in 1991 to counter ANC.

Hani, Chris (1942-1993)—joined ANC Youth League 1957; member of ANC NEC 1975-93; chief of staff, Umkhonto we Sizwe 1987-92; general secretary of Communist Party 1991-93; assassinated April 10, 1993.

Inkatha—founded in early 1970s by Mangosuthu Buthelezi; claims to speak for Zulus; main political force in KwaZulu Bantustan regime set up by Pretoria, became Inkatha Freedom Party in 1991; received funding and support from South African government and National Party.

Jordan, Z. Pallo (1942-)—joined ANC 1960; ANC NEC member; director of ANC Department of Information and Publicity since 1989.

Joseph, Helen (1905-1992)—longtime opponent of apartheid; active in Federation of South African Women; defendant in 1956-60 Treason Trial; kept under house arrest for over a decade.

Kasrils, Ronnie (1938-)—joined ANC and SACP in early 1960s; leader of Umkhonto we Sizwe; currently member of ANC NEC and Communist Party Central Committee.

Kotane, Moses (1905-1978)—ANC leader and general secretary of Communist Party 1939-78.

Kriel, Ashley—Umkhonto we Sizwe fighter; shot by police 1987.

Kriel, Hernus (1941-)—minister of law and order in National Party government since 1991.

Luthuli, Albert (1898-1967)—president-general of ANC 1952-67; Zulu chief.

Mabhida, Moses (1923-1986)—leader of ANC; general secretary of Communist Party at time of death.

Mahlangu, Solomon (1956-1979)—Umkhonto we Sizwe fighter captured and executed by apartheid regime.

Malan, Magnus (1930-)—South African minister of defense 1980-91; following press exposure of secret government funding of Inkatha he was removed, a step long demanded by democratic movement; subsequently minister of water affairs and forestry.

Mandela, Winnie (1934-)—antiapartheid activist; wife of Nelson Mandela, separated in April 1992; head of ANC welfare department 1990-92; resigned all ANC posts September 1992.

Manuel, Trevor (1956-) head of ANC Department of Economic Planning; member of National Executive Committee.

Marks, J.B. (1903-1972)—chairman of ANC National Executive Committee and chairman of Communist Party at his death.

Masekela, Barbara (1941-)—head of staff, ANC Office of the President since 1991; member of ANC National Executive Committee.

Mass Democratic Movement—broad coalition of antiapartheid organizations formed following ban on United Democratic Front; founding conference in December 1989 represented 2,100 organizations with membership of 15 million.

Maxeke, Charlotte (1874-1939)—a founder of ANC Women's League; served as its president for many years.

Meyer, Roelf (1947-)—minister of constitutional affairs and of communication; National Party representative on National Peace Committee and Codesa working group on transitional arrangements.

Modise, Joe (1929-)—commander of Umkhonto we Sizwe since

1965; member of ANC National Executive Committee.

Moodley, Mary (1913-1979)—active in Defiance Campaigns and formation of Congress Alliance in 1950s; trade union organizer; under banning order from 1963 until her death.

Mophosho, Florence (1921-1985)—joined ANC 1952; active in women's movement.

National Party (Nationalists)—ruling party in South Africa since 1948; organized codification of apartheid.

National Peace Committee—multiparty commission charged with overseeing measures to end civil violence; established by September 1991 National Peace Accord.

Ngoyi, Lilian (1911-1980)—helped lead antipass campaign in 1950s; president of Federation of South African Women and ANC Women's League.

Nokwe, Duma (1927-1978)—secretary-general of ANC 1958-69.

Nyembe, Dorothy (1930-)—became chairperson of Federation of South African Women in 1962; sentenced to 15 years' imprisonment in 1969.

Pan-Africanist Congress (PAC)—established 1959 as split-off from ANC, opposing perspective of nonracial South Africa presented in Freedom Charter.

Patriotic Front—formed in October 1991 at Durban conference attended by ANC, PAC, and other antiapartheid organizations.

Plaatje, Sol (1874-1932)—secretary-general of ANC 1912-17.

Ramaphosa, Cyril (1952-)—general secretary, National Union of Mineworkers 1982-91; ANC secretary-general since 1991.

Renamo (Mozambique National Resistance)—right-wing terrorist group set up by former white minority regime in Rhodesia (Zimbabwe) and supported by Pretoria; responsible for hundreds of thousands of deaths in Mozambique.

Shope, Gertrude (1925-)—joined ANC 1954; head of ANC Women's Section 1981-91; president of ANC Women's League since 1991.

Silinga, Annie (1910-1984)—joined ANC during Defiance Campaign in early 1950s; active in Federation of South African Women and ANC Women's League.

Simons, Ray (Ray Alexander) (1913-)—first national secretary of Federation of South African Women; general secretary of Food and Canning Workers Union until banned in 1953; leading member of Communist Party.

Slovo, Joe (1926-)—joined Communist Party in 1940s; general secretary SACP 1986-91; chairman SACP since 1991; Umkhonto we Sizwe chief of staff until 1987; member of ANC NEC.

Smuts, Jan (1870-1950)—South African prime minister 1919-24, 1939-48.

South African Communist Party (SACP)—active in opposition to white minority regime since 1920s; banned 1950-90; part of tripartite alliance with ANC and COSATU.

South African Students' Organisation (SASO)—formed 1969 by black students; first president was Steve Biko.

Tamana, Dora (1901-1983)—longtime activist in ANC Women's League and Federation of South African Women.

Tambo, Oliver (1917-1993)—founding member of ANC Youth League with Mandela in 1944; ANC acting president 1967-77; president-general 1977-91; national chairman 1991-93.

TerreBlanche, Eugene (1944-)—founder and leader of ultraright Afrikaner Resistance Movement (AWB) since 1973.

Tripartite alliance—alliance of ANC, Congress of South African Trade Unions, and South African Communist Party.

Tshwete, Steve (1938-)—imprisoned on Robben Island 1964-79; ANC sports liaison officer, involved in discussions on desegregation of South African sports and reentry of South African athletes into international competition; member of ANC NEC.

Tutu, Desmond (1931-)—Anglican archbishop of Cape Town and antiapartheid activist; winner of 1984 Nobel Peace Prize.

Umkhonto we Sizwe (Spear of the Nation—MK)—formed 1961 as military wing of ANC; Nelson Mandela was first commander-in-chief.

United Democratic Front (UDF)—founded 1983 to coordinate resistance to apartheid regime, uniting over 300 organizations; banned along with 17 other organizations in 1988.

Verwoerd, Hendrik (1901-1966)—South African prime minister 1958-66; a central architect of apartheid.

Vlok, Adriaan (1937-)—South African minister of law and order 1986-91; following press exposure of secret government funding of Inkatha he was removed, a step long demanded by democratic movement; subsequently minister of correctional services.

Xuma, A.B. (1893-1962)—president-general of ANC, 1940-49.

Zihlangu, M.—a founder of United Women's Organisation.

Affirmative action, 51-52, 170
"African Claims, The," 78
African National Congress (ANC): answers criticisms of, 46, 61, 126-27, 153, 155, 178, 186, 225-26, 228; basic objectives, 168-69; Constitutional Committee, 48, 50, 107; democratic principles of, 26, 36, 76-81, 83, 97, 103, 119, 124, 149; founding of, 67, 122, 77, 233; as future governing party, 110, 166-73, 259; generations in, 63-64, 131; history, 54-56, 101, 122-23, 281; among Indians and Coloureds, 111, 222-23, 224-25, 225, 279; internal debates, 69-74, 113, 208, 258-59; internal democracy, 26, 67, 69, 71, 100, 113; as leader of democratic revolution, 24, 67, 101, 102, 146-47, 149, 177; leadership of, 18, 54-56, 69, 73, 113; membership, 32, 64-65, 111, 122-23, 216; as movement of oppressed, 11, 65, 128, 168; not a political party, 127, 157, 168; not reformist, 123; and other antiapartheid forces, 19, 33, 44-47, 66; as people's movement, 65, 101, 111, 115, 123, 135; problems, 63, 65, 69, 102; rebuilding of, 63, 100, 110-11, 252; in rural areas, 111; strategy, 26, 72, 102, 106, 132-37, 138, 225-30, 258-59; unbanning of, 9, 18, 101, 227, 259; underground apparatus of, 54-55, 135, 136, 270; use of intimidation by, 65, 81, 115, 200. *See also* Elections, ANC campaign; Mass action, ANC and; South African government, ANC talks with
African National Congress conferences: consultative (1990), 10, 18, 53-67, 68-74; national (1991), 19, 99-117, 131, 278; policy (1992), 20, 166-73
African National Congress Women's League, 48, 111
African National Congress Youth League, 111, 258-59
Afrikaner nationalism, 76-77
Alexander bus boycott, 187, 277
Algeria, 141
All-party congress, 94, 97, 104, 107-8, 162. *See also* Codesa
Amnesty, 151; of government officials, 20, 240, 241, 279, 280
Amnesty International, 193
Angola, 141; internal conflict in, 40, 73, 230, 236, 249, 279; South African aggression in, 11, 120-21, 137, 142, 272, 274
Antiapartheid movement, in Western Europe and U.S., 41, 141, 179, 250, 255, 262-63. *See also* International solidarity
Antiapartheid struggle. *See* National, democratic revolution
Anticommunism, 101, 114
Apartheid: attempts to salvage, 12, 57, 124, 161, 163-64, 172, 177, 189, 224; basic features, 9, 133-34; as crime against humanity, 34, 40, 147, 188-89, 263, 266; dismantling of, 12, 75, 127, 250; establishment of, 9, 121-22; failure of, 25, 57, 101, 137-38, 151, 258; history of resistance to, 25, 62, 140, 122, 269, 274; ideology, 39, 40, 186; and Jim Crow, 263; laws, 12, 18, 19, 32, 270; social conditions under, 25, 31, 79-80, 218, 228, 242, 254; unreformable, 133-34, 244; white monopoly of power under, 27, 31, 133, 189
Apartheid state, 9, 135; narrow so-

cial base of, 32, 136
APLA (Azanian People's Liberation Army), 215, 278, 281
Armed struggle: political basis of,
26, 102-3, 123-24, 132, 135,
147, 209, 226, 243; suspension
of, 18, 58, 61-62, 112, 139, 154,
190, 205, 271. *See also* Umkhonto we Sizwe
Askaris, 90, 272
Assassinations, of antiapartheid activists, 20, 37, 59, 138, 155, 164,
193-94, 215, 220-21, 239-40,
241, 251, 272, 279
Atlantic Charter, 78
AWB (Afrikaner Resistance Movement), 235, 242, 281
Azapo, 19, 220, 221, 275, 281

Baard, Frances, 49, 281
Bambatha, 122, 274
Bantustans: ANC appeals to, 66,
72-73; as apartheid scheme, 9,
12, 50, 66, 79, 132, 271; corruption in, 222, 278; lack of democracy in, 66, 88, 206; reincorpora-
tion of, 162, 243
Bekkersdal, 59
Bill of rights, 36, 50, 108, 126, 139
Bisho massacre, 20, 204, 206-8,
277-78
Black Sash, 24
Blacks: dispossession from land, 9,
122, 133; lack of rights, 9, 27,
31, 133; as principal force in
struggle, 134; social conditions
of, 25, 31, 79-80, 218, 228, 242,
254; superexploitation of, 9, 133;
in U.S., 29-30, 261-63, 264. *See
also* Apartheid
Boer War (1899-1902), 67, 271
Boesak, Allan, 233, 281
Boipatong massacre, 20, 174-79,
209
Bongco, Washington, 143
Bophuthatswana, 162
Boshielo, Flag, 143
Bosnia-Herzegovina, 265

Botha, P.W., 154, 281
Botha, Pik, 188, 204, 278, 281
Botswana, 93
Boutros-Ghali, Boutros, 188
Britain, 80, 247-48; and South Af-
rica, 67, 122, 247-49, 252, 254-
56
Brown v. Board of Education, 263
Brown, John, 42, 270
Bush, George, 40, 128
Buthelezi, Mangosuthu, 188, 281;
and Mandela, 19, 272. *See also*
Inkatha Freedom Party

Cape Town, 23-24, 224-25
Castro, Fidel, 118, 128, 273
Catala, Ford, 193, 277
CCB (Civil Cooperation Bureau),
90, 194, 272
Chavis, Ben, 263
Chiefs, 25, 233
Chikane, Frank, 233, 281
China, 141
Churchill, Winston, 78
CIA, 120
Ciskei, 162
Civics, 87, 88, 281
Civil rights movement (U.S.), 10,
262, 263
Civil service, 170, 213, 229, 259
Clinton, William, 258
Codesa, 214, 281; Codesa 1 meet-
ing, 19, 146-52, 153-58, 162-63,
183, 185; Codesa 2 meeting, 20,
161, 163-64; deadlock in, 20,
161, 163-64, 172, 181-85, 187,
189, 197; Declaration of Intent,
19, 153, 155, 181-82, 189, 212,
275-76; limited authority of,
149-50, 227, 230; participation
in, 148, 214-15, 275; significance
of, 147-48. *See also* Negotiations
Coetsee, Kobie, 241
Colonial revolution, 77-78, 134
Coloureds, 11, 111, 200-201, 273;
ANC and, 111, 224-25, 279
Commonwealth, 252
Communist Party (SACP), 24,

101, 285; ANC relations with, 24, 114, 126-27. *See also* Tripartite alliance
Communist Party of Cuba, 128
Community Agency for Social Enquiry, 191
Comprehensive Anti-Apartheid Act, 41, 270
Conscription, 172, 276
Conservative Party, 153, 221, 235, 240, 257, 275, 281
Constituent assembly: agreement on, 211, 227; elections to, 126, 139, 149, 163, 183-84; need for, 11, 27, 39, 97, 108, 126, 202, 250; powers of, 183-86, 214, 227
Constitution: democratic, 36, 104, 125, 126, 150-51, 189, 201-2; provisions in new, 48, 51-52, 107-8, 181-82; *See also* Constituent assembly
Corruption, governmental, 164, 220-21, 222, 278
COSATU (Congress of South African Trade Unions), 18, 19, 24, 114, 137, 281. *See also* Tripartite alliance
Councillors, 88, 272
Counterrevolution, 106, 112, 126, 131, 160, 213, 218, 229, 259
Crime, 83-84, 131
Cuba, 118-21, 128. 273-74; and Africa, 120-21, 123, 124, 141, 274
Cuito Cuanavale, 11, 121, 124, 137, 274

Dadoo, Yusuf, 24, 56, 281-82
Daveytown massacre, 87, 91
De Klerk, F.W., 164, 207, 282; amnesty of officials by, 20, 240, 279, 280; and apartheid regime, 72, 153, 154, 158, 177; criticisms of, 71, 138-39, 153-58, 175-79, 210; integrity of, 27, 32, 40, 72; Mandela talks with, 18, 20, 26, 31, 71, 154, 155, 156, 176, 204, 209-10, 211, 278; open letters to, 85-91, 180-87, 190; and political noramalization, 18, 26, 57, 96, 158. *See also* National Party; South African government
Death squads. *See* Assassinations
Declaration of Human Rights, 78, 196
Defence Amendment Bill, 172, 276
Defiance Campaign, 10, 187, 262-63, 277
Democratic Party (South Africa), 221, 282
Democratic revolutions, 78
Democratic rights, 36, 50, 78-79, 103, 108, 126, 139, 182; and free political climate, 12, 27, 125, 151, 162, 205, 209, 212, 259
Democratic, nonracial South Africa, 10, 27, 28, 32, 40, 42, 51, 76, 97, 100, 101, 108, 117, 122, 124, 152, 178, 181, 189, 212, 244, 248, 250, 251; political culture in, 81-83, 93-98, 115, 140, 168
Derby-Lewis, Clive, 235, 240
Dikeledi, Paul, 143
Dingane, 122, 274
Dinizulu, 233, 282
Dlodlo, Theo, 144
Donne, John, 249
Douglass, Frederick, 42, 270
Du Bois, W.E.B., 30, 42, 262, 264, 269

Eastern Europe, 267
Economy, apartheid: distortion of, 37-38, 254; in crisis, 11, 25, 93-94, 151, 258, 260
Economy, postapartheid, 37-38, 167, 168-70, 254-55; foreign investments in, 38, 165, 254; government role in, 37-38; international assistance to, 38-39, 116, 165, 254-55, 258, 266-67; mixed, 38, 254; restructuring, 27, 33, 37-38, 98, 250-51
Education, 79-80, 171, 267

Egypt, 141
Elections: ANC campaign, 13, 21, 108, 110, 126, 205-6, 215-16, 218, 245, 252-53, 257-58; democratic, 19, 39-40, 139, 149, 183-84, 250, 252, 263; and political power, 230, 243-44; scheduling of, 13, 21, 149, 212, 214, 244, 250, 251, 257-58, 263-65
Erasmus, General, 176
Ethiopia, 141
Ethnic divisions, 12, 89, 95, 136-37, 183, 265, 279
Ethnic-linguistic diversity, 32, 97, 182
European Community, 96, 252, 255, 273
Exiles, 12, 18, 58, 64, 94, 105, 125, 212, 227, 259, 271

Factionalism, 69-70, 113
Family, under apartheid, 25, 50, 81
February, Basil, 143
First, Ruth, 49, 239, 279
Fischer, Bram, 24, 282
FNLA, 120, 274
Freedom Charter, 128, 135, 137, 187, 273, 277; nonracial perspective in, 13, 101, 123, 218; social demands of, 168-69, 171
Frontline States, 25, 55-56, 56-57, 141, 269, 282

Gandhi, Mohandas, 223, 282
Garvey, Marcus, 30, 42, 269
GATT, 254
German Democratic Republic, 141
Gluckman, Jonathan, 20
Goldstone, Richard J., 18, 282
Goldstone commission, 20, 193, 206, 209
Gomomo, John, 219
Goniwe, Matthew, 193-94, 239, 277, 279
Government of national unity, 109, 213, 225, 228-30, 258-59. *See also* Interim government
Gqozo, Oupa Josh, 206, 208, 228,

277-78, 282
Granma, 119, 273
Greece, 253
Groote Schuur summit (1990), 18, 58, 60, 138, 155, 271
Group Areas Act, 19, 270
Guevara, Ernesto Che, 120, 274
Gugushe, Gene, 144
Guma, Mduduzeli, 144
Gwala, Harry, 219

Hamer, Fannie Lou, 30, 269
Hani, Chris, 207-8, 219, 226, 236-37, 238-39, 244, 245-46, 282; assassination, 21, 235-37, 239-41, 242, 245, 251, 265
Harare Declaration, 26, 104, 109, 138, 185, 269
Harlem, 29-30
Harris, Peter, 175-76
Health care, 79
Hintsa, 25, 122, 269
Hlekani, Gandhi, 143
Homelands. *See* Bantustans
Homelessness, 25, 50
Hospitals, 44-45
Hostels, 93; need to phase out, 91, 175, 178, 205, 211; and township violence, 19, 86, 87, 95-96
Housing, 12, 31, 79, 171
Human rights, 36, 37, 38, 42, 77-80, 103, 224, 249, 255

Illiteracy, 50, 264
Imperialism, 77; and "new world order," 167
Indemnity Bill, 20, 241, 280
Indians, 11, 111, 200-201, 222-25, 273, 278; ANC and, 111, 222-23, 224-25, 225, 279
Inkatha Freedom Party (IFP), 220, 221, 257, 282; as ally of regime, 125, 126, 138, 162, 195; ANC appeals to, 178, 231-32, 232-33; ANC talks with, 19, 85, 231, 272, 278; government funding of, 19, 126, 138, 157, 162, 164, 179, 275; regionalist demands

of, 230-31; and security forces, 18, 71, 86-87, 89, 174, 176, 191, 195-96, 210, 271; and township violence, 18, 20, 86, 88, 90, 125-26, 174, 191, 195-96, 210, 271, 272
Interim government, 11, 84, 104, 126, 150, 162, 164, 165, 201-2, 211, 212; composition of, 108-9, 139, 186, 213, 250; as government of national unity, 109, 213; life span, 109, 150; and security forces, 97, 139, 241-42, 243, 252; tasks of, 97, 125, 139, 185, 201-2, 213, 215. *See also* Transitional executive council
International Commission of Jurists, 193
International Labor Organization, 56
International solidarity, 11, 140-42, 260; by Cuba, 123, 141; by Frontline States, 25, 56-57, 141; importance of, 25, 63, 109, 115-16, 135; 1993 conference, 21, 217-18; in Western Europe and U.S., 29-30, 41, 141, 250, 255, 262-263; of workers, 93. *See also* Sanctions
Investments, foreign, 38, 165, 254, 266-67
Ireland, Northern, 249
Iscor steelworks, 178, 276-77
Isitwalandwe, 74, 272
Israel, 80

Jefferson, Thomas, 41, 42
Jews, 80, 159-60, 176, 233
Jim Crow, 10, 263
Johannesburg, 86, 93, 265
Jordan, Z. Pallo, 14, 282
Joseph, Helen, 49, 282

KaNgwene, 222
Kasrils, Ronnie, 207-8, 278, 283
Khayiyane, Victor, 143
King, Martin Luther, 30, 42, 269
Koeberg attack, 130-31, 275

Koevoet, 90, 272-73
Kotane, Moses, 24, 56, 283
Kotze, Craig, 178, 277
Kriel, Ashley, 24, 283
Kriel, Hernus, 175, 245, 283
KwaMadala Hostel, 178, 276-77
KwaNdebele, 222
KwaZulu, 88, 194

Land, 9, 122, 133
Land Acts, 19, 122, 270, 274-75
Langa, 132, 275
Lebanon, 265
Lebowa, 222
Liberia, 249
Lincoln, Abraham, 41
Luthuli, Albert, 54, 283
Luthuli Detachment, 55, 130, 143, 270

Mabhida, Moses, 24, 283
Mahlangu, Solomon, 24, 130, 143, 283
Makana, 122
Makaqekeza, Atwell, 145
Make, Cassius, 144
Malan, Magnus, 19, 90, 95, 283
Malcolm X, 30, 269-70
Mandela, Nelson: as ANC leader, 16, 18, 19, 26, 99; and Buthelezi, 19, 72; early years, 16, 77, 83; as future president, 257-58; imprisonment, 16, 28, 29, 34, 37, 41, 81, 94, 120, 218, 260, 269; release from prison, 9-10, 16, 18, 23-28, 29-30, 42; talks with government, 18, 20, 26, 31, 71, 154, 155, 156, 176, 204, 209-10, 211, 278; world travels, 18, 19, 20, 21, 29, 118, 161, 261
Mandela, Winnie, 25, 81, 272, 283
Manuel, Trevor, 283
Marks, J.B., 56, 283
Marshall, Thurgood, 263
Martí, José, 118, 128
Masekela, Barbara, 14, 283
Maseru raid, 144, 275
Mass action: ANC and, 11, 18, 19,

111, 115, 200-201, 230; attacks on, 175, 178, 187, 200; disciplined, 27, 33, 60, 115, 177, 200, 236-37; importance of, 25, 27, 63, 135, 136, 177, 209; and insurrection, 131, 137, 206-207; and negotiations, 65, 108, 138, 201; 1992 campaign, 20, 199-203, 206-7, 230; scope of, 44-45, 111; upsurge of in 1980s, 11, 24, 55, 131, 137
Mass Democratic Movement, 24, 137, 283
Mass media, 45-46, 47, 61, 250; need to open, 150, 243
Matola raids, 144, 275
Maxeke, Charlotte, 49, 283
Meyer, Leon, 144
Meyer, Roelf, 209, 283
Mhlauli, Sicelo, 193, 277
Migrant workers, 93
Mini, Nomkhosi, 144
Mini, Vuyisile, 143
MK. *See* Umkhonto we Sizwe
Mkhonto, Sparrow, 193, 239, 277, 279
Modise, Joe, 226, 283-84
Moegoerane, Simon, 144
Mogabudi, Obadi, 143
Moholo, Patrick, 144
Mokaba, Peter, 219
Molale, Kate, 49
Molaoa, Patrick, 143
Moloisane, Kentridge, 144
Molokane, Richard "Barney," 143-44
Moncada, 118, 273
Monro, General, 95
Moodley, Mary, 49, 284
Mophosho, Florence, 49, 56, 284
Morape, Andries, 143
Moshoeshoe, 122, 274
Mosololi, Jerry, 144
Motaung, Marcus Thagbo, 144
Motlatsi, James, 92
Mozambique, 40
Mphongoshe, Pakamile, 144
MPLA, 230, 279

Multiparty system, 36, 103, 114, 182
Mziwonke, Faldeni "Castro," 143

NAACP (National Association for the Advancement of Colored People), 10, 261-63
Nagorno-Karabakh, 249
Namibia, 93, 113, 272; independence, 11, 18, 121, 137
Natal Indian Congress, 24, 223
Natal province, 18, 230; violence in, 59, 85, 104, 194, 219-20, 223, 232-33, 272; Mandela visit, 219-34
Nation, South African, 84, 123, 150
National, democratic revolution: international impact of, 9, 10, 34, 134, 167, 262-63, 265; new stage in, 9-12, 57, 101-2, 124, 136-37, 259; objectives of, 31, 36, 168-70; role of oppressed in, 10, 67, 128, 134-35; and overthrow of apartheid, 9, 13, 25, 123, 133-35, 244; social character of, 31, 33, 38, 79-80, 171, 266-27; and state power, 103, 104, 106, 135, 229, 243. *See also* African National Congress
National Education Crisis Committee, 24
Nationalism, African, 76-77, 78-79
Nationalization, 38
National Party, 12, 77, 80, 154, 220, 221, 258, 284; and ANC, 154, 177-76, 227; and apartheid, 27, 72, 105, 172; demand for veto by, 20, 161, 163-64, 172, 184-85, 189, 197, 228, 258; election campaign, 176, 205-6, 216; and Indians and Coloureds, 221-22, 224-25; and Inkatha, 126, 157; and interim government, 109, 125; obstacles to negotiations by, 163-64, 172; strategic defeat of, 57, 102; and township violence, 105-6, 176. *See also* de

Klerk, F.W.; South African government
National Peace Accord, 19, 156, 206, 208, 209, 240, 278, 284
National Peace Committee, 215
National Union of Mineworkers (NUM), 92-98
National Union of South African Students (NUSAS), 24, 234
Nazism, 176, 250
Neethling, Lothar, 194
Negotiations, 76, 212, 21, 257; ANC commitment to, 63, 138-39, 197, 202, 205; ANC as initiators of, 26, 31, 39, 70, 124, 147, 154, 158, 220, 226; ANC objectives in, 97, 104, 138, 149, 150-51; ANC suspensions of, 19, 20, 162, 177-78, 211, 276; as arena of struggle, 103, 138, 172, 243; break of deadlock in, 20, 204, 278; government obstacles to, 58, 94-95, 104-5, 125, 138-39, 161, 163-64, 177, 211, 244; Groote Schuur summit (1990), 18, 58, 60, 138, 155, 271; open vs. secret, 27, 70-71, 150; Pretoria summit (1990), 18, 58, 60, 94, 138, 155, 271; removal of obstacles to, 26-27, 31, 39, 58, 60, 62, 104, 125, 191, 202; and township violence, 91, 94, 175, 177, 276; as victory of struggle, 12, 102, 137-38, 243, 259. *See also* Codesa
"Negotiations: A Strategic Perspective," 212-13, 225, 228, 278
Ngoyi, Lilian, 49, 284
Ngudle, Looksmart Solwandle, 143
Njongwe, Lucas Bryce, 144
"Nkosi Sikelel' i-Afrika," 225, 278
Nokwe, Duma, 56, 284
Nonaligned Movement, 56, 147
Nonracialism, 13, 28, 34, 39, 101, 123, 218. *See also* Democratic, nonracial South Africa
Nqini, Zola, 144
Ntuli, Sam, 19, 157, 175, 276

Nyanda, Zwelakhe, 144
Nyembe, Dorothy, 49, 284
Nzo, Alfred, 92

Organization for Economic Cooperation and Development (OECD), 254
Organization of African Unity (OAU), 55, 140, 147

Palestinians, 80
Pan-Africanist Congress (PAC), 220, 221, 275, 278, 284; joint action with, 19, 46
Parks, Rosa, 30, 263, 269
Patriotic Front, 13, 19, 66, 114, 162, 216, 222, 284
Peace brigades, 221, 240
Peasant struggles, 132, 275
Phahle, George, 145
Phola Park, 59
Plaatje, Sol, 262, 284
Police. *See* Security forces
Political power: and elections, 229-30, 243; as strategic objective, 103, 104, 106, 135; white monopoly of, 27, 31, 133, 189
Pondoland, 132, 275
Population Registration Act, 19, 270
Portugal, 253
Powell, Adam Clayton, 30, 269
Power sharing, 20, 213, 225, 228-29, 258
Pretoria summit (1990), 18, 58, 60, 94, 138, 155, 271
Prisoners, political, 64; on death row, 71-72; release of, 12, 26-27, 58, 60, 94-95, 105, 125, 151, 197, 205, 211, 212, 227, 259, 271
Protea, 242, 245, 279

Rabilal, Krishna, 144
Racism, 40, 63; European, 96; institutionalized, 30-31, 50, 78; international fight vs., 30-31, 39, 42, 80, 101, 122, 250. *See also* Apartheid

Ramaphosa, Cyril, 92, 177, 207, 209, 284
Ramushoane, Colonel, 129
Record of Understanding, 20, 211, 212
Red Cross, 179
Reef, 86, 191, 272
Referendum, whites-only, 20, 259, 280
Reformism, 123, 134, 244
Regionalism, 163, 183-84, 230-31
Religious leaders, 25, 233
Renamo, 46, 284
Repression, 11, 80, 82, 187, 226, 244, 275; against ANC, 54-55, 123, 231, 234, 275
Repressive laws, 60-61, 82, 105, 234; repeal of, 58, 82, 101, 197, 259
Right wing. *See* Ultraright
Rivonia trial, 28, 34, 54, 269
Robeson, Paul, 30, 262, 263, 269
Roosevelt, Franklin D., 78

Sabalele, 239
Sanctions: effect of, 11, 41, 259, 266; erosion of, 96, 116, 127-28, 179, 273; lifting of, 165, 260, 266-67; need to maintain, 27-28, 40-41, 96-97, 116, 127-28, 165, 179
Sasol attack, 130-31, 275
Savimbi, Jonas, 230, 279
Seabelo, Morris, 144
Sebokeng massacres: March 1990, 18, 271; July 1990, 18, 59, 71, 87, 90-91, 175-76, 271
Security forces: attacks on southern Africa, 40, 56-57, 93, 120-21, 137, 272-73, 274; covert operations by, 12, 90, 164, 178, 240, 194, 195, 272-73; and Inkatha, 18, 71, 86-87, 89, 174, 176, 191, 195-96, 210, 271; and interim government, 97, 112, 139, 156, 241-42, 243, 252; massacres by, 12, 18, 31, 37, 62, 87, 91, 239, 245, 279; need to purge, 90-91, 178, 213, 229; and township violence, 87-88, 106, 155, 174, 175, 178, 190; and ultraright, 12, 32, 259. *See also* Assassinations; Violence, government responsibility for
Sekhukhune, 25, 122, 269
Self-defense, 112, 131, 134, 232
Self-determination, 77
Separate Amenities Act, 18, 270
September, Dulcie, 239, 279
Sharpeville, 132, 174, 177, 275
Shope, Gertrude, 49, 207, 284
Silinga, Annie, 49, 284
Simons, Ray, 49, 284
Slovo, Joe, 24, 285
Smith, Ian, 142
Smuts, Jan, 262, 285
Social engineering, 50, 79
Somalia, 141, 249, 265
Souls of Black Folk, The (Du Bois), 262, 264
Southern Africa, 11, 73; apartheid attacks on, 40, 56-57, 93, 120-21, 137, 272-73, 274, 275. *See also* Angola; Cuito Cuanavale; Namibia
South African Communist Party (SACP). *See* Communist Party
South African Defence Force (SADF). *See* Security forces
South African government: ANC talks with, 18, 58, 70-71, 76, 91, 177-78, 211, 214, 227, 231, 271, 276; corruption within, 164, 220-21, 222, 278; "double agenda" of, 60, 106, 156-57; illegitimacy of, 61, 84, 150, 153, 158, 177, 243. *See also* Apartheid; Apartheid state; de Klerk, F.W.; National Party; Repression; Security forces; Violence, government responsibility for
South African government, post-apartheid, 213, 243-44, 250-51. *See also* Interim government
South African Police. *See* Security forces

South African Students' Organisation (SASO), 234, 285
South African Youth Congress, 24
Soviet Union, 141
Soweto uprising (1976), 11, 130, 176, 275
Spain, 253
Spear of the Nation. *See* Umkhonto we Sizwe
State of emergency, 82, 212; lifting of, 18, 26, 32, 60, 62, 105, 227, 270
Strikes, 18, 19, 20, 21, 45, 187, 199-200, 238, 277
Students, 233-34
Suffrage, universal, 28, 33, 36, 97, 103, 149, 183, 250, 263
Swanieville massacre, 19, 175, 276
Sweden, 164-65

Table Mountain massacres, 219-20, 232
Tamana, Dora, 49, 285
Tambo, Oliver, 68, 74, 99, 271, 285; as central ANC leader, 24, 54-56; death of, 21, 256, 280
Tanzania, 141
TerreBlanche, Eugene, 221, 285
Terrorism Act, 234
Third World: liberation movements in, 10-11, 170-71
Tolerance, 81-83, 115, 168
Trade unions. *See* COSATU
Transitional executive council, 214, 243, 250, 251-52, 259. *See also* Interim government
Transitional period, 102, 107-10, 125, 182, 213-14, 229-30; duration of, 104, 109, 139, 149, 162, 171, 172, 227-28. *See also* Interim government
Transkei, 132, 162
Transvaal, 104, 132, 175
Transvaal Indian Congress, 24
Tribalism, 136-37
Tripartite alliance, 13, 24, 61, 98, 114, 126, 137, 200-201, 216, 285

Trust Feed massacre, 20, 193, 277
Truth, Sojourner, 30, 42, 269
Tshwete, Steve, 207, 285
Tubman, Harriet, 30, 270
Turner, Rick, 239, 279
Tutu, Desmond, 233, 260, 285

Uganda, 141
Ultraright: attack on World Trade Centre, 21, 265, 280; danger from, 32, 251, 259; government tolerance of, 63, 242; and police, 12, 32, 259. *See also* AWB; Hani, Chris, assassination
Umkhonto we Sizwe, 24, 49, 64, 74, 111, 129-45, 285; attacks on, 153, 155-56, 157, 241; cadres, 112, 131, 142; combat readiness, 61, 112, 131; formation of, 26, 132, 140; martyrs of, 24, 112, 130, 143-45, 283; military actions by, 55, 130-31, 142, 270, 275; and new national army, 112-13, 131, 140; and self-defense units, 112, 136. *See also* Armed struggle
Unemployment, 25, 31, 80, 94, 260
Union Buildings, 199-203, 207
Union of South Africa, establishment of, 61, 67, 122, 148, 230-31, 262, 271
UNITA, 120, 274, 279
United Democratic Front, 24, 285
United Nations, 56, 147, 252; monitoring by, 196-97, 201; and peace force, 221
United Nations Charter, 196
United Nations Declaration on Southern Africa (1989), 109, 190, 196, 197, 253, 273
United Nations Development Program, 254-55
United Nations Security Council, session on South Africa, 20, 179, 188-98, 277
United States, 36-37; antiapartheid movement in, 41, 262-63; blacks

in, 29-30, 261-63, 264; and South Africa, 41, 127-28, 258, 266-67, 270
Unity: of oppressed, 26, 44-47, 114-15, 136-37, 179; within ANC, 74, 113. *See also* Government of national unity

Van der Merwe, General, 176
Van der Westhuizen, C.P., 193-94, 277
Vance, Cyrus, 205
Vanderbijlpark, 242, 279
Venda, 129, 162
Verwoerd, Hendrik, 79, 132, 285
Violence, township, 85-91, 156, 162, 189-98, 219-20; by ANC members, 192-93, 219-20; as attack on democratic movement, 59-60, 88-90, 97, 125, 138-39, 191-95, 202; to block democratic transformation, 12, 60, 95-96, 105, 106, 151, 229, 265; efforts to halt, 19, 63, 85, 90-91, 95-96, 106, 178, 179, 232-34; and ethnic antagonisms, 89, 95, 265; government responsibility for, 20, 62, 87-88, 88-89, 105-6, 125, 138, 155, 175-77, 190, 192, 210; impunity for perpetrators of, 89, 157, 193, 194, 239-40; statistics on, 62, 85, 125, 190. *See also* Inkatha Freedom Party, and township violence; National Peace Accord; Security forces, and township violence
Vlok, Adriaan, 19, 71, 90, 95, 176, 285
Vulindlela, Operation, 55, 270

Walus, Janusz, 235
Washington, George, 41
Weapons, traditional, 90, 175, 205, 211, 278
Webster, David, 239, 279
Whites: ANC appeals to, 11, 27, 32, 67, 167, 178, 213-14, 236; in antiapartheid struggle, 24, 32, 137; violence against, 215, 278. *See also* Apartheid, white monopoly of power under
Wilson, Woodrow, 262
Women: in ANC, 49-50; ANC proposals on, 10, 50-52, 103; and antiapartheid struggle, 25, 48-49; oppression of, 49-50
Working class, 9, 13, 24, 93-94, 98, 133, 200. *See also* Strikes
World Trade Centre attack (Johannesburg), 21, 265, 280
World War II, 77-78

Xhosas, 95
Xuma, A.B., 78, 285

Youth, 25, 237
Yugoslavia, 218, 249

Z Squad, 90
Zaire, 120, 274
Zambia, 93
Zibi, Vuyani, 144
Zihlangu, M., 49, 285
Zimbabwe, 93, 113; Umkhonto we Sizwe in, 55, 130, 142, 143, 270
Zonk'izizwe, 59
Zulus, 95, 233

New International
A MAGAZINE OF MARXIST POLITICS AND THEORY

No. 5

The Coming Revolution in South Africa by Jack Barnes ■ **The Future Belongs to the Majority** by Oliver Tambo ■ **Why Cuban Volunteers Are in Angola** two speeches by Fidel Castro. $9.00

No. 10

Capitalism's March toward Fascism and War by Jack Barnes **What the Stock Market Crash of 1987 Foretold** ■ **Cuba's Revolution Confronts a Crossroads in the Fight for Socialism** by Mary-Alice Waters. Available 1994

No. 9

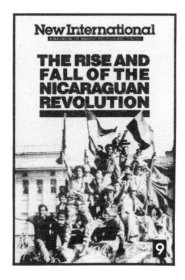

The Triumph of the Nicaraguan Revolution ■ Washington's Contra War and the Challenge of Forging Proletarian Leadership ■ The Political Degeneration of the FSLN and the Demise of the Workers and Farmers Government. $14.00

No. 7

Opening Guns of World War III: Washington's Assault on Iraq by Jack Barnes ■ **Communist Policy in Wartime as well as in Peacetime** by Mary-Alice Waters ■ **Lessons from the Iran-Iraq War** by Samad Sharif. $12.00

Many of the articles that have appeared in *New International* are also available in Spanish in *Nueva Internacional*, in French in *Nouvelle Internationale*, and in Swedish in *Ny International*.

Also by Nelson Mandela

THE STRUGGLE IS MY LIFE

"My political beliefs have been explained in my autobiography, *The Struggle Is My Life*"— Nelson Mandela. Speeches and writings from 1944 to mid-1990. $15.95

NELSON MANDELA: SPEECHES 1990

'Intensify the Struggle to Abolish Apartheid'

Speeches from South Africa, Angola, and Britain following Mandela's release from prison. Includes the Freedom Charter. Booklet $6.00

HOW FAR WE SLAVES HAVE COME!

South Africa and Cuba in Today's World

BY NELSON MANDELA AND FIDEL CASTRO

Speaking together in Cuba in 1991, Mandela and Castro discuss the unique relationship and example of the struggles of the South African and Cuban peoples. Also available in Spanish. $8.95

NELSON MANDELA: ¡INTENSIFIQUEMOS LA LUCHA!

In Spanish. Ten speeches in Africa, Europe, and North America following Mandela's release from prison in 1990. Includes the Freedom Charter. $13.95

HABLA NELSON MANDELA

In Spanish. Includes speeches from the dock in 1962 and 1964, "A Black Man in a White Man's Court" and "I Am Prepared to Die." $9.95

Further reading

APARTHEID'S GREAT LAND THEFT
The Struggle for the Right to Farm in South Africa
BY ERNEST HARSCH
Redressing the forced dispossession of Africans
from the land is central to overturning apartheid's
legacy and carrying through the national, democratic
revolution in South Africa. Booklet $3.50

THOMAS SANKARA SPEAKS
The Burkina Faso Revolution, 1983-87
The president of Burkina Faso, murdered in 1987,
tells the story of the revolution that unfolded in this
West African country as peasants and workers
began confronting hunger, illiteracy, and other
conditions perpetuated by capitalism. $18.95

TO SPEAK THE TRUTH
Why Washington's 'Cold War' against Cuba Doesn't End
BY FIDEL CASTRO AND CHE GUEVARA
Why the U.S. government is determined to destroy
the example set by the socialist revolution in Cuba
and why its effort will fail. Introduction by
Mary-Alice Waters. $16.95

TWO TACTICS OF SOCIAL DEMOCRACY IN THE DEMOCRATIC REVOLUTION
BY V.I. LENIN
Written in 1905, this work explains the strategy
that enabled an alliance of workers and peasant to
overturn the monarchy, landlordism, and capitalist
rule in Russia. $5.95

DEMOCRACY AND REVOLUTION
BY GEORGE NOVACK
The limitations and advances of various forms of democracy in class society,
from its roots in ancient Greece through its rise and decline under
capitalism. Discusses the emergence of Bonapartism, military dictatorship
and fascism, and how democracy will be advanced under a workers and
farmers regime. $18.95

AVAILABLE FROM PATHFINDER. SEE FRONT OF BOOK FOR ADDRESSES.

From Pathfinder

February 1965: The Final Speeches
BY MALCOLM X

Speeches from the last three weeks of Malcolm X's life, presenting the still-accelerating evolution of his political views. First volume in the chronological series. $17.95

To See the Dawn
Baku—First Congress of the Peoples of the East

How can peasants and workers in the colonial world achieve freedom from imperialist exploitation? How can working people overcome divisions incited by their national ruling classes and act together for common class interests? These questions were addressed by 2,000 delegates to the Baku congress, representing two dozen peoples of Asia. They met at a time when the young workers' and peasants' republic in Russia gave hope of a new dawn for the world's toilers. Complete proceedings. $19.95

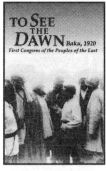

Cosmetics, Fashions, and the Exploitation of Women
BY JOSEPH HANSEN, EVELYN REED, AND MARY-ALICE WATERS

How big business uses women's second-class status to generate profits for a few and perpetuate the oppression of the female sex and the exploitation of working people. $12.95

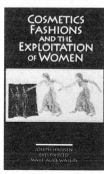

The Communist Manifesto
BY KARL MARX AND FREDERICK ENGELS

Founding document of the modern working-class movement, written in 1847. Explains how capitalism arose as a specific stage in the economic development of class society and how it will be superseded through the revolutionary action on a world scale of the working class. Booklet. $2.50

Teamster Rebellion
by Farrell Dobbs
The 1934 strikes that built a fighting union movement in Minneapolis and helped pave the way for the CIO. $15.95

Dynamics of the Cuban Revolution
by Joseph Hansen
To understand the first socialist revolution in the Americas, Hansen says, "it is not necessary to begin from zero. The problems presented to Marxist theory by the uniqueness of the events were solved at the time." This compilation, written with polemical clarity as the revolution advanced, presents the conclusions that guide fighters everywhere. $19.95

The History of the Russian Revolution
by Leon Trotsky
The social, economic, and political dynamics of the first victorious socialist revolution, as told by one of its principal leaders. Unique in modern literature. Unabridged edition, 3 vols. in one. 1,358 pp. $35.95.

The Jewish Question
A MARXIST INTERPRETATION
by Abram Leon
Traces the historical rationalizations of anti-Semitism to the position of Jews as a "people-class" of merchants and moneylenders in the centuries leading up to the domination of industrial capitalism. Leon explains how in times of social crisis renewed Jew-hatred is incited by the capitalists to mobilize reactionary forces against the labor movement and disorient the middle classes and layers of working people about the true source of their impoverishment. $17.95

PATHFINDER